Thai Women in the Global Labor Force

Thai Women in the Global Labor Force

CONSUMING DESIRES, CONTESTED SELVES

MARY BETH MILLS

Rutgers University Press

New Brunswick, New Jersey, and London

Seventh paperback printing, 2012

Library of Congress Cataloging-in-Publication Data

Mills, Mary Beth, 1962–
    Thai women in the global labor force : consuming desires, contested
selves / Mary Beth Mills.
        p. cm.
    Includes bibliographical references and index.
    ISBN 0–8135–2653–1 (cloth : alk. paper). — ISBN 0–8135–2654–X
(pbk. : alk. paper)
    1. Women—Employment—Thailand.   2. Migrant labor—Thailand.
3. Women—Thailand—Social conditions.   I. Title.
HD6192.55.M55 1999
331.4'1279593—dc 21   98–44992
                                                                       CIP

British Cataloging-in-Publication data for this book is available from the British Library

Portions of Chapters 5, 7, and 9 are reprinted by permission of the American Anthropological Association from *American Ethnologist* 24:1, 1997. Portions of Chapter 8 are
reprinted by permission of the Overseas Publishers Association, Amsterdam B.V., from
Identities: Global Studies in Culture and Power 5(3), 1998.

Manufactured in the United States of America

CONTENTS

v

FIGURES

ACKNOWLEDGMENTS

This book is the product of many years of research, reflection, and dialogue, and more people than I can mention here have had a hand in shaping my experiences, observations, and understandings along the way. Among these, I owe special thanks to the staff at Friends of Women Foundation in Bangkok who offered friendship, advice, and practical assistance in great measure; I am deeply in their debt. In particular, I wish to thank Kamolrat (Pranee) Monthongdaeng, who was my research assistant and without whose tireless help, cheerful demeanor, and endless patience the fieldwork portion of this study would have been much more difficult and far less productive. Most of all, I am indebted to the residents of Baan Naa Sakae and to the many women and men from this and other rural communities whom I met in Bangkok. They let me into their homes and lives with a generosity and kindness that I had no right to expect but without which I could never have completed this study. Although it cannot adequately express my gratitude, I hope that this book can convey my deep respect and admiration for these individuals and their struggles to live with dignity and meaning amid daunting circumstances.

I am very thankful for the institutional sponsorship, the friendly support, and keen interest that my work received in Thailand from Dr. Juree Vichit-Vadakan of the National Institute for Development Administration and Dr. Amara Pongsapich at Chulalongkorn University Social Research Institute. I wish to thank the National Research Council of Thailand for granting me the necessary research permissions to pursue this project. Additional encouragement and kind assistance came from Dr. Akin Rabibhadana, then at the Thailand Development Research Institute, from the research staff members of the Research and Development Institute at Khon Kaen University, and from faculty at Srinakharin Wiroj University in Mahasarakham. In Khon Kaen, Dararat Mettariganond and Patcharin Lapanun were especially generous with their time and energy. I owe particular thanks to the staff of PLAN International in the Khon Kaen, Mahasarakham, and Borabue offices. They provided valuable assistance at several stages of my research in Isan. Throughout my time in Bangkok, I was graciously received and assisted by staff members at several Thai non-governmental organizations, including the Asian Cultural Forum on Development, the Ecumenical Coalition on Third World Tourism, the Project for Migrant Youth, and the Union for Civil Liberties.

During the research and writing of this book, I was fortunate to receive financial support from several sources. My time in the field was funded at different stages by the following: a National Science Foundation Doctoral Fellowship, a Social Sciences and Humanities Research Council of Canada Doctoral Fellowship, a Fulbright-Hays Doctoral Dissertation Research Abroad Grant, a Social Science Research Council Dissertation Research Grant, and a Luce Foundation Research Grant (through the Center for Southeast Asian Studies at the University of California, Berkeley). I am also grateful for travel support from the Colby College Social Sciences Division, which allowed me to make a follow-up trip to Thailand in the summer of 1993. Additional time and support for data analysis and writing came from a post-doctoral fellowship at Yale University, the Program in Agrarian Studies (1995–96), and from a Colby College sabbatical extension grant (1996–97). For all these sources of assistance I am truly grateful.

The writing of this book has also benefited from innumerable conversations with teachers, colleagues, and students. Special thanks are due to my teachers at the University of California, Berkeley, especially Herbert Phillips, Aihwa Ong, and Michael Watts, whose encouragement and insight guided me through the early stages of this project. I wish also to thank Penny Van Esterik, who has been an ongoing source of inspiration and encouragement. During the past decade, I have been exceedingly fortunate to share in the pleasures and challenges of several vibrant intellectual communities. My exchanges with these friends and colleagues—particularly at the University of California, Berkeley, the Program in Agrarian Studies of Yale University, and Colby College—were enormously important in helping to clarify my thoughts and sharpen my prose. For key sources of support and constructive criticism at different stages of the research and writing, I owe special thanks to Arun Agrawal, Jennifer and Paul Alexander, Lynda Banks, Jiemin Bao, James Barrett, Kim Besio, Catherine Besteman, Christine Bowditch, Saowalak Chaytaweep, Louise Cort, Pamela DaGrossi, Susan Darlington, Jen Estes, Donna Goldstein, Jill Gordon, Linda Green, Mary Grow, Joan Harkness, Zhang Hong, Constantine Hriskos, Nina Kammerer, Peter Korat, Sureerat

Lakhanavichian, Leedom Lefferts, Kay Mansfield, David Nugent, Nancy Peluso, Pauline Peters, Jesse Ribot, Nina Glick Schiller, James C. Scott, Leslie Sharp, Sarah Ann Smith, Nayana Supapung, Patricia Symonds, Peter Vandergeest, and Ara Wilson. My thanks also to Michael Corr and Arline King-Lovelace for their map-drawing artistry. Finally, the suggestions of Diane Wolf and of Martha Heller, my editor at Rutgers University Press, as well as Diana Drew's thorough and efficient copy editing, provided valuable guidance in bringing the manuscript to its final form. I am grateful for all the interest and support, critiques and commentaries I have received from these and other sources. I must emphasize, however, that the arguments presented in this book are my own and any shortcomings or errors are entirely my responsibility. Portions of this book, particularly parts of Chapters 5 and 7, were previously published in an article, titled "Contesting the Margins of Modernity: Women, Migration, and Consumption in Thailand," which appeared in *American Ethnologist* (vol. 24, no. 1 [1997]: 37–61). Parts of Chapter 8, here substantially revised, appeared in an article, titled "Gendered Encounters with Modernity: Labor Migrants and Marriage Choices in Thailand," published in *Identities: Global Studies in Culture and Power* (vol. 5, no. 3 [1998]:301–334). Permission to reprint is gratefully acknowledged.

I also have debts to acknowledge of a different order. I am, like the women of this study, a daughter; my parents, Howie (whom I miss deeply) and Geegee, were and are my teachers, counselors, and friends. Their gifts of love and the love of learning, their keen sense of justice in a world of profound inequalities, inspired me to take paths that they might not always have expected but which they always embraced with enthusiasm. I would not be who or where I am without them.

Sarah Ann Smith has been friend, elder sister, travel companion, mentor, and colleague—a constant source of inspiration, intellectual challenge, love, and laughter. I am grateful for her many gifts but especially here for sharing with me her love of Asia and of Thailand.

James Barrett has encouraged and strengthened me through the ups and downs both of writing and of daily life; his inexhaustible confidence, humor, and generosity (as well as probing questions) renewed my too-often flagging spirits and sustained my energy and commitment to bring this book to completion.

Thai Women in the Global Labor Force

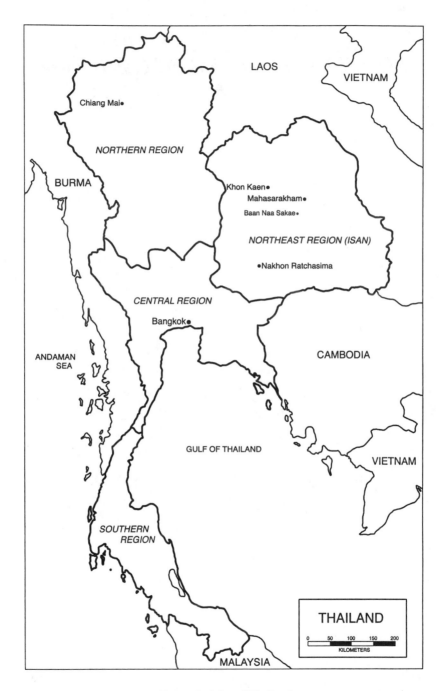

FIGURE 1. Map of Thailand.

CHAPTER 1

Women, Migration, and Thai Experiences of Modernity

⚋✛⚋

Clutching her bags, a young woman jumps down from the rear of the bus as it slows and pulls over onto the road's red gravel shoulder. The conductor barely waits until her feet hit the ground before shouting "Go on!" to the driver. The bus lurches back onto the pavement and speeds off into the early morning sun. A cloud of red dust rises in its wake. Brushing at her printed T-shirt and new blue jeans, Nok crosses the highway. She moves toward a dirt road that bears the deep grooves and potholes carved by the last rainy season. There is a lone noodle shop at the crossroads; Nok can hear the shopkeeper and her family preparing for the day's trade. She stops at a small shelter a few paces away. She will wait there for a motorcycle-taxi or a passing truck to take her the rest of the way home. Just a few more kilometers to Baan Naa Sakae and the long night's ride from Bangkok will be over.

It is good to be back, to hear the familiar Lao phrases of home, to smell the fresh, clean air of Isan. Better still to leave behind the city's noise and dirt, and the boredom of her factory job, sewing the same seam in an endless stream of garments, hour after hour, shift after shift. Still, it is a long way from the Thai capital to her home village in this northeastern province. Making the trip is always an effort. Especially traveling alone, although, after six years of working in the city, she knows how to take care of herself. And how to ignore the speculative glances of fellow passengers who see in her new clothes and fashionable haircut evidence of a less respectable occupation than factory work. Her parents at least will be happy to see her; she has brought the money that they asked her for in their last letter. She is not sure if it will be enough for what they need. There are always so many expenses: medicine for her mother's stomach problems, fertilizer for the new rice crop, building materials for the house . . .

Maybe in a few more years she will come home to stay. That, too, would please her parents. They were already hinting about it on her last trip home, talking about the son of a neighboring family who is hard-working and at the age to settle down and marry. Since her elder brother married last year and moved away to his wife's village, she knows that her parents would welcome a son-in-law to help with the heavy work in the rice fields and cassava plots. It's hard to think of her parents still working so hard all the time; this last year she could only make it home for a few days to help transplant the rice. And at twenty-three years of age, Nok knows she is getting old to start a family; every month or so it seems that another of her friends in the city leaves the factory to go home and get married. She would like to marry and have a family, of course, but to become like her mother? All stooped and worn from the long days of work in the fields, her skin burned dark and ugly from the hot sun?

Well, she is not ready for that, not yet, maybe not ever. Living in Bangkok is certainly difficult, the factory dormitory is hot and crowded and she often gets stomach aches and has trouble sleeping. But she earns steady money. Her job at the factory is dull, but living in the city is not; there is so much more to do and see there than at home. Bangkok is full of life, full of progress. Everything is so convenient there: running water and electricity, shops and markets on every corner and buses running all day and most of the night. And after work no one to tell her where and when she can go out with friends, no one to look askance or gossip if she talks with a young man or even goes out to meet him alone. . . . But if she were to stay in the city would it be any better? What if she married and then her husband left her? That's what happened to her friend last year; now San has to work on her own in the city while her mother back in the village raises San's little baby. It's happened often enough to other girls at the factory. But if Nok doesn't marry, doesn't have children, who will take care of her when she's too old to keep working in the city? . . . A motorcycle taxi drives up to the shelter, its engine breaking into Nok's thoughts. After a few words to settle the fare, she climbs up behind the driver who guns the motor and roars away.[1]

$\mathcal{N}$ok is one of the hundreds of thousands of young rural women whose labor in Bangkok manufacturing and service jobs has helped to fuel Thailand's dramatic economic growth over the past two decades. Led by booming industrial and manufacturing production, annual GDP growth averaged well over 10 percent in the late 1980s, falling only slightly in the early and mid-1990s (Pasuk & Baker, 1995:152–53; Warr, 1993:53, 56–57). During these years many observers, both inside and outside the country, hailed Thailand as one of Asia's "newly industrialized countries" (or NICs in the common shorthand of the region), soon to join the ranks of Asia's more established economic "tigers"—such as Taiwan, South Korea, Singapore, and Hong Kong. In 1997, after the research for this book was completed, Thailand's record of rapid growth stumbled abruptly. A currency crisis led to the sharp devaluation of the Thai currency, the *baht*, and triggered a series of financial setbacks that soon spread to other countries in the region. Analysts and other commentators quickly pointed to structural imbalances and inadequate regulatory measures, which the high profit margins of preceding years had obscured. However, long before the events of 1997 led to questions about Thailand's standing in the global marketplace, the evidence of serious dislocations was apparent for those who looked more closely at the nation's so-called economic "miracle."

Despite years of high growth, the benefits of Thailand's economic successes were never evenly distributed. The most dynamic sectors of the Thai economy—export-oriented manufacturing and service industries—have long been concentrated in urban areas, particularly in and around the country's primate and capital city of Bangkok. Similarly urban-rural income disparities have widened steadily since at least the 1970s (Medhi, 1993). Moreover, the cheap labor that sustained this urban-based accumulation came largely from the agricultural periphery, the daughters and sons of Thailand's majority peasant population.[2] In particular, rural women—unmarried and between the ages of fifteen and twenty-five—constituted the preferred work force for many urban employers. Although many thousands of Thai migrants lost their Bangkok jobs in the months following the financial crisis of 1997, the long-term importance of rural (and especially women's) labor for urban industry is unlikely to abate. Indeed, the availability of a vast pool of inexpensive and mobile (i.e., easily replaceable) workers remains one of Thailand's key selling points as planners and politicians struggle to reassure international investors and to restore the nation's image as an up-and-coming player in the global marketplace.

Few if any communities in rural Thailand, and especially in the economically disadvantaged and predominantly Lao-speaking Northeast (Isan), have remained untouched by the flow of village youth into urban employment. Migrants to Bangkok from all over Isan as well as many people still living in the countryside frequently assured me that "There is no one left [in the village] but old people and little children." Certainly not all young people leave their villages for the city; however, the rates of youth migration from Isan households into urban employment—whether for a few months or several years—makes it more accurate to ask not *whether* adolescent children will go to Bangkok but *when.*

This book is about this youthful mobility as I observed it in Bangkok and in the community of Baan Naa Sakae between 1987 and 1993, the peak years of Thailand's economic boom. Although I examine the process of labor migration generally—its effects both on movers and on those left behind—my focus is on the mobility of young rural women. Young women's labor migration is at once a powerful vehicle for—and an expression of—profound social and personal transformation. Conventionally, rural Thai women's geographic mobility has been more restricted than that of men, especially before marriage; yet, over the past two decades, women (and particularly young unmarried women) began moving into Bangkok at rates generally equal to that of their male counterparts; at times, young women migrants have exceeded young men on the move by nearly two to one.[3] Although young Thai men are also important participants in contemporary rural-urban migration circuits, male mobility has clear historical precedents in rural Thailand. These include long-standing patterns of masculine adventuring travel (*pay thiaw*) as well as other forms of mobility exemplified by itinerant Buddhist monks, cattle salesmen, and a variety of traveling venders (Kirsch, 1966; Anchalee & Nitaya, 1992: 169). By contrast, young women's mobility represents a sharp departure from established patterns of feminine behavior and notions of appropriate activities for women, especially unmarried daughters. Consequently, as young women enter new fields of urban employment, they and their families confront changing understandings of gendered roles and social values. Labor migration highlights points of conflict within existing household relations as well as the ongoing production or reworking of these relationships in new ways. These struggles reveal not only the individual circumstances and needs of particular migrants and their families but also the effects of more wide-ranging structural and ideological tensions within Thai society as a whole.[4]

On the one hand, women's labor migration points up and is itself produced by powerful structures of inequality in Thailand, including the social and economic subordination of rural producers within the national political economy. However, there is much more involved in women's labor migration than a response to rural-urban disparities of income and employment opportunities. Female migrant labor also engages critical ideological dimensions of women's participation in the Thai urban-industrial boom. At the same time that women's labor figures prominently in the nation's high rates of economic productivity, Thai women also represent evocative symbolic resources, particularly in the mass media. In contemporary Thailand, women—and especially women's bodies—are widely portrayed as symbols of progress and modernity. Such representations glamorize urban life and livelihood in ways that help to sustain the steady flow of migrants into city jobs; they also help to obscure the lived experiences of exploitation, including physical and economic hardship, with which urban workers must contend. For most migrants, then, living and working in Bangkok brings them into contact with a dramatically different side of Thai modernity than that portrayed in the seductive images dominating the popular culture.

The contradictions this situation poses for women migrating to Bangkok and their families back home are real and direct. In the course of moving between village and city, migrants must negotiate not only shifts in space but also shifting identities and social relations. For many in the countryside, the mobility and independence of young women is seen both as a potentially valuable economic resource and as a source of conflict, especially when women's mobility challenges customary expectations about gender roles and household authority. Consequently, women's rural-urban migration illuminates both how social relations of domination and exploitation are reproduced as well as how they are negotiated, contested, and reworked in individual experience. Women's mobility highlights the participation of migrants and their families in powerful cultural discourses about Thai modernity, or what in Thai is called *khwaam pen thansamay*, "being up-to-date." The resulting conflicts and tensions are most clearly expressed and mediated through ideas and practices of gender and gendered identities.

In the chapters that follow, I examine Thai experiences of rural-urban labor mobility, especially the movement of young women like Nok. I focus on the consequences of labor migration for rural youth and for their village families. Based on ethnographic research in both the Bangkok metropolis and in rural Isan, this study addresses each end of the labor circuit, incorporating city and village contexts as equal parts in the whole migration experience. At the same time, however, this is a specific ethnography. It focuses on one sending community in northeast Thailand, Nok's home village of Baan

Naa Sakae. Throughout the text I move back and forth between the wider Thai context and the lives and practices of the residents of Baan Naa Sakae. This alternating focus traces the complex intersections between broad structures of power and historical processes of change on the one hand, and local experiences and agency on the other. By situating my analysis of labor mobility in this way, I do not mean to claim that the people of Baan Naa Sakae represent all rural producers or labor migrants in Thailand or even those from other ethnic-Lao communities in Isan. Rather my goal is to see how patterns operating at national and even global levels are played out in a particular setting, in the lived experience of specific people. Similarly, this is not an attempt to analyze "Thai culture" as a monolithic phenomenon or entity but to explore social and cultural processes of continuity, change, and conflict as they are played out in the lives of young women and their families in northeast Thailand.

This study offers one perspective through which to approach the analysis of social and economic transformation in Thailand. It is not the only way in which this may be done nor does it attempt to address the experiences of Thai society as a whole. Like any case study, it is limited in scope; nevertheless, this work builds on more general understandings that changes are not simply imposed from without but may be actively received and engaged by people on the ground. Young women's rural-urban labor migration in Thailand cannot simply be explained as an economic response to uneven development, although this is not an irrelevant factor. It is also, and just as important, a dynamic field of social practice and cultural production through which people constitute, rework, and at least potentially contest understandings about themselves, their relationships with others, and their places in the wider world.

Women, Migration, and the Global Economy

At one level, the mobility of rural Thai youth represents one more instance of how the contemporary global economy consistently relies on rural migrants, and especially women, in countries around the world as the foundation of a cheap and compliant work force. As technologies of communication and transportation have made capital investment more and more mobile, the search to reduce costs of production has led manufacturers farther and farther afield. One result has been the rapid shift of labor-intensive industrial production from the United States and Western Europe, with their historically well-organized (and predominantly male) work forces, to new and highly dispersed sites around the globe.[5] Anyone reading the manufacturer's label on a new pair of blue jeans, a tape deck, or any number of mass-produced items for sale in North American shopping malls can begin to map the outlines of this international assembly line. Labels claiming "Made in Mexico [or China, El Salvador, Sri Lanka, Dominican Republic, Philippines, Guatemala, Seychelles, Indonesia, Mauritius, Thailand]" offer some indication of an otherwise hidden geography of production. Even less obvious, however—because it leaves no visible sign for the consumer—is the fact that the item in question was most likely cut, sewn, and/or assembled by a woman and that she most likely earned no more than a few cents an hour.

Current political and economic debates, especially in relation to the advent of the North American Free Trade Agreement, have brought increasing public attention to the movement of U.S. industries "offshore"—especially to the heavily feminized work forces of the Maquiladora projects along the U.S.-Mexico border. The Maquiladora are, literally, "subcontracting" enterprises in which hundreds of corporations—whose managers usually live and work in U.S. cities—have built factories just south of the U.S.-Mexico border. There companies employ Mexicans, most of them women, to produce inexpensive textiles and electronic goods for retail sale to U.S. consumers. But this is only one of the dozens of sites of new industrialization in countries around the world that rely on cheap (and predominantly female) labor to attract international investment. In the Caribbean, Latin America, Asia, and Africa nearly two decades of research has documented the gendered employment patterns in export-oriented manufacturing ventures. The reliance on female labor is especially pronounced in the textile and electronics industries that have dominated the shift to globally dispersed production sites.[6]

In part, women's labor is attractive to international capital investment because of persistent assumptions by employers regarding what kind of workers women make. Employers often expect that young women without a family of their own to feed will have a limited commitment to wage employment, that they are only in the labor market for a few months or years prior to marriage. Consequently, women workers are more likely to put up with low pay, limited benefits, and long-term job insecurity. Their youth and gender also suggest a work force already schooled in obedience to (parental) authority, hard work, and the patience and dexterity required for many domestic chores (such as weaving and sewing).[7] As a result, women's character and skills are often seen to be particularly well-suited to the fine detail and endless repetition of textile and electronics assembly work.

Moreover, the rural origins of many new workers, and their ongoing ties to agricultural communities, may increase their attractiveness to urban industry. Like labor migrants in many parts of the world, women and men working in Bangkok commonly remit part of their earnings to rural families. At the same time, however, they may receive from these village households supplements of rice or other foods and even cash. Children born to urban workers are frequently sent home to be raised by grandparents or other kin in the countryside. Rural households provide care and support to migrant members in cases of illness, unemployment, or other crises they may encounter while working in the city. In effect, then, rural households practicing small-cash and subsistence-crop production provide an unacknowledged subsidy for urban industry. Not only are they the sources of a highly flexible pool of labor through out-migration, but the continuing economic ties between workers and their village homes bear part of the cost of maintaining and reproducing this work force. This allows urban employers to keep wages low, which, in turn, makes long-term urban employment less tenable for migrant workers and reinforces patterns of temporary and circular migration (Porpora & Lim, 1987).[8]

Of course, the present-day importance of rural and migrant women's labor to capitalist production is nothing new. During the first decades of the nineteenth century, young women, fresh from New England farms, provided the initial labor force for the textile mills that drove the industrial revolution in the northeastern United States. As production expanded and the pace and discipline of industrial labor intensified, Yankee women began to leave the mills only to be succeeded by generations of immigrant girls and women.[9] Similarly, in Meiji Japan, cotton and silk thread mills employing Japanese farm daughters initiated that country's rapid industrialization in the late 1800s and early 1900s (Tsurumi, 1990). Throughout the history of industrialization, manufacturers have often sought out female workers, especially where production conditions are characterized by low pay, high turnover, and a labor-intensive, highly repetitive work process.

But if the pattern is not new, what strikes contemporary observers is the extent to which it now replicates itself in the most diverse regions of the globe. The recruitment of young women into industrial wage labor is now commonplace in countries and communities where a generation ago female employment outside agriculture was often limited to small-scale vending, domestic service, or prostitution. From Mexico to Java, from Bangladesh to Guam, women work for low wages producing T-shirts, televisions, and computer chips—items that will be sold not in their own communities but rather will be shipped to the high-consumption economies of North America or

Western Europe. The pattern is so pervasive and its effects so widely felt that it has given rise to such catchphrases as "the New International Division of Labor" (NIDL), "Global Feminization" or "the Global Assembly Line" (Nash & Fernandez-Kelly, 1983; Standing, 1989; Bonacich et al., 1994).

Such terms are useful, indeed essential, in recognizing and beginning to analyze the broad social and structural consequences of global industry and capitalist expansion. But in focusing on the generalized processes of a world economy, increasingly described as a regime of "flexible accumulation," one risks losing sight of the people and the lives that underlie aggregate models (see Harvey, 1989). Certain features of late twentieth-century capitalism are striking in their rapid proliferation—the internationalization and easy mobility of capital, greater flexibility in the recruitment of labor and strategies of labor control, the separation of managerial and production processes not only between classes but also across national boundaries.[10] However, constructing a global analysis of such trends may reveal very little about the diverse experiences of work and population mobility to which these broader processes give rise.

Unquestionably, women's labor migration in Thailand may be understood as a part of the Global Assembly Line; however, for Thai migrants (or Mexican maquila workers or Sri Lankan free trade zone operatives), such abstractions become meaningful only from the vantage point of their own experiences and beliefs, as shaped by their particular historical and cultural contexts. Furthermore, if young women in Thailand or elsewhere appeal to urban and industrial employers as a presumably quiescent and inexpensive labor force, this tells us neither why women themselves take up wage work nor how they construct their experiences of it. Cynthia Enloe (1989) makes the obvious but often overlooked point that young women throughout the world enter and stay in new types of employment—despite low wages, harsh labor discipline, and unhealthy working conditions—not solely for the money earned but also to achieve more complex social goals: "Without women's own needs, values, and worries, the global assembly line would grind to a halt" (Enloe, 1989:16–17).

As local arenas of social and cultural production increasingly intersect with global processes of capitalist expansion and mass-market commodification, the "needs, values, and worries" of Thai women revolve not only around familiar meanings of family and economic survival but also around newly imagined needs and possibilities, often conveyed through technologies of mass communication. This book explores the varied "needs, values, and worries" that promote the movement of rural Thai women into Bangkok employment. These, I argue, are informed not only by local gender and household relations but, just as significantly, by dominant cultural discourses about Thai modernity and progress. Attention to these complex motivations as they converge and collide in the course of migration may, in turn, illuminate women's diverse, often ambivalent responses to their urban sojourns.

Women and Migration in Thailand

When I began my research on rural-urban labor migration I was predisposed to see young women moving into Bangkok as the unwitting victims of Thailand's headlong pursuit of national development. Eager to attract foreign and domestic capital investment, by the 1980s the Thai government had made urban-based export manufacturing and an international tourist industry the cornerstones of its economic planning. Crucial to the success of these policies was the steady availability of a cheap and easily replaceable labor force. Consequently, it seemed to me that young women and men moving into Bangkok employment from an impoverished countryside bore much of the burden but enjoyed few of the benefits of the nation's drive for "development" (*kan phatthana*) and "progress" (*khwaam caroen*). Poorly educated and inexperienced, they were ill-equipped to challenge employers and other authorities. Low wages, unhealthy working conditions, inadequate legal protections, arbitrary and unfamiliar forms of labor discipline—these constituted a baseline of exploitation to which rural-urban migrants had little choice but to submit.

These assumptions, while not entirely without merit, very quickly collided with the strength of purpose and sense of personal agency that characterized the urban careers of the women and men whom I met. Rural migrants (both female and male) do confront significant obstacles in the city. As I discuss further in Chapter 6, wages are low and the conditions in which migrants must work and live are commonly stressful and often physically hazardous. The dangers and exploitation that migrant women suffer are nowhere more apparent than in Thailand's internationally infamous commercial sex industry. Prostitution is both illegal (though it is openly promoted through a wide range of legal enterprises—bars, nightclubs, massage parlors, and the like) and, with the advent of the AIDS epidemic, potentially fatal. Yet those employed in factories or as domestic servants also face serious hardships and often earn considerably less pay. Whatever their occupation, migrant workers can rarely influence their terms of employment and, in cases of abuse, may have little recourse beyond seeking a different post or returning to their village homes. Nevertheless, generalized conditions of structural disadvantage and economic exploitation explain neither the complexity of women's migration experiences, nor the meanings that women and their families give to rural-urban labor mobility in their own lives. They are neither victims pure and simple nor free and unfettered actors. Rather, they must be understood as conscious agents, making decisions and pursuing goals within—and, at times, despite—their often difficult circumstances.

Studies of labor mobility, both in Thailand and elsewhere, often focus on migration as a response to rural poverty.[11] Moreover, the movements of individuals are often viewed as directed by the economic decisions of larger households. There is no doubt that conditions of indebtedness, cash dependency, and scarce sources of credit underlie patterns of labor out-migration from peasant communities all over the world. The deployment of unmarried daughters' (or sons') labor may be one option available to peasant households seeking to increase their cash income. But models that rely on rural poverty and household economic strategies are not always able to account for the varied dynamics of migration in particular situations. In addition, more complex understandings of households—that they are sites of conflict, competing interests, and contested authority—challenge interpretations of women's employment and migration that presume the functional, strategizing unity of the household. As Diane Wolf's recent comparison of Javanese and Taiwanese workers has shown, the ability of parents to direct the labor and control the wages of working daughters is an empirical question, the answer to which may vary widely both between and within specific cultural settings (Wolf, 1992:174–78).

In the case of Thailand, analyses of youth migration that focus on household decision making are liable to obscure more than they explain. As the material in Chapter 4 highlights, household obligations are an important aspect of labor mobility but these are by no means the only, or even the most important, considerations. Almost all the migrant women I came to know spoke of desires to help rural kin as part of why they came to Bangkok but very few claimed to have been sent or otherwise persuaded by parents to take up urban employment. On the contrary, most young women were adamant that it was their decision, and this opinion was rarely contradicted by their families back home. Indeed, some parents I knew actively disagreed with their daughters' choices. Even when, as was usually the case, parents supported the labor migration of their children, they had no means to ensure that urban wages would be sent home. Although most rural families recognized the potential economic benefits from labor migration, complaints about infrequent or inadequate wage remittances were a common refrain in rural communities. Furthermore, the financial needs of rural households varied, as did the uses to which urban wages were put. Labor migration in Thailand involves not just members of poorer families; urban employment attracts rural youth from families at nearly all income levels. Consequently, Bangkok wages remitted by absent daughters and sons may be an important source of household subsistence income but, just as often, urban wages may enable rural families to purchase more and newer commodity items to enhance their comfort and status within the village community.

Beyond conventional ideals of filial obligation and the economic difficulties of rural households, labor mobility also reflects young women's (and others') powerful desires for acquiring the personal status associated with Thailand's modern, urban centers. Working and living in a city, especially in the capital city, Bangkok, provides young people with the cash wages and social opportunities to participate in new experiences and forms of entertainment and to acquire the commodity emblems—such as blue jeans, television sets, cameras, and other items—that represent claims to modern sophistication and self-identity. The consumption desires and practices of rural-urban migrants reveal the powerful cachet that cultural markers of modernity carry in present-day Thailand. For more than a century, state policies and public rhetoric have made explicit the national goals of political and economic "modernization." The country's apparent achievements, particularly during the peak years of the recent economic boom, heightened popular awareness of (and desires for) being modern or "up-to-date" (*thansamay*) among people at all levels of contemporary Thai society. At the time of my research through the late 1980s and early 1990s, whether in rural or urban locales, ideas about "old times" and "new times," *samay kôn* and *samay may*, provided powerful conceptual models for assessing local and national experiences of social and economic change. Similarly, the commodified signs and symbols of *thansamay* consumption and display were increasingly essential markers of individual, household, and/or community claims to status among both village and city dwellers. Within this wider context, rural women's labor migration responds not only to the material realities of agricultural underdevelopment, it also engages these influential meanings and cultural practices of Thai modernity.

Thai Modernity: Experience and Cultural Discourse

What I mean here by "Thai modernity" requires some explanation. The term, "modernity," is itself widely used but is not easily or consistently defined.[12]

Part of the confusion is that modernity encompasses a variety of meanings, some more descriptive, others more prescriptive. In one common usage, modernity defines a particular form of political and economic organization, particularly that associated with the contemporary nation-state and industrial capitalism. In this sense, modern societies are characterized by such features as bureaucratic rationalization, standing national armies, and an economy oriented toward production for commodity markets and reliant on complex technologies and industrial labor discipline. This kind of modernity refers to the presence of particular institutional structures that exist today (though not always in the same way or to the same degree) in every part of the globe.

In contrast to this descriptive sense of modernity, a related but different usage refers to a prescriptive ideal in which the pursuit of modern social forms and institutions is hailed as a movement toward socially valorized goals of "progress," "growth," and "advancement." In this sense, modernity represents a break between past and present as distinctive ways of life, contrasting the achievements and forward-looking potential of modern life against the failings or disadvantages of backward-looking "tradition." Not surprisingly, in many societies both past and present, such ideological constructions of modernity have tended to accompany and support modernity in its more descriptive sense, i.e., the expansion of nation-state political forms and capitalist economies (Foster, 1991; see also Hobsbawm, 1983).[13]

Increasingly, however, contemporary scholars of modernity seek neither to represent it in terms of a particular, objective reality nor to reveal its functions as a purely symbolic system. Rather, what attracts their attention is how structures and symbols of modernity combine to produce new forms of experience. Marshall Berman offers an unusually evocative portrait of this:

> To be modern is to find ourselves in an environment that promises us adventure, power, joy, growth, transformation of ourselves and the world—and, at the same time, that threatens to destroy everything we have, everything we know, everything we are. Modern environments and experiences cut across all boundaries of geography and ethnicity, of class and nationality, of religion and ideology: in this sense, modernity can be said to unite all mankind. But it is a paradoxical unity, a unity of disunity: it pours us all into a maelstrom of perpetual disintegration and renewal, of struggle and contradiction, of ambiguity and anguish. To be modern is to be part of a universe in which, as Marx said, "all that is solid melts into air." (1982:15)

Berman's portrayal of modern experience as both creativity and disruption describes a phenomenon that is at once shared yet is nowhere the same. This "unity of disunity" suggests what a number of scholars have begun to argue: that modernity, however homogeneous it may appear as a global phenomenon, takes on highly varied forms and meanings in any specific context.[14] Experiences of modernity are commonly linked to the structures and ideologies generated by an increasingly global political economy; yet these emerge in different forms and provoke different responses across time and space. What results, as Michael Watts has said, is the "production of . . . new, local modernities" out of the historical experiences and the cultural and symbolic resources available to people in particular settings (Pred & Watts, 1992:18). Modernity in this sense is not singular but multiple. It is not a structure or ideology imposed from above or outside but a process of engagement and local negotiation that is everywhere historically and culturally contingent. Consequently, the concept of modernity, as I employ the term in this study, must be understood to be a specifically Thai modernity.

Even so, there is no particular set of institutions or ideas that clearly define modernity in Thailand. Rather, it is more easily understood as a powerful field of popular discourse and cultural production. The meanings and practices of modernity constitute a discursive arena through which people make claims or express ideas concerning themselves and their society, and about which they may or may not agree.[15] In contemporary Thailand, discourses on modernity permeate much of everyday life. People from all parts of the country and of diverse class backgrounds are familiar with and employ a language of modernity in order to discuss and at times critique directions of social and cultural change.[16] These debates emphasize images and standards of newness and new times (*samay may*), as well as ideas concerning progress (*khwaam caroen*), and development (*kan phatthana*). However, the most prevalent phrase denoting (often divergent) goals or styles associated with modernity is the notion of being "in step with the times" or "up-to-date" (*khwaam pen thansamay*).

A national (and nationalist) rhetoric that celebrates Thai progress and development has had a powerful influence on popular images of and ideas about modernity; nevertheless, the meanings and practices of *thansamay* Thai society are not necessarily experienced or understood in the same way by everyone. For example, members of the urban elite, scholars, and policy makers frequently debate whether national political and economic development has meant too much modernity (i.e., at the expense of traditional values). The nuances of such debates, and their accompanying nostalgia for an authentic Thailand (one that often invokes the simpler ways of an imagined and historically distant peasantry), are often very different from the experiences of modernity with which Thailand's contemporary peasant producers must contend. The images of urban wealth and commodified progress that pervade Thai popular culture establish models of consumption and social status that, however difficult for rural residents to achieve, are impossible to ignore. In particular, the ownership and display of new technologies and consumer commodities are increasingly valued as symbols of modern success and social status throughout Thailand. Rural-urban migration is one vehicle through which women like Nok and their rural families encounter, mediate, and attempt to rework these meanings of modernity in their own lives. Their efforts, as I examine in the following section and in later chapters, often take the particular form of claims to and struggles over identity.

Being *Thansamay*: Identity and the Experience of Thai Modernity

Experiences of modernity, as Berman clearly recognized, are commonly associated with the emergence of new identities and/or the reworking of old ones. This stems from the profound (though always locally specific) ways that the structural and ideological transformations of modern societies alter the everyday lives and perceptions of individual members. Arjun Appadurai has described the rise of "global cultural processes" in these circumstances as effecting a parallel transformation of the social imagination:

> [T]he imagination has become an organized field of social practices, a form of work (both in the sense of labor and a culturally organized practice) and a form of negotiation between sites of agency ("individuals") and globally defined fields of possibility. . . . The imagination is now central to all forms of agency, is itself a social fact, and is the key component of the new global order. (1990:5)

Of course claims for the imagination as a fundamentally new component in human social creativity should not be overdrawn; nevertheless, experiences of modernity for many people—including young Thai migrants—are informed by the availability of newly imagined (and imaginable) identities and social relations. All around the world, new and increasingly global technologies of mass communication have had particularly important and wide-reaching effects on how people think about themselves and their surroundings.[17] As Chapter 5 addresses in more detail, women's rural-urban labor migration is closely tied to the production of such "imagined" possibilities in the dominant Thai culture. In effect, their geographic mobility is informed by what Henrietta Moore has called "fantasies of identity," that is, "ideas about the kind of person one would like to be and the sort of person one would like to be seen to be by others" (1994:66). For young Thai women, the imagined possibilities of migration and urban employment are intricately bound up with culturally produced meanings about and images of Thai modernity.

Ideological constructions of modernity are disseminated to and received by the broader population through various urban- and elite-controlled means of cultural production: commodity markets, mass media, government bureaucracy, standardized school curricula, to name but a few. For example, state agents and other representatives of power and privilege in Thailand exhort rural producers to participate in government programs, to comply with new policies, or support new forms of consumption in order to "develop" (*phatthana*) their communities for the advancement and "progress" (*caroen*) of the society as a whole.[18] Nevertheless, more than a century of state-sponsored programs of modernization and national development has only increased the concentration of wealth and power in urban and elite hands. At the same time, residents of Thailand's agricultural periphery remain marginal figures within the national community; not only are villagers denigrated as supposedly backward and unsophisticated peasants but many face additional difficulties as members of ethno-linguistic or regional minorities. Despite and perhaps because of their common exclusion from the material benefits of economic modernization, many rural farmers must grapple with dominant narratives of national progress as standards of success that few can hope to achieve.

However, as in any interaction with hegemonic cultural forms, there is always some slippage between dominant meanings or ideals and the ways that people encounter and interpret them in everyday life. Such breaks between received meanings and lived realities can provide space for alternate understandings and messages to be produced "from below": that is, for people in subordinate and marginal positions to construct new ideas and to challenge or rework existing ones (Roseberry, 1989:47). In rural Thailand, as elsewhere, these gaps between image and experience offer opportunities for what Aihwa Ong has referred to as "cultural struggle," processes by which people receive and contest dominant cultural "meanings, values and goals" (1991:281). The results may sustain or reproduce existing structures of power but they may also alter popular interpretations of the dominant social order and lead to shifts in the perceived quality of social experience. Such changes are generally subtle, but they have the potential to produce more profound social and cultural transformations.

In this study I am concerned less with dominant portrayals of modernity, as these are formulated in Thailand's arenas of social and political power. Instead, I ask how the meanings and practices of being *thansamay* are received and engaged by subordinate groups. Given their position within the wider society, rural producers and their migrant daughters and sons, have little choice but to participate in the powerful discourse of Thai modernity. While they often do so in ways that reproduce dominant symbolic and social relations, this is not always the case. Ideas about being *thansamay* occupy a central place in the cultural repertoires of young migrants and their rural families, but these are not static concepts; rather, Thai modernity constitutes a strategic field for the production and negotiation of meanings about the world and one's place in it. In the case of women's rural-urban labor mobility, these symbolic strategies and the material practices that they entail almost always concern claims to and conflicts over gendered identities.

Gender and Cultural Struggle

Gender categories present powerful tools for understanding social life in almost every culture. In any given setting, gender constitutes a complex and historically constructed system of beliefs and social relations built on but not determined or limited by the "fact" that (most) human bodies have one of two recognizable sets of sexual organs and that these have different functions in the physical reproduction of the species. The content of gender symbolism, however, varies widely. Most gender systems can be analyzed in terms of basic concepts such as maleness, femaleness, anatomical sex, and sexuality but their cultural elaborations take highly divergent forms and give rise to dramatically different expectations concerning appropriate social identities, roles, and behaviors. Nevertheless, whatever the meanings and values attached to gender categories in any given context, these are generally believed to be not cultural constructs but "natural" or inherent characteristics of human behavior. This naturalized aspect of most gender systems and of the gendered identities they prescribe for social actors may be fertile terrain for conflict and struggle. When new social forms and practices arise, which alter or challenge conventional gender relations and beliefs, the cultural conflicts that result may be felt as profound stresses or tensions either of personal identity and day-to-day relations or within the social order itself.

The construction of gender in Thailand (and indeed throughout Southeast Asia) differs significantly from gender systems that are more familiar to people in Western Europe or North America. In Thailand, as in many Southeast Asian cultures, gender identity does not determine an individual's social identity along rigid or easily predictable lines.[19] Women are excluded from the most culturally celebrated positions of authority and value—ordination into the community of Buddhist monks—and are generally absent from prestigious arenas of political leadership and formal office. However, at the level of everyday interaction in villages like Baan Naa Sakae, men and women as husbands and wives share responsibility for many domestic tasks and farm chores. Practices such as equal inheritance of land by daughters and sons, marriage payments from the groom to the bride's family, and a preference for post-marital residence in the wife's home (at least in the initial stage of a union) give women access to economic and emotional resources that are unusual in many other parts of the world. Scholars have debated the extent to which men and women enjoy complementary or unequal status in Thai society (see Keyes, 1984; Kirsch, 1982, 1985; also Hanks & Hanks, 1963; Van Esterik, 1982a); however, most Thai village ethnographies depict a variety of factors such as relative age, wealth, education, and occupational position as markers of social identity and status that are at least as significant as differential gender roles and expectations.

Although gender distinctions may appear muted in the context of day-to-day social interaction, gender meanings and identity have an important place in northeastern Thai cultural beliefs and practices. This is especially true for the socialization and supervision of young people, and of young women in particular. In Isan communities, gender meanings are manifested subtly but directly through behavioral norms that limit direct physical contact between men and women and emphasize the special need to control the movement of young female bodies (see Chapter 5). These gender-specific body codes make clear associations between spatial mobility and sexual activity. This linkage draws, in turn, on key cultural understandings about the differential moral status of male and female sexuality. In general, spatial mobility is perceived as a natural and appropriate characteristic for men, while women's bodies and their movement are subject to far greater restrictions.

Approached from this perspective, the movement of young women into urban wage work challenges customary gender ideals in rural communities. At one level, the migration of rural women into Bangkok may be seen as appropriate gender behavior—the acts of dutiful daughters upholding their obligations to help support parents and younger siblings. However, employment in the city not only provides young women with access to cash income but also to an experience of independence and self-sufficiency that no previous generation of rural women has ever shared. Consequently, their mobility raises tensions that are absent or much less problematic in the case of migrant sons. Parents and other elders give expression to these conflicts in the form of ongoing fears that urban autonomy will undermine the sexual propriety and moral safety of young women living away from home. These worries are exacerbated by the fact that within the dominant culture, women and women's bodies represent powerful images of modernity and moral degradation. The active, mobile, beautiful, *thansamay* woman is celebrated and promoted in a variety of modern settings—the entertainment media, beauty contests, shopping malls, beauty salons, nightclubs, and cafes; at the same time, many of these contemporary venues are linked directly or indirectly with Thailand's commercial sex industry (Van Esterik, 1988). The widespread portrayal of young women as symbols of modern status and as objects of consumption contributes to feelings of ambivalence toward their movement into urban employment.

Although urban wages are a valued economic resource for many households, women's new geographical mobility and income-earning power challenge the economic and moral authority of parents and of men in general over female productive and reproductive capacities. Whether by their own intent or otherwise, the experience of migration involves both the movers and those left behind in choices about what they want for themselves, their families, and their communities. In practice, most villagers have only a narrow range of options—choosing between employment in domestic service or in a garment-making sweatshop; electing to spend remittances on housing repairs or sending a child to school. Nevertheless, Bangkok-based styles and images of conspicuous consumption permeate Thai society and serve as standards of prestige and success that residents of villages like Baan Naa Sakae find as difficult to ignore as they are to emulate. Living and working in Bangkok brings women like Nok and their families face to face with the commodified meanings and practices of being *thansamay*; the gendered tensions and cultural struggles that result offer insight into not only the reproduction of power and cultural authority in contemporary Thailand but also the ways in which these can be negotiated, contested, and (if only partially or temporarily) transformed. This ethnography examines these processes from the perspectives of peasant producers in Thailand's rural periphery and their mobile daughters, a generation of young women who have seen and experienced Thai modernity at its heart, the Bangkok metropolis.

*T*he chapters that follow develop these issues through ethnographic material gathered during nearly two and a half years of fieldwork in Bangkok and in Baan Naa Sakae. The discussion divides roughly into two sections. The first—Chapters 2, 3, 4, and 5—focuses on the rural setting, the point of origin and for many young women the endpoint of labor mobility. The second part—Chapters 6, 7, and 8—examines the experiences of young migrants in the city, their encounters with the creative disorder, the excitement, and the alienation of life in Bangkok, and the decision of when (or, in some cases whether) to return to their village homes.

Chapter 2 situates the experiences of people in Baan Naa Sakae in relation to the recent history of Thailand as a whole. More than a century of national political and economic transformation has had a profound impact on the lives of people in Baan Naa Sakae. Incorporated as citizens within a newly imagined national state modeled on Central Thai (Bangkok) standards of a "Thai" identity, the village's residents continue to be identified (and to identify themselves) as members of a marginalized regional and ethnic minority (as Lao or Isan people—*khon lao, khon isaan*), subordinate to the hierarchical and often arbitrary authority of a distant Thai state and its agents. At the time of my research, residents still grew the staple crop of glutinous rice primarily for their own consumption, but this did not obscure the deep dependence of Baan Naa Sakae residents on forms of production oriented toward a cash economy—including out-migration for wage labor. Indeed, the economic and political pressures confronting villagers since the early decades of the twentieth century have prompted a sharpening of internal differentiation, as some village households have benefited to a much greater degree while others have lost ground.

Chapter 3 brings us into the heart of Baan Naa Sakae, describing key aspects of community life. The chapter focuses special attention on local consumption practices, particularly as these reveal local residents' encounters with the dominant meanings and standards of Thai modernity. Village residents' basic consumption needs and expectations reflect profound material transformations in the rural economy; yet, along with ceremonial and other periodic household expenditures, they also reveal how dominant discourses of Thai modernity are present in nearly every aspect of community life. A close examination of three arenas of material and symbolic consumption in Baan Naa Sakae—rice, houses, and household ceremonies—illustrates how mass-market commodities are incorporated into village practices. As markers of *thansamay* style and status, commodity items represent not only their owner's material wealth but also an increasingly important form of cultural capital. Commodified images and ideals shape the aspirations and desires of community members, including the decisions by young women and men to enter urban employment.

Chapter 4 examines tensions within Baan Naa Sakae households that contribute to and are amplified by high levels of labor mobility. Ties between parents and children in Isan, as throughout Thailand, are defined by powerful values concerning age-hierarchy and "debts of merit" (*bun khun*). As cash income has become increasingly important to Baan Naa Sakae households, labor migration offers adolescent daughters and sons an important means to demonstrate their gratitude for their elders' sacrifices and to fulfill their obligations to help support parents and siblings. Urban wage work, however, is also desired by rural youth in order to participate in the adventure and modernity of urban life. The new clothes and other signs of urban sophistication displayed by migrant siblings and friends cultivate youthful desires not to be left behind by their peers. The contradictions and conflicts arising between household bases of identity and the powerful, seductive standards of Thai modernity create a series of tensions and expectations that combine to encourage the city-ward movement of village youth. Nevertheless, young women's mobility raises anxieties for parents; these concerns are absent, or much less problematic, in the case of migrant sons.

Shifting understandings about gender and gendered bodies underlie both the migration decisions of rural women and the ambivalent responses of their village families. Chapter 5 examines cultural constructions of gender in Baan Naa Sakae, focusing on pervasive discourses of and about gendered bodies and their mobility. Isan villagers, like most Thais, recognize a sharp sexual double standard: They accept and even value sexual experience in men, but view women's sexuality as a source of moral ambivalence and potential danger. Consequently, appropriate gender roles and behaviors seek to restrict physical contact between young women and men by constraining the spatial mobility of daughters, keeping them more closely tied to the parental household and village community. However, glamorous images of modern women and mobile urban lifestyles dominate Thai popular media and represent powerful competing models of gender identity for many rural youth. Motivated in part by these images of *thansamay* femininity, the movement of young women into urban wage work poses new challenges to customary gender ideals and identities.

Chapter 6 shifts the focus of analysis from the countryside to the city, examining the obstacles and opportunities that migrants encounter as neophyte wage laborers. While touching on the conditions faced by domestic servants (and, to a lesser extent, commercial sex workers) the chapter concentrates on industrial employment, particularly textile manufacturing, which has been the primary destination for young women moving from Baan Naa Sakae. Here the aspirations and hopes of rural youth collide immediately with the chaotic reality of city life. The exploitation and structural discrimination that women face within the urban labor market limit their choices significantly. As new forms of labor discipline and authority in the workplace confront popular portrayals of women and women's bodies as symbols of progress and modernity, young migrants in Bangkok encounter a series of sharp dilemmas.

Chapters 7 and 8 look at the responses of women to their experiences while in the city. As in the village, migrants' consumption practices serve to highlight the power that images and ideas about modernity exert on women's own assessments of the urban sojourn. Chapter 7 explores migrants' decisions about how and where to spend their wages. Migrants' consumption activities reflect the underlying tensions of their urban employment as they try to pursue newly imagined identities as modern women while still upholding economic and moral responsibilities to rural kin. As consumers, workers attempt to balance competing demands on their earnings but can rarely achieve more than a partial and temporary resolution.

The contradictions of the migration process emerge most clearly in young women's ideas about and the choices they make regarding marriage and sexuality, the subject of Chapter 8. While some elect to stay in the city permanently—sometimes to marry there, but just as likely remaining single—most women prefer to plan a return home at the point of marriage. The ambivalence young women express about their time in the city reflects the gap between dominant meanings of modernity in Thailand and young women's lived experiences of labor mobility and wage employment. Ultimately, however, the choices migrants make in attempting to resolve these differences tend to reproduce rather than challenge the structures and symbols that underlie their marginalization and exploitation within the wider society.

Finally, the last chapter addresses the broader implications of this case study. Although rooted in the particular historical and cultural dynamics of the Thai context, young women's experiences of agency, accommodation, and struggle as Bangkok wage workers suggest the role that ideologies of modernity and gender identity may play in the reproduction and discipline of cheap, migrant labor in similar contexts of rapid industrialization. The lives and aspirations of the migrant workers I knew in Bangkok and Baan Naa Sakae speak to the ways that experiences of subordination may both constrain and open new avenues for thinking about and acting in the world. Their stories illuminate the complex articulations and disjunctures between the "local" and the "global," points of tension and transformation that are increasingly and unavoidably central features of our lives, wherever and whoever we may be.

Modernity, Identity, and the Ethnographic Experience

Before turning to the stories of Baan Naa Sakae and its residents, I must first situate myself in relation to the research process and the ideas I present in this book. Ethnographic research is always an extremely personal endeavor and its outcome—an attempt to understand "other" lives and practices—is necessarily filtered through the ethnographer's own peculiar interests, emotional responses, and cultural sensitivities. This study will no doubt reveal as much about me as it does about migrants in Bangkok and their rural families in Isan; however, I hope that this ethnography is more than a disguised confessional or autobiography. Ethnographic knowledge is neither purely objective nor subjective but, rather, intersubjective. It is less a product formed and finished by the participant-observer than it is a process of communication in which both "anthropologist" and "informants" seek to establish relationships, define expectations, and negotiate the ways and meanings of their interactions. Fieldwork, therefore, engages people in the construction and interpretation of their own and others' identities (see, for example, Kondo, 1990). The arguments I present here are shaped by the shifting narratives of these mutual encounters, as I and the people I met attempted to express who we thought we were and how we perceived each other. This book constitutes one part of that unfinished dialogue, an ongoing process of definition and interpretation of self and other.

My acquaintance with the people of Baan Naa Sakae and others discussed in these pages unfolded like the steps of an intricate dance, a constant drawing together and moving apart, as we sought mutually intelligible and acceptable positions of interaction. And it was through this process that my attention was directed to discourses on modernity as recurrent themes in local understandings. At first glance, these issues seemed tied to my own presence in Baan Naa Sakae; yet, over the course of a year, I came to see that images and ideas about modernity were more pervasive concerns for community members. References to and discussions of *samay may* and *thansamay* ways were constant features of my interactions with people from Baan Naa Sakae, both in the village and in Bangkok. In part, this reflected my obvious status as a white, well-educated, presumably wealthy foreigner (*farang*) from an urbanized, already "developed" country. To many people in the village, I was a living representative of the prestige and possibilities that being *thansamay* could entail.

My entry into Baan Naa Sakae—which was facilitated by an introduction from a local community development organization—was greeted in much these terms: Many residents viewed my interest in studying their community as a sign of its growing progress. Not only was I a symbol of modernity but my presence was felt by many to increase local access to sources of expertise and material resources which could promote community economic and social development. To my own way of thinking, I had little to offer the community in return for their patience and hospitality beyond dispensing small amounts of cold medicines, contributing as generously as possible to ceremonial funds and events, and teaching an occasional English class at the village primary school. My halting efforts at this last task were received by the local teachers and the community with far more grace and appreciation than they deserved. However, my visibility as a foreigner was a valued resource in and of itself, a kind of bargaining chip that community leaders could use to increase their own access to state officials and economic patrons in order to negotiate greater disbursements of government funds and other desired benefits. Consequently, I received a steady stream of unsolicited (and, to my mind, inconvenient and at times annoying) invitations to attend a wide range of official and semi-official events and ceremonies. These requests came on occasion from more powerful officials and people of influence in the surrounding district but mainly from more prominent and ambitious members of the village who (it seemed to me) hoped my presence would increase their own status and therefore access to local authorities. I, in turn, developed a strong aversion to my identification as a modern *farang*, not the least because it was of such advantage to more privileged community members.[20]

My *farang*-ness also set an initial baseline of social, cultural, and emotional distance between myself and everyone else in the community. A few residents found this the only identity to which they could relate and addressed me throughout my stay as *acaan* ("professor") or more often *hua naa* ("leader" or "boss"), the same title given to community development workers and other outside "experts" with whom villagers must deal from time to time. However, with most members of the village and especially with those who became closer friends, points of commonality did emerge in our encounters to serve as a basis for sympathy and communication. The particular circumstances of my presence in Baan Naa Sakae—I was alone and far from my home—offered clear parallels to the experiences of many residents who remarked again and again how my experience was "just like when I [or my son, daughter, or spouse] was away" working in Bangkok or elsewhere. Other aspects of my situation—such as linguistic difficulties, travel experiences, homesickness, and the concern my own parents felt during my absence—were seized on by myself and others as similar points of shared knowledge.

In the course of my residence in Baan Naa Sakae, my status as a relatively young (I was then in my late twenties) and unmarried woman became the basis for a mutual effort to define me as a "daughter of our village." This was a self I felt more at ease with than "rich foreigner"; it was agreeable to many village residents, too, since it provided them with the authority as my elders and "parents" to enlist my cooperation in and contributions to community events and ceremonies. Ultimately, of course, distance and difference remained. I was always and inescapably *farang*, but more important, unlike permanent residents of Baan Naa Sakae, my active participation in the community was defined from the start as temporary—I would be leaving after a year. Indeed, the statement frequently made in my presence—that I was *khon baan hao* ("a person [from] our community")—was at least partly aimed at instilling a sense of obligation on my part toward the interests of the community and its members.

This book represents one component of that obligation, both to the people of Baan Naa Sakae and the many others both in Isan and Bangkok—scholars, officials, staff members of non-governmental organizations, and especially labor migrants—without whose patience and generosity this research could never have been completed. One aim of this study is to represent the needs and experiences of those in Thailand—young rural women and their families—whose voices are rarely heard in debates about social change and its consequences. In these pages, I have sought to convey some portion of the rich experiences, the emotionally textured contexts, and the multilayered conversations that shaped our interactions. Their stories attest to the strength and creativity of people seeking to forge meaningful lives amid complex and often distressing circumstances.

CHAPTER 2

Village and Nation

=+

Baan Naa Sakae

I saw the village of Baan Naa Sakae for the first time on a November morning in 1989. Approaching by motorcycle along the gravel access road, my initial view was of a dense cluster of wooden houses, their tin roofs bristling faintly with television antennas. Rice paddies stretched away from the village in all directions; ripening grain shimmered in the day's heat. The shallow bottomland rose gradually into the sloping, irregular contours of upland fields; the leafy tops of cassava plants and tall, thin stalks of kenaf (a plant grown for its sturdy fibers and used in making jute and burlap), edged up to stands of trees and tangled brush covering the few small hills on the horizon less than a kilometer away. The road ran along the western edge of the community past the grounds of Baan Naa Sakae's Buddhist temple (*wat*) and headed south toward several other villages. A half kilometer beyond the *wat*, a stretch of tall trees and a brick gate marked the entrance to the grounds of the village primary school.

A community of just under one thousand people, Baan Naa Sakae differed little from the nearly two dozen villages I visited in central Isan while searching for a rural base for my research.[1] Members of almost every household identified rice farming as their main occupation, although this was supplemented in most cases by cash cropping and, more often than not, by wage labor. Wage labor was predominantly linked to labor migration, especially by the community's young people, unmarried women and men who most often sought work in Bangkok and a few other urban centers. The decision to make Baan Naa Sakae my primary research site came about as a result of these similarities rather than because of its particular or unique features.

FIGURE 2. Harvested rice fields at the edge of Baan Naa Sakae.

The deciding factor, as it happened, was the availability of housing in Baan Naa Sakae for myself and my research assistant, Mon.[2] On the southern edge of the village stood two wooden houses, built as teachers' residences for the local school. One of these was empty. In December 1989, with the permission of the village headman and the local school principal, Mon and I moved our belongings into this small two-room structure.[3] Baan Naa Sakae would be our home for the better part of the next year.

Thailand's northeast region, Isan, comprises a third of the country's geographic territory as well as a third of its population. The large majority of the region's inhabitants speak a range of dialects that are more closely related to the speech of lowland Laos than to that of central Thailand (though still part of the same Tai language family) and reside in small clustered villages like Baan Naa Sakae. The Northeast has long been perceived both by Thai and outside observers as the country's most impoverished region and the one most isolated from the rapid growth of Bangkok's booming industrial economy. But during the time I spent in Baan Naa Sakae, it was impossible to think of it as a community on the periphery either of Thai society or the national economy.

In contrast to the economic and cultural isolation that characterizes images of Isan in both Thai popular culture and national policy discussions, the people I came to know in Baan Naa Sakae were deeply engaged in relations and activities linking them to much wider national and even international political and economic arenas. For example, most village households were involved in some form of cash-crop production, particularly of cassava and kenaf, for sale on the world market. Moreover, temporary and circulating migration to Bangkok—especially by unmarried youth—involved nearly three-quarters of the community's 200 households. In addition, almost one-half of the community's adult men had either worked or attempted to work overseas as contract laborers. However, the benefits and the risks of these activities had significantly different effects on village families. As Chapter 3 reports in more detail, a few households in Baan Naa Sakae enjoyed substantial wealth while others struggled simply to get by.

Despite noticeable economic disparities within the community, the residents of Baan Naa Sakae were well aware that they lived in what was considered the nation's poorest and least "developed" (*phatthana*) region. Agricultural yields for the region were among the lowest in the nation, due in part to generally poor, sandy, often saline soils. Regional rainfall was also irregular; Isan as a whole has the highest incidence of drought of any region in the country. Baan Naa Sakae farmers estimated that three years out of every seven were dry years, resulting in reduced rice harvests for many village families.[4] Furthermore, although peasant communities in other parts of Thailand—particularly in the central delta around Bangkok—were already producing rice for international markets in the late nineteenth century, cash cropping in Isan (primarily dry-field crops such as cassava and kenaf) did not become widespread until after World War II (Keyes, 1967; Hanks, 1972; Hong, 1984). Even in the late 1980s and 1990s, Baan Naa Sakae households continued to grow the staple crop of glutinous rice primarily for their own use.

This persistence of staple rice agriculture as a noncommercial activity fueled popular images of Isan as an economic backwater. Despite the importance of cash crops to most Isan households, Bangkok observers noted the region's lack of a significant industrial base and an average per-capita income that consistently trailed all other parts of the country. On these counts Isan certainly appeared to have little in common with the frenzied economic growth taking place in other parts of Thailand in the late 1980s and early 1990s, especially in and around the capital city.[5]

People in Baan Naa Sakae, however, were sharply aware of their links to distant places and powers. Basic features of everyday life—such as cash-

FIGURE 3. Baan Naa Sakae farmers transplant rice seedlings into a rain-flooded field.

crop production for world markets and radio and television broadcasts—collapsed the physical distance between rural residents and centers of power in Bangkok and the world beyond. The frequent and lengthy absences of family members—daughters, sons, husbands, or wives—who were away working in Bangkok or elsewhere gave particular force to local awareness of connections to the wider society. But through these connections, villagers also confronted their status within the dominant urban culture as "country bumpkins" (*khon baan nôôk,* literally "people on the outside") living on the nation's cultural and geographic periphery far removed from the *thansamay* achievements of urban Thai life.

If national standards of "progress" (*khwaam caroen*) and "development" (*kan phatthana*) tended to exclude rural Isan, members of Baan Naa Sakae were nonetheless deeply engaged with notions of *thansamay* progress and prestige. In particular, the attractions and necessities of *thansamay* commodity consumption played a crucial role in community life and underlay many migration decisions. As I argue in Chapters 3 and 4, Bangkok's status as the center of Thai modernity was an important factor attracting young labor migrants to the city. Nevertheless, this symbolic hierarchy reflects a long history of rural-urban relations in Thailand, a history marked by long-standing inequalities between Bangkok as the site of elite culture and political authority on the one hand, and the rural countryside, the home of the country's major- ity population of small peasant producers on the other. Beginning in the late nineteenth century, fundamental shifts in the Thai political economy both multiplied and intensified the ties between rural communities like Baan Naa Sakae and the wider Thai society. Over the course of the twentieth century, the residents of ethnic-Lao communities throughout rural Isan experienced a collective transformation into Thai citizens, subordinate to the centralized authority of the Thai nation-state. A closer look at this history is essential to understanding both the high rates of labor out-migration from Baan Naa Sakae in the 1980s and 1990s and the meanings given this mobility by migrants and those left behind.

A Century of Transformation

The territorial and political entity known as "Thailand" is in many ways a modern invention. Until the mid-nineteenth century, Siam, a kingdom cen- tered in the Chao Phraya River valley, was a dynastic power not unlike other mainland Southeast Asian polities. Ruling from their city-court center of Bangkok, the Chakri monarchs of Siam claimed cosmological and temporal authority (backed by military strength) over a broad hierarchy of smaller statelets and principalities. These weaker local powers had their own princes or strongmen rulers who owed yearly tribute payments to the Siamese kings. Tribute demands took the form of either corvée labor service (including mili- tary conscription), owed by the adult male population, or annual shipments to Bangkok of valued agricultural or forest products. Royal authority ema- nating from Bangkok (or from Ayuthaya and Sukhothai, the court-city cen- ters of earlier Siamese kingdoms) was based less on direct control of specific territories than on a ruler's power to command and, when necessary, compel the loyalty and tribute offerings of local lords (*cao*), particularly in regions more distant from the court center, to Bangkok's overrule. Commoners (*phray*), who worked the land, produced the crops to supply tribute payments, and filled the ranks of military conscripts, did so not out of a perceived citi- zenship in a Thai or Siamese nation but through personalistic ties (including various forms of servitude, debt bondage, and slavery) to specific overlords who had their own place in a wider patronage hierarchy. The transformation of these linked polities into the contemporary Thai nation-state—what Benedict Anderson has termed an "imagined community" of ethnic-national citizenship within a sharply bounded territory—only came about in the wake of relatively recent challenges to the sovereignty of indigenous Southeast Asian rulers (Anderson, 1991; Thongchai, 1994).

During the nineteenth century, expanding European interests in Southeast Asia posed new threats to indigenous rulers and state formations throughout the region. Pressed on one side by the British in Malaya and Burma and by the French in Indochina (today's Vietnam, Laos, and Cambodia) on the other, Siamese rulers confronted a form of geopolitics predicated on clear and definable borders where none had existed before. The Chakri dynasty succeeded in evading European conquest—the only indigenous Southeast Asian monarchy to do so—but to preserve their sovereignty Bangkok's rulers oversaw a radical political transformation, from a geographically fluid dynastic polity to the territorially based nation-state, or what Thongchai Winichakul (1994) has called the "geo-body" of the nation.

Beginning in the mid-1800s, the Chakri monarchy embarked on an ambitious program of administrative reform. Wary of possible European colonial designs on Siam, King Mongkut (r. 1851–1868) and his successor King Chulalongkorn (r. 1868–1910) oversaw the comprehensive restructuring of state administration. These reforms were modeled after Western bureaucratic institutions, and European advisors often played important roles in their design (Hong, 1984; Wyatt, 1982).[6] By the early 1900s the outlines of the modern nation-state were in place: a centralized bureaucracy staffed by salaried civil servants, a standing army based on universal male conscription, a codified legal and judicial system, and the abolition of slavery.[7] During this same period of administrative reform, rapidly expanding trade relations with both China and European powers prompted the Siamese Crown to develop an extensive system of taxation over local commercial and export trade. The right to collect different taxes was allocated to powerful nobles and followers of the Siamese Court. These "tax farms" ensured a steady flow of cash into the Crown treasury and were also profitable for the collectors, who retained a portion of the funds they raised in return for their services. Tax farm revenues boomed, and the Crown treasury came to rely less and less on the tributary system of forced labor and payments in kind funneled through intermediary nobles. This weakened the hold of local aristocrats over peasant producers and freed many of the latter to move into new territories to open frontier lands for agricultural and commercial production.

These effects were felt initially and most rapidly in the rice lands of the Chao Phraya River delta provinces surrounding Bangkok. By the 1870s, this river basin was developing into one of the premier rice-producing areas of Southeast Asia. Rice became the primary export commodity of the Siamese economy. A more independent peasantry provided the centralizing state with an alternate tax base (a head tax on small producers) thereby enabling the Crown to reduce its reliance on both tax farms and the powerful families that had controlled the most important of these (Hong, 1984; Pasuk & Baker, 1995:95–109).

Toward the end of the nineteenth century, as they consolidated power over what is today the central region of Thailand, the Chakri rulers began to extend the same "modernizing" administrative reforms into outlying territories, challenging and ultimately destroying the semi-autonomous bases of power for local lords and nobility in these outlying regions. Among these peripheral zones was the predominantly Lao-speaking northeastern territory, known today as "Isan."[8] This region attracted increasing attention from Siam's rulers during the 1800s but it was not until the early twentieth century that Isan residents felt the full force of Thailand's bureaucratizing rule.

Bordered to the north and east by the Mekong River and to the west and south by low mountains (the latter crossing into present-day Cambodia), Isan forms an expanse of uneven terrain known as the Khorat Plateau. An area of sparse population, the Khorat Plateau remained largely ignored by surrounding state powers until settlement in the region began to rise sometime in the seventeenth century.[9] Although some of these settlers were Thai-speakers who moved into the region from the south, many more were ethnic Lao moving across the Mekong River to find new land. Settlement was slow and only gradually expanded into the interior of the Plateau (Keyes, 1976:46–47). Today descendents of these pioneers constitute the region's majority population along with smaller pockets of Khmer-speaking groups and other ethnically distinct minorities.

Prior to the twentieth century, political organization in the Khorat Plateau took the form of small domains (*müang*), each consisting of a local lord (*cao*) and his followers, perhaps a few thousand people. The latter owed their lord regular tribute payments either of agricultural produce or of corvée labor service (sometimes both). The *cao* passed on a portion of this production to his own overlords, most often rulers in or loyal to the court in Siam. The political loyalties of these small principalities became a point of concern to the rulers in Bangkok in the early 1800s, when the vassal states of Vientiane and Campasak (parts of present-day Laos) sought to escape Siamese domination and attempted to extend their own authority over the Khorat Plateau. In the late 1820s, Bangkok dealt a crushing military defeat to these defiant Lao states, sacked the city of Vientiane and forcibly resettled much of the populace loyal to Vientiane's rulers across the Mekong into Isan. Bangkok further strengthened its authority over the area by granting dozens of new *müang* to local nobles and their kin who had supported Bangkok against the Lao princes. These families received their authority from the king in Bangkok, so they owed allegiance (and annual tribute) directly to the Crown (Keyes, 1976:47–50). Around the turn of the century, however, the Crown began to extend to the Northeast the same administrative reforms it had begun in the central part of the country.

In 1893, the system of semi-autonomous domains was replaced by a series of administrative units dividing the region into three "circles" or *monthon*.[10] Each *monthon* was further subdivided into a four-tier hierarchy that remains the basic structure of local administration today: provinces (*cangwat*), districts (*amphoe*), subdistricts (*tambon*) and villages (*muubaan*). In the process, the rulers of the former *müang* lost their power as independent lords, although some moved into positions within the Thai civil service, for example, as provincial governors or district heads. Though still wielding authority, these new *khaaratchakan* (civil servants) were subject to direct supervision by Bangkok officials; they also received fixed salaries rather than, as in the past, retaining a portion of the tribute and taxes they had collected for the Crown.

This extension of centralized control over the Northeast was aided substantially by new forms of transportation and communication. Railway construction reached the town of Nakhon Ratchasima (at the southern edge of the Khorat Plateau) in 1900; it continued northward to Khon Kaen by 1933 and eastward to Ubol Ratchathani by 1928. Long-distance travel in the region was no longer restricted to ox-cart caravans or those on foot. In addition, telegraph services were available in some parts of the Northeast beginning in the early 1890s and continued to expand rapidly thereafter (Keyes, 1967: 18–19). Nevertheless, Bangkok's increased presence in the region did not proceed without resistance. The most dramatic response to new patterns of state control occurred in 1902 with the widespread millenarian uprising known as the Holy Men's Rebellion. Some of the leaders of this very loosely organized rebellion were members of local ruling families whose power was threatened by the new administrative reforms (Pasuk and Baker, 1995:227–228; Chattip, 1984). Their followers, however, included many hundreds of ordinary peasants hard hit by the imposition of new cash taxes. Not surprisingly, the superior forces and arms of Bangkok troops, aided by newly opened railroad and telegraph lines of communication, soon crushed open opposition. Although small revolts recurred occasionally to annoy state forces over the next few decades, they posed no serious threats to the absorption of the region and its inhabitants into a national system of administration.

In establishing a centralized, bureaucratic basis for governing their kingdom, Siamese rulers laid the groundwork for the eventual demise of the absolute monarchy. Growing numbers of Western-educated military leaders and other high-ranking civil servants came to resent the concentration of ministerial and fiscal power in the hands of royal princes and a few powerful noble families. In 1932, a group of educated commoners took over the state in a swift and bloodless coup. After some initial uncertainty, they proclaimed their continuing loyalty to the Chakri Crown but now in the form of a constitutional monarchy. The country's new leaders continued many of the political and economic policies of their royal predecessors, moving to further centralize state administration and expanding the civil service (Wyatt, 1982). Though adopting certain aspects of European-styled electoral democracy, for many decades real power rested in the hands of a series of military strongmen.[11]

In 1939 the country's new leaders replaced the name "Siam" with a new national identity: "Thailand." This change in name made explicit the shift in political authority from the absolute power of Siam's dynastic rulers to the imagined community of a nation-state governed by and for the Thai people (Anderson, 1991; Thongchai, 1994). However, the shift in name from Siam to Thailand signaled a projected rather than an actual ethnic-national polity. The population of the former Siam was diverse, including not only groups— such as Lao (Isan), Shan, and various other Tai-language speakers[12]—related by custom and language to the central Thai, but also significant numbers of Chinese, Khmer, Mon, Malay, and a host of other minorities. These latter groups were most populous in the more remote uplands along Thailand's northern and western borders. Moreover, much of this ethnically and linguistically diverse population had only recently been made subjects of Bangkok's direct rule, and their experiences of state authority remained that of an autocratic but often distant power. For many, if not most of its citizens, the "Thai nation," as an object of personal loyalty and identification, was a new concept. However, important guidelines for building a "national" community were already in place. During his reign from 1910 to 1925, the sixth Chakri monarch, King Vajiravudh, vigorously promoted a vision of ethnic Thai nationalism focusing on the symbolic triad of "Nation, Religion, and King" (*chaat, satsana, phra mahakasat*). This influential formulation neatly codified a nationalist ideology that had begun to emerge under the centralizing policies of his predecessor, King Chulalongkorn. But the developing rhetoric of Thai nationalism at court and within government circles spread more slowly to the rest of the country. Following their overthrow of the absolute monarchy in 1932, Thailand's new leaders used expanding communication and transportation technologies and, with particular success, the gradual extension of mandatory primary schooling to promote nationalist sentiments among the country's dispersed and predominantly rural population. This inculcation of a national identity has remained an important policy of the Thai state throughout this century. However, from the perspective of residents in Baan Naa Sakae and villages like it, official instruction in national loyalties has been accompanied by other equally powerful lessons concerning their marginal status as peasants (*chaaw baan*) and peripheral *khon baan nôôk* amid the modernizing and development successes of the nation as a whole. In the remainder of this chapter, Baan Naa Sakae's own story illustrates these conflicting dynamics within the Thai nation-state's extension of direct authority over its rural citizens.

Early Settlement and State Authority

Baan Naa Sakae was founded in the early 1900s, just as the Siamese Crown began to extend centralized forms of administration into its northeastern territories. Initially, five families cleared land for a permanent settlement at the site of an old hunting camp. Homesteading of this sort was a common settlement practice throughout turn-of-the-century Isan, prompted both by a growing scarcity of land in the most fertile and accessible areas of the region and new legal restrictions on land tenure—such as the Land Law of 1901 defining land as a legal commodity to which access could be controlled through a system of title deeds (Keyes, 1976:54–55). These pressures may have provided all the motivation necessary for the founders of Baan Naa Sakae to seek out new farm land in a more remote location; however, it is possible that the original settlement of Baan Naa Sakae took place in an effort to avoid the attention of state officials. According to some villagers, Baan Naa Sakae had its beginning when a "bandit" (*nakleng*) and his kin made the hunting camp their permanent home in an attempt, though ultimately unsuccessful, to escape government pursuit.

Whatever the motivation of these initial pioneers, they were joined within a few years by more settlers. Soon a dozen or so households formed the core of a small community. Maeyaay Lin,[13] at age seventy-seven, recalled that her family moved to Baan Naa Sakae sometime before 1920. Traveling by ox-cart from a village about twenty kilometers away, their journey required two days' hard travel through the forest, a trip that now takes less than thirty minutes by car or bus. Despite this distance, Baan Naa Sakae was quickly incorporated within the administrative hierarchy of the emerging national state. Already in 1914, only a few years after the first arrival of permanent settlers, local officials appointed a village headman (*phuuyaaybaan*). Like *phuuyaaybaan* in the present, Baan Naa Sakae's first headman was responsible for keeping community records, assisting government officials in the collection of the annual head taxes (now land taxes), recruitment for corvée labor service (now military conscription), as well as arresting bandits, thieves, and other troublemakers. After 1932, with the transition to constitutional government, the *phuuyaaybaan* was made an elected office initially for life, later until age sixty. Though headmen could and did voice local concerns to state authorities, their lengthy terms of service often meant that office holders' own interests lay in encouraging local compliance with state policies and programs. In this manner, the *phuuyaaybaan* linked Baan Naa Sakae to the full hierarchy of state agents and institutions emanating from the centers of national power in Bangkok.

Schooling for Citizenship

By the middle years of the century, mandatory primary education had begun to forge even more direct links between residents of Baan Naa Sakae and the wider nation. In addition to instruction in basic literacy and numeracy, the standardized curriculum of the state-run village school emphasized respect for new symbols of Thai nationalism and the responsibilities of loyal citizens. The state's goal of universal primary education was first promulgated in the 1920s but it took many years for implementation to reach a significant proportion of the country. As in communities throughout the country, Baan Naa Sakae's Buddhist temple served as the initial site of instruction; Buddhist monks were the first teachers.

Historically, village *wat* were centers of education, providing villagers with the tools of literacy and instruction in Buddhist doctrine; however, access was largely limited to boys and men who sought ordination as novices and monks. Beginning in the 1930s, only a decade or so after the residents of Baan Naa Sakae had established their own *wat*, the Thai state entrusted village temples and their resident monks with the task of instructing rural children of both sexes. The state-mandated curriculum was divided into four grade levels and included both secular and religious subjects. By mid-century, lay teachers and monks were working together in the village school, holding classes in the *wat*'s large *saalaa* or ceremonial hall.

In the 1960s, a separate school building was erected on the village's southern outskirts, ending direct involvement of the local *wat* and monks in the secular education of Baan Naa Sakae children. A decade later, the number of mandatory years of instruction rose from four to six; as of 1990, Baan Naa Sakae's primary school boasted a full staff of eight professional teachers in charge of over 150 children in six grades and an optional kindergarten year.

Thai schools serve as powerful instruments defining the status and position of rural producers within the national hierarchy, inculcating attitudes of deference to state authority, while also distinguishing the practices of rural "tradition" from contemporary values of "development," "progress," and other goals of the "modern" Thai nation.[14] In the words of one observer, state-run education plays a key role "in preparing villagers to accept a subordinate position in the centralized bureaucratic world of the Thai nation-state" (Keyes, 1991:89). In Baan Naa Sakae the success of this drive was clear. Although village residents referred to their local language and customs as "Lao" or "Isan," their pride of membership in a particular community (*khon baan hao*, "people of our village") and in a distinctive cultural region (*khon isaan*, "isan people") existed alongside clear assertions of identity as Thai citizens (*khon chuat thai*).[15]

Students in Baan Naa Sakae, as in schools throughout the country, enter a powerful crucible for the formation of attitudes and beliefs about what it means to be "Thai." The standardized national curriculum provides students with early and repeated lessons in the symbols of Thai nationalism and the meanings of Thai citizenship. Lessons in civic studies and Thai history emphasize the symbolic triad of Nation, Religion, and King (*chaat, satsana, phra mahakasat*). These are reinforced by daily rituals of homage as when each morning students line up by class to raise the national flag, recite Buddhist precepts, and sing the national anthem. Teachers at the village school instruct the children of Baan Naa Sakae from an early age in these unifying expressions of their "Thai" citizenship, while enforcing a style of interaction that emphasizes the deference of students to all in authority above them. As Charles Keyes has noted for Thai schooling more generally, students soon internalize standards of deferential behavior that serve as a powerful model for future dealings with official figures and state agents throughout their adult lives (Keyes, 1991).

In varied ways, students at Baan Naa Sakae's school learn the subordination of village-based knowledge and skills to national forms of expression and sources of authority. Among the most important lessons learned by young students is the primacy of standard (i.e., Central or Bangkok) Thai, the language of the state and of urban society, over the Lao tones and vocabulary of their local speech. As in every Thai school, Central Thai is the language of instruction in Baan Naa Sakae and its use in the classroom is strictly enforced—although I often observed teachers and students alike speaking Lao in more informal situations, at recess, or outside of school hours.

This privileged status of Central Thai over the more familiar speech of family and community life is also reinforced in numerous settings outside the village. Encounters with institutions or agents of the national society—for example, government officials, bank officers, teachers, doctors—almost always require an ability to communicate in standard Thai. Any documents involved in such interactions—tax receipts, loan papers or other contracts, instructions for the use of medicines, newspapers, and so forth—are printed in standard Thai (and often employ a vocabulary far beyond that conveyed in a primary education). These linguistic demands are especially clear to those who travel outside the Northeast, including labor migrants, who have to use the standard dialect or risk being misunderstood if not actively ridiculed for their ignorance as *khon baan nôôk*.

State Regulation and Everyday Life

The authority of the Thai state and the emphasis placed on a national Thai identity for all citizens is repeated in numerous ways for Baan Naa Sakae residents long after their school years are behind them. Pictures of the King and Queen adorn the walls of almost every home and every day begins with the headman's broadcast of the Thai national anthem over the village loudspeaker. Other instances convey similar messages (some subtly, some more forcefully), underlining the subordinate position of rural producers within a national hierarchy of power and status. Like all Thai citizens, residents of Baan Naa Sakae are subject to state systems of documentation, including household registration papers recording births, deaths, and changes in permanent residence; and national identity cards required for all citizens over fifteen years of age. The economic activities and livelihood of village members are also bounded by legal restrictions and obligations to the state. In some cases these obligations are specific to particular ages or statuses, as in the annual lottery draft of twenty-one-year-old men for military service. The state also defines rights and access to land through a complex system of land deeds and titles ranging from simple use rights to full ownership.

At the time of my research, land regulations affected residents of Baan Naa Sakae in several ways. In 1954, more than a generation after the village was founded, the state designated a large area in Mahasarakham province as "national reserve forest" (*paa sanguan*). This area included land surrounding Baan Naa Sakae and several neighboring communities. Even though, by the late 1980s, little of the original forest remained, the reserve forest designation meant that no full title deeds (*chanot thii din*) could be issued despite residents' long history of settlement and cultivation. Rather, villagers first had to apply for a limited use rights deed, which could later be upgraded to a limited property title (*nôô sôô saam*). Many of these latter documents were issued to Baan Naa Sakae families during the mid-1970s (under the reform government of Kukrit Pramot). In 1987, district records reported that approximately 80 percent of Baan Naa Sakae land was held under *nôô sôô saam* titles. These titles were transferable by sale or inheritance but had not always been acceptable as collateral for private bank loans. About one-half of Baan Naa Sakae farmers were members of the government-run Bank of Agriculture and Agricultural Cooperatives from which, as *nôô sôô saam* holders, they could borrow for some purposes at relatively low interest rates; however, many in the community continued to rely on more informal credit, often extended by wealthy district merchants whose interest charges were much higher— commonly 5 percent to 10 percent per month.

During my time in Baan Naa Sakae, local residents were also subject to a recently imposed ban on forest logging. Officially designed to halt large-scale depletion of timber resources around the country, the ban nevertheless made the customary use of remaining forest areas around Baan Naa Sakae subject to state oversight and punishment. Suddenly, felling trees to use as lumber for house building or repairs, or to make charcoal for daily cooking needs, was potentially illegal and subject to fines by the Forestry Department. But these and other punitive sanctions that the state imposed on common village activities—such as gambling, or brewing homemade rice beer and liquor—were not always equally applied. Many residents spoke openly of their own or others' efforts to deflect state fines or avoid the more onerous duties of citizenship through ties to influential patrons, perhaps a wealthy merchant in the district town, or by making strategic and often substantial "gifts" to key officials. For example, in 1990, families who wished to buy their sons' names out of the draft lottery had to come up with a significant sum of money, about 6,000 *baht* ($240 U.S.) or the price of an adult water buffalo.

Periodic visits to Baan Naa Sakae by state officials offered further striking illustrations of the hierarchy of power and influence that marked most relations between residents of Baan Naa Sakae and representatives of the Thai state. During my research, a number of state agents came through Baan Naa Sakae: district agricultural and community development officers, police, supervisors of local elections, education officials, and more. The public rhetoric of these officials commonly urged local cooperation with government programs and policies in the name of national "development" (*phatthanaa*) and "progress" (*caroen*). When speaking to village gatherings, many officials employed a vocabulary of "democracy" and "participation," but these expressions were contradicted both by the fact that most spoke in the authority-laden tones of Central Thai rather than in the local Isan dialect, and by long-standing patterns of deferential behavior that characterized interactions between villagers and civil servants. Community leaders often prepared special refreshments (including store-bought beer and alcohol) in advance of official visits. In one case, Baan Naa Sakae's recently elected headman received word that assistants to the District Governor would be arriving to address community members that evening. He scrambled to find a neighbor who would sell him a chicken so that his wife could prepare a special meal, paying a high price because of the short notice, and rushed to inform the members of the village council. The dozen or so council members waited in the headman's house for several hours but the delegation never showed up. Finally, they ate the chicken themselves. The district delegation did come to Baan Naa Sakae a few days later but offered no explanation for the delay.

Economic Integration

In addition to their historical incorporation within the political hierarchy of the Thai nation-state, the livelihood of Baan Naa Sakae residents had long been involved with wider economic relations, especially regional networks of trade and commerce. Community members traded in district market towns, even when this meant carrying goods for long distances on foot or by ox-cart. Elderly residents also recalled that traveling merchants visited Baan Naa Sakae periodically, even in the early years of settlement. In late nineteenth and early twentieth century Isan, itinerant traders, often Chinese, Vietnamese, or Shan (from Northern Thailand and Burma) followed regular trading routes across the region (Keyes, 1967; Paitoon, 1984:100–109; Pasuk & Baker 1995:49–50). Some traders went from village to village bartering manufactured items—cloth, thread, knives and other metal products, kerosene, and matches—for local products such as salt, silk, spices, or rice, which could be sold at a profit in Northeastern or Central Thai markets. As commercial rice production took hold in the central plains during the late 1800s, Isan cattle and buffalo traders, *naay hôôy*, became frequent visitors to the delta region where there was an expanding market for their northeastern-raised draft animals (Pasuk & Baker, 1995:23). The same railroads, telegraphs, and roads that had helped to extend the reach of centralized state administration, gave an equal impetus to regional trading networks and other commercial relations linking Isan to other regions of the country and to Bangkok in particular.

Infrastructure improvements also enabled Isan's rural producers to forge new and closer economic relations with farflung markets, driven by the demands of the national and even the international political economy. The development of regional infrastructure in Isan was sharply influenced by growing political and military conflicts in neighboring Laos, Cambodia, and Vietnam. From the 1950s to the 1970s, the United States made significant economic and military investments in Isan. The U.S.-funded Mitraphap highway, constructed from 1955 to 1961, ran from Bangkok north to the Mekong River; another branch extended east from Khorat city to Ubol Ratchathani near the border with Laos and Cambodia. These remain the primary transportation corridors for the region. In the 1960s, the United States built several airbases in Isan to support its expanding air operations for the Vietnam War and also gave increased aid to rural electrification plans.[16]

The expanding network of railroads and roads provided more efficient transportation of goods, just when expanding world markets for agricultural products—including cassava, a dry field plant that grows well in the poor soils of Isan—brought more and more Isan farmers into cash cropping. Although commercial agriculture had been a foundation of rural production in Central Thailand since the late 1800s, cash crops were slower to reach the glutinous rice-farming communities of Isan. The new highway system being built in the 1950s and 1960s made the timely delivery of goods to markets more feasible. Farming households throughout the Northeast put more and more land into new commercial dry-field crops and cleared new areas that had been too high or uneven to retain the water needed for glutinous rice. Cassava came first to Baan Naa Sakae in the 1960s. At first the new crop produced strong yields; coupled with high world prices, cassava produced solid profits for the first local families who planted it. Others followed in quick succession and by the early 1970s almost every household in Baan Naa Sakae was raising some cassava for sale. When international prices fell and initial rates of return for cassava dwindled, local farmers added kenaf and other cash crops. By the late 1980s, the main commercial crops planted in Baan Naa Sakae were still cassava and kenaf, along with lesser amounts of yam beans, cashews, and sugar cane.

Mass Media: Consuming the Nation

Alongside cash-crop production for global markets, new technologies of mass communication also spread rapidly after World War II, incorporating local communities into an expanding national audience. Radio broadcasting began in Thailand during the 1930s; army and state-controlled stations were soon set up in many regions of the country. By the 1970s, television, again tightly controlled by military or government agencies, began to achieve national coverage. By the end of the 1980s, television was almost universally accessible throughout rural Thailand.[17] The extension of electric power lines to many rural areas made the use of televisions, radios, and many other commodity items and appliances (fans, irons, refrigerators) increasingly attractive. Baan Naa Sakae was connected to the regional power grid in the early 1980s, and by 1990 well over half the community's households owned a television (at least a small black-and-white set), supplanting battery-operated radios as the main source of electronic media in the community. Media broadcasting provided residents an immediate connection to events and ideas of the larger nation, images that often emphasized the central importance of Bangkok. The evening's "national" news focused on the activities of the royal family, military and civilian leaders, events that most often took place in the capital city of Bangkok, and less commonly in major provincial capitals or overseas. Politicians and other prominent figures, usually dressed in Western-style suits and filmed in luxurious hotel or government meeting rooms, dominated these "important" news stories. When rural areas or communities were mentioned in these broadcasts, it was almost always in relation to either charitable visits to or inspections of outlying regions by members of the royal family, stories describing the results of floods or other natural disasters, or "human interest" tales about unusual or amusing local customs or beliefs.

Fictionalized television dramas, as well as many commercial advertisements, commonly invoked parallel contrasts between urban sophistication and rural backwardness. For example, night after night I watched, alongside others in Baan Naa Sakae, television dramas interspersed with frequent commercials, many of which portrayed upper-class urban households and their servants. The latter were usually depicted as migrants from the countryside, often from Isan. These servants served as stock figures of comic relief, foolish because of their spirit beliefs or other "superstitions" or for their ignorance of domestic technologies and consumer conveniences (electric rice cookers, microwave ovens). Another common image, especially in "action" dramas, was the portrayal of ruffians and thugs in the "rough" dress of peasant farmers, usually identified by their *phaakhaomaa*, a long piece of plaid cotton cloth worn around the waist or head by many rural men and a common part of male attire in Baan Naa Sakae.

These media images provided people in Baan Naa Sakae with forceful representations of their lesser status and subordinate position in Thai society. As members of a regional minority (*khon isaan, khon lao*) and as peasant farmers, residents of Baan Naa Sakae were well aware that they neither enjoyed an equal status nor received the same material rewards as other more prestigious segments of Thai society, especially members of the urban elite.

The relevance of these distinctions for people in Baan Naa Sakae was certainly not new. For most of the twentieth century, and with increasing emphasis after World War II, the rhetoric and policy of the Thai state had stressed goals of national development (*kan phatthana*) and progress. Although *kan phatthana* proposed to benefit the entire Thai nation, in practice state energies and funds were concentrated on the promotion of industry and infrastructure in and around the capital city. This urban bias in government policy and practice only strengthened popular understandings of village and city as fundamentally different modes of life and distinctly separate economies. However, the growth of mass communications technology and the rapid expansion of television, in particular, brought these contrasts to life for Baan Naa Sakae's residents in striking new ways. Television projected Bangkok's cosmopolitan styles and modes of social interaction into Baan Naa Sakae homes on a daily basis. At the same time, increasing labor migration meant that more and more women and men in Baan Naa Sakae had personal experiences of urban life and work, experiences that had little in common with the bright images of *thansamay* commodity consumption and self-expression portrayed on national broadcasts.

Meantime, the wages of Baan Naa Sakae's migrant daughters and sons had begun to play an increasingly important role in the local acquisition of these new commodity items. The 1950s and 1960s were the years during which rural-urban labor migration between Isan and Bangkok began in earnest. Reports of labor mobility from Isan extend back to the late 1800s, when some Northeastern men traveled southward, often in caravans of cattle merchants, to seek work as seasonal agricultural labor in the rice fields of the Chao Phraya delta (Pasuk & Baker, 1995:23; Lightfoot et al., 1983). However, large-scale movements of rural producers from Isan or elsewhere into urban wage labor did not begin until after World War II.

Labor Migration

Throughout the nineteenth century and the first half of the twentieth, Bangkok's labor needs were supplied almost entirely by immigration from mainland China. Chinese migrants found employment as dock workers and porters for the export trade, construction workers for an expanding railroad system and port facilities, and in emerging urban manufacturing and service industries. During these same decades, growing numbers of the Thai peasantry escaped or were legally freed from obligations of service to local nobility and other overlords. But rather than entering urban occupations, the vast majority moved to open up new agricultural frontiers, founding new settlements such as Baan Naa Sakae, putting new land into production, and supplying the rice—and to a lesser extent sugar and other crops—demanded by the expanding export trade. In 1949, however, Chinese sources for the urban labor force abruptly ended when the Thai government banned all immigration from the newly communist state. Bangkok employers turned quickly to the nation's rural hinterland to fill their labor needs. More than any other region, these first migrants—the majority of whom were men—came to Bangkok from the rural Northeast. By the late 1950s, certain occupations, most notably pedicab drivers (as with drivers of motorized taxis today), were already dominated by in-migrants from Isan (Textor, 1961). While some settled permanently in Bangkok, the majority sought employment on a temporary basis, often for a few months during the dry season (i.e., January-May) after the rice harvest and before the next planting.

Residents of Baan Naa Sakae did not participate in these earliest streams of migrants to Bangkok; however, in the 1960s a number of young men sought work in the regional cities of Khon Kaen and Udon Thani, where the opening of U.S. airbases (to support American involvement in the Vietnam War) prompted booms in construction and in services for the foreign troops. At the same time, the first labor recruiters from Bangkok began to appear in the local area. These agents induced a few young women from Baan Naa Sakae to take jobs in the capital as domestic servants. Then in the 1970s urban industries began to recruit workers directly from the countryside; sometimes prospective employers even provided buses to transport new employees to the city. Increasing numbers of Baan Naa Sakae's young people, especially young women, began to leave for these new manufacturing jobs.

For a time in the 1980s, lucrative opportunities for overseas labor contracts redirected some of this flow (although only among the community's adult men) toward countries in the Middle East, and later to Singapore and Brunei. The chance to make enough money in a relatively short period of time (two to four years) to build a new house and purchase major commodity items prompted the movement of many Baan Naa Sakae men into overseas labor. Even though high entry fees meant that overseas migrants carried a heavy debt into their contracts, many were willing to take the risk. Some lost the gamble. In 1990 nearly 20 percent of the men who had been, or tried to go, overseas reported being cheated, usually by an agent who absconded with the prospective migrant's fee. Several men had serious accidents or became ill while abroad; four were killed. Of those who made it overseas without serious mishap, most spent their first year working only to pay off their agent's fee; not until the second year did they earn anything for themselves. By the time I arrived in Baan Naa Sakae, falling exchange rates, rising agency fees (averaging $1,500 to over $2,000 U.S. in 1990), and significant losses suffered by some village households had substantially reduced local interest in overseas contracts. Meanwhile, the movement of young people into Bangkok jobs had grown from a trickle to a steady out-flow.

In 1990, labor migration—especially to Bangkok—involved members from almost every household in the community. Out-migration was particularly common among unmarried youth; yet many of these daughters and sons made only irregular, and in some cases negligible, financial contributions to their families in Baan Naa Sakae. Even for many of Baan Naa Sakae's poorest households, contributions from migrants' wages more often supplemented household income than provided for basic subsistence needs. Phô Lum and Mae Phim, echoing the experiences of many Baan Naa Sakae parents, reported that their eldest daughter's remitted wages were most useful in aiding large periodic or one-time expenditures, such as seasonal farming costs—fertilizer purchases, hiring transplanting or harvest labor. Migrants' wages were also used to cover other occasional expenses—notably education costs for younger siblings still in school: books and uniforms at the beginning of term as well as tuition and other fees for those studying beyond the primary level. More often, however, migrants in Bangkok and their families in Baan Naa Sakae cited the contributions that urban wages made to more conspicuous forms of household consumption: financing house construction and repairs, helping to fund household and community-based merit-making ceremonies, as well as supporting a wide range of mass-market commodity purchases, from televisions and electric fans, to motorcycles, refrigerators, and mechanized plows.

The extensive participation of Baan Naa Sakae residents in national and international labor migration circuits is one (but by no means the only) consequence of the profound political and economic transformations that Isan's rural producers have witnessed during the past century. The experiences of Baan Naa Sakae residents, as migrants and wage workers, highlight their incorporation within and subordination to the economic and cultural hierarchies of the Thai nation-state. Members of Baan Naa Sakae identify as Thai citizens yet are keenly aware of their marginal status as *khon baan nôôk* within the national community. As migrants and as consumers of market commodities—issues addressed in the next chapter—villagers seek to negotiate their status within the wider Thai society. The uses to which village residents put urban and overseas wages—particularly the acquisition and display of market commodities as emblems of style and status—represent one way to challenge their continuing exclusion from the *thansamay* successes of the nation's urban centers of power and wealth. At the same time, commodity consumption in Baan Naa Sakae points to tensions over disparities of wealth and status within the village itself. These conflicts, in turn, shape the complex motivations of labor out-migration and the meanings given this mobility by both migrants and their families.

CHAPTER 3

Cash, Commodities, and Modernity

⚍⊹

"Today life is more convenient but now everything is money."
—Maeyaay Sii

*A*t the time I arrived in Baan Naa
Sakae, the political and economic transformations of the preceding decades
had left their mark on almost every aspect of community life. This chapter
examines one particular dimension of that legacy: the role and significance
of money and commodity consumption. The consumption needs and expectations of residents reflected the profound dependence of Isan farmers upon
national and international circuits of commodity production and exchange;
at the same time, local consumption patterns revealed how urban identified
standards of Thai modernity had entered into the everyday imagination and
social interaction of community residents. The rising cash costs of everyday
subsistence, as well as commodified forms of status competition between village households, sustained disparities of wealth and power within the community. However, the proliferation of *thansamay* images and commodified
styles in Baan Naa Sakae also reflected a general recognition among local
residents that as rural producers they remained excluded from dominant constructions of Thai modernity and progress.

This chapter examines both the material and symbolic practices of commodity consumption in Baan Naa Sakae and the influence these had upon
rising household demands for cash income, including wages earned through
labor out-migration. Cash and commodities represented powerful standards
of material success against which village residents judged their own and their

neighbors' claims to *thansamay* status. And, as Chapter 4 explores in greater detail, the demands and desires that shape villagers' actions, not only as agricultural producers but also as consumers, play a critical role in local migration decisions, including the nearly universal movement of rural youth into urban employment.

From my first days in the community, I was struck by the importance of cash for Baan Naa Sakae residents; earning it, holding onto it, spending it—these were central, critical concerns for everyone. Most families in Baan Naa Sakae earned money through a variety of economic activities from cash crops and cattle raising to seasonal wage labor and petty trade. Some households were considerably more successful in these efforts than others. Sharp economic differences divided the community, and these divisions were obvious not just to me; residents of Baan Naa Sakae clearly distinguished between those in the community who "had money" (*mii ngoen*) and those who did not. Importantly, it was the presence or absence of money that was the key here, and while land ownership or occupation might indicate the likelihood of household wealth, what counted and what people emphasized was the availability of cash income and what it could buy.

However it was earned, in Baan Naa Sakae money was essential for every aspect of economic and social activity. Not just a means for satisfying basic household needs, money was also seen as an important resource used to maintain dignity and respect within the community. When one of the poorest couples in Baan Naa Sakae came to blows and briefly severed their often-stormy relationship (though only for a few weeks), gossip about the event focused on their chronic money problems. As one woman stated, whose household was financially comfortable: "When there's no money, any little thing can lead to a break; when there's money, neither small nor big matters drive you apart." For some in Baan Naa Sakae the need for money represented a crushing weight and a constant strain; for others money was the foundation of their personal ambitions and hopes; for everyone money was a critical measure of social as well as economic standing.

Elderly residents often emphasized the heightened importance of cash transactions in contemporary society compared to the time of their youth. In 1990 Maeyaay Sii, a woman in her mid-sixties, recalled:

> "Life was hard before (*samay tae kii*) but there was plenty of food and other necessary things (*bô üt bô yaak*). We made everything that we used: cloth and clothing, baskets, and cups, fish traps, everything. [Compared to today] we didn't have very much. There were no roads

to the village so people traveled by ox-cart or on foot. And no shoes. If we ever had to take things to the market, we had to walk the whole way to town without shoes! It's true, today life is much more convenient (*saduak*) but now everything is money. Now you can't live a day without spending money. And in the village, money is hard to find."

Similar claims of greater self-reliance and autonomy in the past, of hard work rewarded by an abundant environment were common among men and women over age fifty, and it seems likely that these perceptions were at least partly rooted in an older generation's nostalgia for the "better" times of their youth. But whether or not the past was as plentiful as some elderly villagers recall, residents of Baan Naa Sakae asserted without exception that their present lives were much more intensely engaged with cash and commodities than in the past. And while the pursuit of a cash income and the purchase of commodity items in the Baan Naa Sakae of 1990 was a matter of great necessity for the daily subsistence of many village households, the importance given to cash and commodities also reflected the status associated with *thansamay* patterns of consumption. A wide variety of market commodities, new technologies, and urban-identified styles (particularly in clothing, food, housing, and entertainment) were greatly appreciated and desired in the community, not only as evidence of their owners' material comfort and convenience but also as emblems of being *thansamay*, in step with the styles and practices of modern Thai society. As I argue below, manufactured and purchased commodities in Baan Naa Sakae represented not only material wealth but also symbolic resources—"cultural capital" (Bourdieu, 1977, 1984)—with which residents negotiated identity and status within the community. In varied contexts and with differing abilities, people in Baan Naa Sakae deployed and manipulated commodities to display and establish claims about themselves and their relations with fellow villagers.

Though desired by all, commodified comforts and conveniences posed much more difficult standards of consumption and display for some members of the community than for others. As the divergent concerns of the following households illustrate, life and livelihood in Baan Naa Sakae involved different choices for those who had money than for those whose access to cash was much more uncertain.

Phôyaay Phum, age sixty-one, the widowed father of six sons and one daughter, headed one of Baan Naa Sakae's more comfortable households. He lived in a spacious wooden house with his twenty-seven-year-old married daughter, Kham, her two girls, aged nine and three, and Phôyaay's youngest son, age ten. Kham's husband was away working in Libya, on the third year of a four-year contract. The two eldest of Phôyaay Phum's sons were married and had moved out to live with their wives in separate households in Baan Naa Sakae. Although none of his older children ever studied beyond the minimum required primary education, three of his younger sons had completed high school. Of these three, all were unmarried and in their early twenties; one was away doing military service and the other two traveled back and forth to Bangkok where they found a series of jobs, primarily as factory workers. These two sons only brought back small amounts of money from their city jobs and even Kham's husband did not send regular monthly contributions, although his yearly visits home were always occasions for major purchases of household goods. But as Phôyaay Phum argued: "Whatever they give is enough. We get by just fine (*bô üt bô yaak*)."

In fact, by local standards Phôyaay Phum's family was prosperous. He owned over one hundred *rai* (forty acres) of agricultural land, more than four times the regional average of twenty-five *rai*, and substantially more than the holdings of most families in Baan Naa Sakae. Only a quarter of the community owned more than forty-five *rai* and fully one-third owned less than twenty *rai*.[1] Furthermore, much of Phôyaay Phum's land was located in more fertile and well-watered areas surrounding the village, adding to their value and productivity. Together with his children (all of whom would inherit a share of the household land), he grew cassava as a cash crop and enough rice that there was usually a surplus to sell for ready cash. Their substantial land holdings also allowed the family to graze several head of cattle year-round. They owned nine head of cattle and the previous year had sold three calves, at about six or seven thousand *baht* per head.[2] As was true for many other land-rich families in Baan Naa Sakae, livestock provided a steady income while also serving as a reserve of wealth that could be converted into ready cash in an emergency. "Cattle are the farmer's bank," said Phôyaay Phum's neighbor, Phôyaay Dan, himself the owner of more than a dozen head of cattle.

Phô Lat, forty-eight, and his wife Mae Sahn, forty-six, headed a slightly less prosperous household than Phôyaay Phum. Although their land holdings were more than most—forty-five *rai* of land planted in rice and cash crops—they no longer owned any cattle. "We had to sell them all when Phô Lat tried to find work in Singapore—the employment agent ran off with the money and we were left with the debt," Mae Sahn explained.[3] Despite this setback, they owned a comfortable wooden house in good repair. Almost as large as Phôyaay Phum's home, it easily accommodated the couple and their young-

FIGURE 4. Cattle pass concrete water cisterns and some of the village's newer houses on their way to morning pastures.

est child, a small boy of six years, as well as their two, unmarried, older children when they were home. Both had begun working in Bangkok a few years after completing their primary schooling. Their eldest son, Sanit, age twenty-two, had just left for Bangkok after the end of the rice harvest. He found a job working with one of Phôyaay Phum's sons at a bicycle factory. Sanit had been to Bangkok several times but he usually worked there only for a few months during the dry season, returning home (though with limited savings) to help his parents at the start of the main growing season. Their twenty-year-old daughter, Phan, had been working in Bangkok much longer, for four years, coming home only two or three times a year for brief visits. Both children sent money home occasionally but it was not a key source of household income. Phô Lat and Mae Sahn produced enough rice to have some left over for sale in a good year in addition to their cash-crop sales (mainly cassava and yam bean). Three years before, Phô Lat had purchased a mechanical plow on installments and, by hiring himself out to plow others' land, they had very nearly paid off this new investment.

The relative comfort of these families contrasted sharply with the difficulties facing poorer residents of Baan Naa Sakae, especially the one-third of village households owning less than twenty *rai* (eight acres) of farming land. Phô Lum, forty-four, and Mae Phim, forty-five, for example, headed one of the few households in the village that owned no farming land at all. Their house was small, and roughly built; several floorboards and parts of two walls needed replacement. They rented twenty-one *rai* of land owned by Mae Phim's sister who lived in the nearby district town of Baan Phai, where she and her husband worked as sweepers for the local sanitation department. Because it was land owned by a close relative, Phô Lum and Mae Phim paid rent in kind—one-third of their annual rice harvest—but even so they did not always produce enough rice to last through the year. Although in 1990 it looked like they might have enough, the previous year they had had to buy nearly 6,000 *baht* of rice, incurring a debt they had not yet paid in full.

None of their four children completed more than primary schooling. One son, age eleven, was still in primary school; the other three—daughters, Pom, aged twenty-four, Sang, seventeen, and a nineteen-year-old son, Beh, had all spent varying amounts of time working in Bangkok. Sang worked in the capital for one month before quitting her job sewing garments in a small sweatshop; unhappy with the harsh working conditions, she came home and swore never to return to the city. Instead, she found work on a construction crew in the local district town. Beh went to Bangkok and worked at a series of jobs in small factories, but after a year he had returned home empty-handed. Pom, however, worked for three years in Bangkok in a furniture factory, and for three years before that in a restaurant in Chiang Mai. She had sent money home every few months but had recently left Bangkok to prepare for her marriage to a young man from another province. His family was better off and so, when the wedding took place, Pom moved from Baan Naa Sakae to her new husband's home village in Roi Et province.

In addition to the periodic remittances that Pom and, to a lesser extent, Sang had contributed from their wages, both Phô Lum and Mae Phim took on day labor in the fields of other villagers. Local wage work of this sort was not always easy to find except for short periods at transplanting and harvesting time. Wages during these seasons were relatively high (45–50 *baht* per day in 1989–90, $1.80–$2.00 U.S.) but agricultural work at other times of the year was irregular and more poorly paid (30–35 *baht* per day in 1989–90, $1.20–1.40 U.S.). However, Phô Lum and Mae Phim did have some more substantial assets than most landless and land-poor families in Baan Naa Sakae; they owned six head of water buffalo. Most years, this gave them two calves to sell, bringing about 3,000 *baht* each. The mature stock was worth about 6,000 to 7,000 *baht* per head. "But we would only sell one [of the mature buffalo] in an emergency," said Mae Phim. Kept for breeding, their buffalo were also rented out as draft animals to other families who had no beasts of their own for plowing.

In Baan Naa Sakae land-poor families, like Phô Lum's, often had a hard time making ends meet. They had to supplement subsistence rice production and small amounts of cash crops with occasional day labor and perhaps wage remittances from a daughter or son working in Bangkok. These families were also less likely to have cash savings, or ready access to cheap credit. This was a major source of concern for Mae Kaew, age forty-one, who worked thirty *rai* of poor quality land, sharing the often meager harvest with an elderly mother and several unmarried siblings. Mae Kaew's own husband was ill and unable to do much heavy field work; their two children were still in school. The younger, a girl of twelve was completing her final year of primary school. The elder, a boy of fourteen, was enrolled in the district high school. Mae Kaew admitted that she would not have been able to afford the additional school fees and expenses for him without the regular cash assistance of two of her younger, unmarried sisters who worked as domestic servants in Bangkok. But cash for school fees and other "extras" were not the only needs Mae Kaew struggled to fulfill. Every year the rice they harvested was never enough to supply the needs of both Mae Kaew's and her mother's households. Though she had spent many years working in Bangkok when she was younger, now Mae Kaew took all the day-wage labor she could find in Baan Naa Sakae and periodically went to work harvesting fruit in another province. Like others among Baan Naa Sakae's poorest residents, Mae Kaew cultivated the favor of wealthier neighbors, often helping to harvest and thresh their rice without pay "because then we can ask them for help [for rice or small loans] when we need it."

The debts poor households incurred were a constant worry. If these accumulated, land-poor households had little to cushion them from outright dispossession. This vulnerability was revealed most dramatically not long after I moved into Baan Naa Sakae, when one of the community's poorest residents, Mae Tan, mother to five children, was forced to sell her last remaining plot of rice land (15 *rai*) to pay off debts. Owning no house or land on which to build in the village itself, she and her children had been living in a shack in the compound of a wealthier cousin. But losing their rice fields was the final blow: Mae Tan and her children left Baan Naa Sakae and moved into a slum area in the regional city of Khon Kaen, joining Mae Tan's estranged husband who worked there as a pedicab driver. I was unable to trace them afterwards.

Mae Tan's household offered the most extreme example of economic insecurity in Baan Naa Sakae (indeed one that could not be sustained within the community but was forced out).[4] By contrast, the most secure members of the community were not always those, like Phôyaay Phum, with the most extensive land holdings; members of the village elite also included several households that combined agricultural production with salaried posts in the civil service, primarily as teachers, police, or government clerks. Khruu Wirat was one of ten such civil servants living in Baan Naa Sakae in 1990. A primary school teacher (*khruu*) and principal of the school in a neighboring village, Khruu Wirat, age forty-nine, had married a woman native to Baan Naa Sakae, Mae Khao, forty-four. They owned forty-five *rai* of land but rented two-thirds of it to a poorer relative of Mae Khao's. Khruu Wirat's monthly salary and the rice they grew on their remaining fifteen *rai* of good rice land provided a relatively comfortable income for the family, which included two unmarried daughters in their early twenties.

Civil service jobs were coveted by others in Baan Naa Sakae and valued by their holders not simply for the steady income. Salaries were not particularly high; a starting teacher's salary in 1990 was approximately 4,000 *baht*, or $160 U.S. per month, and raises were generally small and irregular. However, government employees and their families had access to significant benefits that were the envy of most people in Baan Naa Sakae. Khruu Wirat, in addition to his regular monthly salary, could take out low-interest loans and received a variety of benefits, such as health care and high-school tuition wavers for their children. These advantages allowed Khruu Wirat and other civil servants in the village to finance additional commercial activities; for example, Mae Khao and the wives of two teachers at the Baan Naa Sakae primary school all operated small shops from their village homes, selling small amounts of produce, dried goods, alcohol, and cigarettes. Another teacher's family raised pigs for market.

In addition, more than half the Baan Naa Sakae households with civil service incomes, including Khruu Wirat's family, had built (or were in the process of building) large new houses. These invariably included a ground-level story enclosed with concrete block walls in a style more reminiscent of urban architecture than most village homes. These same families owned a wide variety of major commodity items, including color televisions, refrigerators, fans, motorcycles, and, in one case, a pickup truck. Few children of government workers ended their education at either the primary or the high school level; in 1990, for example, Khruu Wirat's two daughters, Nang, age twenty-five, and Duang, twenty-two, were both studying for their bachelor's degrees at Mahasarakham Teachers College. Nang had worked in Bangkok for over a year after finishing high school—"I did it for the experience"— before returning home to continue her studies. Both she and her sister hoped to find civil service jobs when they graduated.[5]

The varied situations of these and the many other households I came to know in Baan Naa Sakae, offered a complex picture of rural income and labor mobility. The need for cash income propelled most village families into a variety of economic activities, from agriculture to wage labor to petty commerce as well as labor migration. However, the economic necessity of the latter was not always immediately obvious. Bangkok wages might make a real difference to households like Mae Kaew's and Phô Lum's who struggled to get by; however, urban jobs attracted even members of prosperous families like the children of Phôyaay Phum and Phô Lat. Clearly these wealthier households did not rely on the wage remittances of daughters and sons to cover critical household expenses or subsistence needs. However, for families "with money," migrants' wages might still represent a potential cash reserve that could be drawn upon for various purposes, including the purchase of new, prestigious, commodity items.

Adopting commodified styles and practices represented a claim to sophistication of taste and knowledge through which villagers could assert a positive self-image in opposition to their portrayal in the dominant culture. At the same time, however, access to markets and consumer commodities, transportation fares, electricity and water bills, all entailed regular and sometimes large amounts of cash outlay in order to maintain even a minimal level of conformity to these new standards of community existence. The desirability of doing more was clear to everyone but it was a realistic possibility only for some. Not surprisingly, then, resentment and conflict were the consequences of visible economic disparities in Baan Naa Sakae. Theft was an ongoing concern for wealthier families, a few of whose houses resembled urban buildings not only in form but also in security measures (e.g., barred windows or a locking metal grille across the front entry). While the rich protected their belongings with lock and key, poorer families grumbled about stingy neighbors and exchanged occasional barbed comments. But these rarely escalated into more open confrontations. Most poor villagers, like Mae Kaew, depended on wealthier households to give them wage work and small loans, and could not afford to antagonize potential patrons.

Cash, Convenience, and Community Progress

Cash transactions were, in fact, routine features of daily life for village households. Most of these involved the purchase of small amounts of food, soap, and other items at a local store. Several families in the community ran small shops out of the ground floor of their homes. Of the nine such businesses operating in 1990, three sold a limited range of items (mainly dried and packaged foods), while six kept a regular stock of both fresh and packaged food, alcohol, tobacco, soap, and other household items. All were privately owned and self-financed, usually with capital from a family member who was either working overseas or, more often, had a salaried civil service position.

A variety of traders, sometimes several in a day, stopped in Baan Naa Sakae before moving on to other villages nearby. Some came on foot, carrying baskets of dried fish, small trinkets, or items of clothing. More often, traders drove pickups, riding slowly around the village while announcing their wares over high-powered loudspeakers attached to the truck's roof. Goods offered for sale in this manner ranged from trinkets and cosmetics to a variety of foods and condiments, as well as more expensive commodities such as woven matting for floors, heavy wooden furniture, even refrigerators and portable gas stoves. Some offered to accept rice in barter, but more expensive commodity items were always sold on a cash basis, often through installment plans of quarterly or twice-yearly payments. Even when merchants asked for rice rather than cash in exchange for their goods—usually for food products such as dried chilies or fish—most people in Baan Naa Sakae preferred to pay cash, well aware that the amount of rice demanded as payment could approach three or four times the market value of the items sold.

Nor were Baan Naa Sakae residents limited in their purchases to the wares offered at local stores or by traveling merchants. Early each morning two or three *songthaew* ("two-bench" buses made from freight trucks converted to passenger use) passed Baan Naa Sakae along the state-maintained dirt road heading north to the paved highway. They followed a regular route to the main market town in a neighboring district. For a few *baht,* anyone could make this trip or transfer to a regular bus at the paved highway for a longer journey. The same *songthaews* passed the village on their return in the late morning or early afternoon, but travelers who wished to reach the village later in the day had only to wait near the highway for one of the freelance motorcycle taxis or flag down a passing pickup truck whose driver might be willing to take fares up the dirt road leading to the village. Nonresidents could travel to and from Baan Naa Sakae with similar ease and regularity.

One regular visitor to Baan Naa Sakae was the district postal carrier who delivered all mail for the community to the home of the *phuuyaaybaan*. Often the day's letters included notes from village residents writing home from Bangkok or abroad, sending news of their welfare and possibly money orders or bank transfers of remitted wages.

Beyond the access and ease of transportation provided by the road, the extension of electricity to Baan Naa Sakae in 1982, dramatically increased the range of commodity items that residents considered integral to community life. By 1990 even the poorest households had an electric hookup (sometimes feeding off a neighbor's line) to power, if nothing else, a single electric lightbulb. Other homes boasted a variety of electrical appliances ranging from radios and fans to tape decks, televisions (preferably with color screens), refrigerators, rice cookers, and, in one case, a video cassette player.[6] In addition, commodities and market relations affected even such fundamental acts as bathing and elimination. Over the preceding decade, private concrete-block wash houses with squat toilets had replaced local ponds and outlying fields as the sites for tending to personal needs.

The initial campaign to build these sanitary facilities in Baan Naa Sakae was part of a national effort spearheaded in Mahasarakham province by a Thai nongovernmental organization, the Population and Development Association (PDA). Villagers used their own labor for construction but had to pay for materials, although the PDA subsidized some costs through no-interest loans. In 1990, these *thansamay* conveniences were enjoyed by over 80 percent of Baan Naa Sakae households.

Commodities and cash also played a part in local access to drinking water. Ensuring an adequate supply of water for drinking and cooking, particularly during the long dry season from February to June, had long been a concern for every household in the community. But over the preceding decade, access to safe and abundant water had eased for most of the community, especially for families with greater financial resources. Four times in the 1980s, the regional office of the Population and Development Association had offered technical and some financial assistance to families in Baan Naa Sakae (as well as other villages in the area) who wished to construct large concrete cisterns to collect rain water. Materials cost over four thousand *baht* (about $160 U.S.), a significant sum (especially when a day's wage for agricultural labor ranged between thirty-five and fifty *baht*), and construction required a dozen or so people to work together for one to two days. Villagers supplied the labor and the PDA encouraged groups of households to work together, rotating their efforts to build a cistern for each participant.

By 1990, more than half of the community had benefited from these projects. As Mae Kao said: "Now in the rainy season we can store enough clean water in the cistern to use [for drinking and cooking] the whole year." However, one-third of village families had been unable either to afford the construction costs or to provide the necessary household labor. Families like Mae Kaew's still relied on an older technology, collecting rainwater in giant earthenware urns. "We would need another two urns to have enough water to get through the dry season; and if we are not careful to keep the urns covered, if an animal gets in and drowns, the water can be spoiled. Every year we run out and have to go find a spring." There were several springs in the local area, but none were considered as healthy and clean as rain water and some springs often ran dry during the hottest months of the year.

Although concrete cisterns meant that many families no longer had to worry about their drinking water, other water needs required continuing effort. With the exception of a few of Baan Naa Sakae's wealthiest families, like those of Khruu Wirat and Phôyaay Phum who had managed to build two cisterns for themselves, every household in the community had to haul bathing and washing water from one of two nearby ponds, often on a daily basis. My own efforts to this end were soon a familiar and entertaining sight to our closest neighbors, as I huffed and puffed behind a borrowed wooden cart, loaded with large plastic containers, heading to and from the nearest pond. However, not long after Mon and I moved in, the community began construction of its first piped water system, again with the financial and technical assistance of the PDA. Villagers who participated would have water piped to a spigot in the yards of their homes, but they had to pay a preliminary subscription fee (200 *baht*, $8 U.S.) as well as contribute labor for the several months of construction. Though this water pumped from deep underground was untreated and not safe to drink, most community members welcomed the new source as more convenient and cleaner than the stagnant and often murky local pond water previously used for bathing, laundry, and other needs. Other residents were suspicious and reluctant to embark on a project that they thought might never be realized. Phô Lum and Mae Phim initially refused to participate, afraid that if the project fell through, they would have lost their subscription fee; more important, as with other families dependent on day-to-day wage labor, they feared the many days of unpaid labor would place a severe strain on their resources.

Phô Lum's suspicions were not at all allayed by the fact that the project coincided with a local election campaign. Construction began just as the old village headman turned sixty, the mandatory age for retirement. Prospective candidates for his post and their boosters, primarily members of Baan Naa Sakae's most prominent and richest families, all claimed credit for bringing the piped water project to Baan Naa Sakae (e.g., through their connections with the local office of the PDA, local government officials, or friendship with the project engineers). They also took on the attractively high-profile supervisory tasks of organizing work rosters and overseeing the collection of subscriptions.

The actual labor for the project—pouring concrete, raising the large water storage tanks, digging and laying pipelines—was supplied by men and women from the rest of the community. At the peak points in the construction, this meant that each household had to contribute the labor of one adult every day for two or more weeks at a stretch, an especially difficult sacrifice for poorer families. Considering the connection of the project to local elections, some, like Phô Lum, worried that once the elections were over the construction efforts would come to an end. As the project continued, however, and construction began in earnest, Phô Lum and Mae Phim decided to approach the school principal who was in charge of the subscriptions. After the principal refused their request to join, Phô Lum asked me to intervene: "The principal won't listen to us and it is humiliating to beg. Maybe you can talk to him?" The principal was reluctant to make an exception for a family whose "lack of faith and laziness kept them from participating until they knew the project would be a success." He did eventually allow Phô Lum and Mae Phim to join, but charged them a fine "for the labor they have not contributed." Grumbling about an expense they could ill afford and the hard hearts of those "with money" who "lacked sympathy" for their poorer neighbors, Phô Lum and Mae Phim paid: "Otherwise, we'll be left behind while everyone else in the village moves ahead."

When the piped water began to flow in late October of 1990—replacing daily trips to local ponds by a new monthly water bill—everyone in Baan Naa Sakae praised the increased "convenience" and "comfort" (*saduak, sabaay*) of the new technology. Piped water, everyone agreed, signaled the growing "development" and "progress" (*kan phatthana, khwaam caroen*) of the community as a whole. Baan Naa Sakae was moving closer to the standards of national development. Despite the general enthusiasm for this latest evidence of local progress and the successful results of the community's hard work, a few suspicions lingered that the project's benefits would not be equally distributed. In particular, complaints began to circulate when Phô Lat's son, recently returned from Bangkok, was selected to oversee the collection of water-use fees. A number of poorer families pointed to Phô Lat's close ties

FIGURE 5. Baan Naa Sakae residents provide the labor to build water tanks for a community piped-water system.

to the new headman's family. As Phô Lum said: "Phô Lat is one of the *phuuyaaybaan*'s supporters. People like that always eat together"—suggesting that these more powerful community members would soon be "eating" the water funds as well.

Rice and Commodified Subsistence

Metaphors of eating draw upon local residents' awareness that divisions of wealth and status in the village were sustained by unequal access to cash and other resources. But in Baan Naa Sakae the concrete, mundane act of eating—particularly eating rice—also illustrated the way that cash and commodities not only mediated claims for status and power in the village but also were essential components of household survival. Rice, or more properly glutinous rice, is the staple food of the northeastern diet. In 1990 Baan Naa Sakae households still produced rice, first and foremost, for their own consumption. Only if there was a surplus crop or a pressing need for cash was rice taken to market for sale. Most villagers identified themselves as wet-rice farmers, even if cash cropping or some form of wage or salaried work provided the bulk of household cash income. The seasonal cycle of rice production—planting and transplanting at the beginning of the wet season (June-August), harvesting and threshing at the end of the rains (November-December)—defined the fundamental rhythm of community life.

Rice was *the* staple food for people of Baan Naa Sakae, without which life could barely be sustained and would not flourish. Whether in Thai or Isan speech, to be hungry, is literally "to be hungry for rice."[7] People in Baan Naa Sakae hungered especially for the heavy, glutinous "sticky" rice (*khaaw niaw*), the staple grain throughout the northeast region. Eating sticky rice was an important part of their identification as ethnic Lao people. Traveling outside of the Northeast usually means eating the lighter rice of central and urban Thailand (*khaaw cao*, literally "rice of the lords"). As nourishment, villagers felt this latter kind of rice was far from satisfactory. "It does not stay in the stomach. You cannot eat and be filled (*bô yuu thôông, kin bô im*)." Eating *khaaw cao* can also denote physical weakness; villagers who consulted doctors at private clinics or government hospitals in the district town were often told to avoid the heavier sticky rice as part of their therapy. Residents of Baan Naa Sakae cited the apparent inability of Central Thai people, and especially urban-dwellers, to digest sticky rice with ease as a mark of their inferiority in comparison to the Lao peoples of Isan. Thus rice, particularly sticky rice, nourished both the body and a local self-image as a strong and sturdy people.

As food, sticky rice is a basic necessity of life. But people in Baan Naa Sakae grew rice for more than its nutritional properties. Rice was important as a means of exchange and as an essential ingredient of community social interaction and ritual activities. Unmilled rice could be exchanged for a variety of goods, although this form of barter had been more common in the past. Families with a rice surplus could sell it for cash or lend it to needy relatives and neighbors. Despite the prevalence of wage labor and other cash transactions in most areas of community life, rice still formed the basis for patron-client ties on which some of the poorest Baan Naa Sakae families relied in bad years. Thus Mae Kaew explained that she and her husband continued to "help" certain households with their harvest and transplanting needs, even though they might earn a better wage working elsewhere. "We help them so that we can get rice when we need it." A bad rice harvest is the harbinger of real hardship and several poor crops in a row may be little short of disastrous. A number of villagers recalled how, some twenty years previously, following a seven-year-long drought, many families had to go begging in other communities to get enough rice to eat.

Sufficiency in rice was, therefore, the foundation of a secure subsistence and a surplus offered the potential for material accumulation. Rice was also a crucial factor in the arena of spiritual accumulation. Cooked rice offerings to Buddhist monks earned religious merit for the donor. Early every morning the monks and novices at the village temple—whose numbers varied during my fieldwork from three to eight depending on the season—walked around the village with their alms bowls. Villagers, typically older women, awaited the monks with freshly cooked sticky rice, and small portions of prepared foods (eggs and fruit often). These they placed in each monk's alms bowl. Rice, as the most important food, was offered first.

Rice offerings were also essential features of most ritual events, both household and community-wide ceremonies. Festival meals held at the temple, wedding and funeral feasts, healing rites as well as offerings to the village guardian spirit and other local spirits—all such rites and ceremonies associated (often self-consciously) with local or regional traditions—required rice either to be eaten and/or to be manipulated ritually in various cooked, raw, and unmilled states. Individuals gained religious merit from offering rice to monks or in the context of Buddhist rites. In a similar fashion, generosity with rice was both a measure of hospitality and a meritorious act toward fellow villagers and visitors from outside the community. Having an ample supply of rice was, therefore, critical not only to sustain life but to fulfill social obligations of hospitality and to earn religious merit.

Although rice itself was not grown as a cash crop in Baan Naa Sakae, cash and a wide range of market commodities entered into both its production and consumption within the village. Due to a plentiful harvest the previous year, most Baan Naa Sakae households had a sufficient supply of seed rice for their planting needs in the 1990 growing season, but other important inputs had to be purchased. Because of high market prices, most households applied fertilizer and pesticide only in small quantities, and sometimes not at all, despite the fact that villagers felt these were important to guarantee a high yield in the sandy, marginally saline soils of the area. Many families had their own water buffaloes with which to plow, but others had to hire buffaloes every year or engaged the services of a fellow villager who owned an "iron buffalo," a small mechanized plow designed for small paddy fields and wet-rice agriculture.

The cost of material inputs was not the only requirement for cash investment in Baan Naa Sakae agriculture. Farm labor, too, was often mobilized through wage payments. Villagers spoke of their reliance in earlier generations upon voluntary exchange labor (*long khaek, haa raeng*) in which friends and neighbors worked together "helping each other" (*sôôy kan*, Lao; *chuay kan*, Thai). Phô Chuay recalled, "In the old days (*samay kôn*), we would help each other with everything: transplanting and harvesting, not just rice threshing like today. And when someone was building a house, people came to help; they didn't hire construction teams as people do now." But in 1990 *long khaek* work parties, with the exception of rice threshing, were rare in Baan Naa Sakae. Wage work had replaced most forms of cooperative labor, whether in rice production or any other type of farm or non-farm task.

For the most part, residents of Baan Naa Sakae actively preferred exchanging labor for a wage rather than for payment in kind or expectations of future assistance. Voluntary labor and other forms of "help" may contain an element of exploitation, at least for the poorest villagers who, like Mae Kaew, felt compelled to "help" richer families in order to ensure access to the latter's resources in times of hardship.[8] One woman explained her preference for waged work over exchange labor: "If someone comes asking for people [as exchange labor], then I have to go. It's how we do things here. But if it's wage work, I can go or not as I please." Wage work implied no longer-term obligations between the one hired and the one hiring. Nor did it necessarily imply any status differences; a person paid for work in someone else's field one day might hire labor to work on their own field the next.

The approximately one-third of village households with limited farm land (twenty *rai* or less) or those who had a large number of adult workers might get through the rice season using only household labor. Those with more land to till, and especially the one-quarter of families with land holdings of forty-five *rai* or more, usually had to hire help at transplanting and harvesting time, the peak periods of labor demand in wet-rice agriculture. Workers were hired on a daily basis either from other Baan Naa Sakae households or from neighboring communities.[9] The wage for a day's work in Baan Naa Sakae ranged from 30 *baht* to 45 *baht* ($1.20–$1.80 U.S.) in 1990, depending on seasonal demand. Even when voluntary labor was still used, most often for rice threshing parties immediately following the harvest, this "old-style" (and for most participants, highly enjoyable) organization of labor entailed significant cash costs for the host. Although most of the food supplied to feed workers was produced by the host (rice, home-brewed rice liquor, chickens, and ducks), cash expenses were considerable. Most households that held a *long khaek* party to thresh rice after the 1989 harvest claimed that they spent 500 *baht* ($20 U.S.) or more, much of which went for the purchase of store-bought liquor. In the case of many poorer families, hosting a threshing party in proper style required more cash expenditure than they could reasonably afford. Not surprisingly many chose to forgo this form of labor mobilization. A final production expense involved the transportation of the rice from the fields back to the village by truck. In 1990 nine families in Baan Naa Sakae owned short- or long-bed freight trucks, usually purchased with earnings from overseas migration. Each charged a flat rate of 100 to 150 *baht* per load for carrying rice in from the surrounding fields.

The consumption of rice was equally intertwined with the purchase of market commodities. The 1989 harvest was good and most Baan Naa Sakae households reaped sufficient rice to supply their own consumption needs for the year. Similarly, villagers with stands of forest remaining on or near their holdings gathered wood to make their own charcoal for cooking. But almost all other components of rice preparation were market commodities. Metal pots for cooking, china dishes, glass, metal or plastic cups, metal spoons and forks were standard—replacing (except for some picnic-style meals in the field) the banana leaves, coconut shell, and bamboo utensils that previous generations often produced for themselves. Even the woven bamboo baskets, used for steaming rice and for a variety of storage purposes, were now almost always purchased, either in the district market or from itinerant merchants. Only a handful of elderly men continued to practice the once-common craft of basket weaving by collecting their supplies from the dwindling stands of local bamboo.

Rice was the staple food and no meal was complete without it; however, the quality of a meal was also judged on the variety and types of dishes prepared to be eaten "with rice" (*kap khaaw*). Chicken, duck, pork, and, most especially, beef were more prestigious foods, reserved for special occasions when some of the household livestock might be slaughtered. In addition, the rural northeastern diet is well known throughout Thailand for its wide range of protein sources, culled from forest and field. Fish, either fresh from local ponds or in the form of a preserved paste (*plaa raa*, Thai; *plaa taek*, Lao), was probably the most common addition to Baan Naa Sakae meals; however, depending upon the season, villagers' meals might include items such as frogs, lizards, beetles, snails, red ants and ant eggs, or silk worms. These seasonally available delicacies were valued for their special flavors as well as their association with local ingenuity and cultural identity. Nevertheless, much of what people in Baan Naa Sakae ate came to them via commodity transactions. In the long dry season, especially, the small stores in Baan Naa Sakae did a steady trade in basic food items. Children sent by their mothers to buy the ingredients for the evening meal were a common sight in the late afternoon as they returned home carrying small plastic bags with a few eggs, salt

FIGURE 6. An exchange labor (*long khaek*) party threshes rice in the fields of their host.

or dried fish, or vegetables. In addition, the basic condiments and flavorings, without which food is "tasteless" (*cüüt*) and hardly worth eating, were largely purchased. Bottled fish sauce, refined cane sugar, monosodium glutamate (none of which were or had ever been produced in Baan Naa Sakae) were essential ingredients in almost every dish. Even the pungent fish paste, *plaa taek,* that provides the quintessential flavoring of Isan food, was no longer produced by anyone in Baan Naa Sakae and had to be purchased. Other major condiments—garlic, lime, chilies—were grown in small quantities by some local families but this was rarely enough to supply household needs year-round. Most Baan Naa Sakae households regularly bought these and a variety of other food products either on trips into the local market town or in Baan Naa Sakae itself from traveling salesmen or at one of the village shops.

Rice, Ritual, and Commodified Display

In the context of village social interaction, rice marked important continuities between residents' actions in the present and their historical imagination. Whether as a product of people's labor or an object of physical and spiritual consumption, rice and its uses were linked quite explicitly to the preservation of local tradition and a valued Isan or Lao cultural identity.[10] For example, rice offerings by individual households were an important part of most community celebrations and rituals, including the annual series of festivals (*ngaan bun*) of the northeastern ritual cycle (see also Tambiah, 1970; Condominas, 1975). On these occasions, villagers gathered at the temple or in certain cases at the shrine of the village guardian spirit—both of which represented sacred space common to all community members. A variety of household-based ceremonies, often focusing on major life-events such as ordinations, marriages, or memorial feasts for the recently deceased, supplemented the yearly cycle of community religious rites.

However, this close association between rice, religious merit, and community ceremonials was also heavily mediated by money and commodities. Rice remained an essential component of food offerings to Buddhist monks but a variety of market items were also standard features of merit-making ceremonies. Offerings made to individual monks at ordinations, or at annual *thôôt kathin* or *thôôt phaa paa* ceremonies, usually included both cash and a range of purchased goods: robes, soap, toilet paper, laundry detergent, and packaged or powdered drinks such as sweetened milk and Ovaltine. One villager who had migrated to the northern city of Chiang Mai, where she had done very well, returned on a visit to Baan Naa Sakae, bringing with her a color television set as an offering to the temple monks. In addition, when monks were invited to preside over special ceremonies in the homes of particular village families—such as at funerals, house blessings, or memorial and merit services for deceased relatives—they were given offerings of money, served bottles of Pepsi, Coca-Cola, and other soft drinks, plus rice and the best food the family could muster.

Moreover, expressions of community solidarity and ethnic-regional identity also involved the mobilization of prestigious symbols and resources associated with urban, *thansamay* styles and practices. Thus, for example, during the ritual procession of the *songkran* water festival, villagers carried the temple's primary Buddha image through the village in the back of a large freight truck rather than on the temple's older hand-held palanquin. Furthermore, no community event was complete without the use of a microphone and public address system. Similarly, like most aspects of social life in Baan Naa Sakae, the success of ritual celebrations was increasingly dependent upon the mobilization of cash and market commodities.

Nowhere was this more obvious than in the demonstrations of hospi-

FIGURE 7. Monks are offered food and drink after chanting blessings at a Baan Naa Sakae household merit-making ceremony.

tality necessary to major household rituals such as weddings, ordinations, and memorial celebrations for deceased relatives (*bun caek khaaw*).[11] Most villagers linked these occasions with the upholding of valued local customs, including explicit associations of ethnic Lao identity. One of the most prominent and self-consciously ethnic-regional features of these ceremonies was usually the performance of a *baay sii suu khwan* (although in memorial ceremonies for the dead different rites were required). This ritual is of animist origin and seeks to bind the soul-essence (*khwan*) of key participants to their bodies in order to ensure health and happiness. Its focus is the *baay sii*, a large ornament made of banana leaves and flowers. In Baan Naa Sakae the *baay sii* was usually constructed by a group of older women (often while their younger counterparts were preparing large amounts of food for the expected guests). The rite itself was presided over by the community's ritual expert (*môô sut*), an elderly man in his seventies who chanted blessings inscribed on old palm-leaf texts in a variety of ancient Thai and Lao scripts.

However, in tandem with these links to a local sense of ethnic tradition, these same ceremonies were also occasions to display household wealth and status, primarily through an elaborate deployment of market commodities and related *thansamay* practices.[12] For instance, the host family frequently announced their plans to hold a major ceremony by distributing invitations enclosed in matching envelopes, mechanically designed and printed in the district town. Guests then used the envelope to hold monetary merit offerings, or, in the case of a wedding, cash gifts for the bride and groom. In addition to the expected holiday foods—particularly beef dishes, rice noodles with a fish or chicken curry, and boiled rice confections—the host usually offered guests an abundant supply of commercial liquor and soft drinks. Truly prestigious events included an evening of entertainment, preferably performed by a professional drama or musical troupe, or a feature-length movie shown on a giant open-air screen. This component of the celebration alone might cost the host family anywhere from ten thousand to fifty thousand *baht* ($400 to $2,000 U.S.). At the very least the hosts would try to rent an electronic sound system so that a microphone and amplifier could broadcast taped music and the speeches of hosts and honored guests as widely as possible throughout the village. The lavish style with which the wealthiest village families were able to conduct these ceremonies was appreciated and praised by all participants.

Individually, the majority of Baan Naa Sakae households could not replicate these festive achievements but, under some circumstances and through cooperative effort, even poor families might share in the prestige of these "up-to-date" displays. For example, a number of years before my fieldwork, an elderly and revered village monk died. His closest relations included a cluster of some of Baan Naa Sakae's poorer families, for whom the expenses of an elaborate memorial were prohibitive. However, in this case they were able to draw on the whole community (because of the deceased's status as a monk) to hold a major memorial ceremony and to fund the construction of an elaborate shrine on the temple grounds that featured a life-size plaster statue of the monk in a meditation pose. Although this was a community effort, the memorial ceremony and shrine remained sources of special pride among the monk's kin. It was a public statement that they, too, could mobilize the same symbols of status and success as their wealthier and more powerful neighbors. In general, however, such opportunities were rare for poorer villagers whose material constraints clearly limited their ability to participate in the symbolic manipulation of commodities as status markers. While unwilling to abandon the field entirely, Baan Naa Sakae's poor were generally spectators at the ceremonial successes of their neighbors. Indeed, their place as guests was often secured only by "helping" out with the preparations.

Thansamay Style and Village Houses

Household ceremonials not only required the use and display of a wide range of market commodities; as important occasions of hospitality between villagers, they also placed on display the most prominent sign of family status: the house. In the past, the size of a house, particularly the number of supporting wooden pillars which marked out its length and width, was the primary point of comparison. Built well above ground, Isan homes were not usually divided into rooms, although a few small sleeping and/or storage chambers might be built along a wall or in a corner. A large and spacious interior allowed for greater air circulation in the hot weather and also was a measure of the number of guests the household could accommodate for ceremonies and other events to display hospitality. These "old" houses, most of which were built from ten to twenty-five years ago, were made of hand-hewn wood. Only the second story was enclosed, leaving the ground level open as a work area, a place to relax and visit with neighbors as well as to store tools and keep cattle or water buffalo safe at night. Even the more private second story often had part of one or two walls open to the air. While this allowed for better ventilation in a hot climate, it also left the internal activities of the household partially open to public view.

New houses constructed in Baan Naa Sakae, especially during the last decade, marked a departure from this older pattern to embrace a range of more "modern" styles. More than size or spaciousness, what was most valued in these newer homes was the degree to which the building approximated architectural models more commonly found in urban settings. Rather than the number of pillars, the use of modern construction materials and finishing evoked the greatest admiration. Thus, the houses judged "most beautiful" in Baan Naa Sakae were those that had incorporated such materials as concrete pillars, specially cut and shaped doors and windows, machine-tooled wooden railings and eaves, glass windows, and, most desirable of all, a finished ground level with concrete block walls and a poured concrete floor. These newly constructed homes of wood and concrete stood in stark contrast not only to the roomier but roughly worked, older houses but also to the humble wood and bamboo shacks of Baan Naa Sakae's poorest families. Easily overshadowed, the homes of the village's poor hugged the village margins or hid in the shadow of more fortunate neighbors.

The manner of building had changed as well. Older-style houses were often built using the labor of household members, relatives, and neighbors, under the supervision of someone skilled in these matters. Most new houses in Baan Naa Sakae were constructed by a team of hired builders. The more "urban" in style the house, the more its owners required the services of skilled carpenters, brick layers and electricians to ensure the proper installation of doors, windows, concrete walls and floors, and electrical outlets.[13] Consequently, these houses were extremely expensive by village standards and it was no easy feat to raise the money required for such displays of conspicuous consumption. Labor costs alone could exceed 10,000 *baht* ($400 U.S.). One particularly elaborate house, erected in 1990, reportedly cost its owners over 100,000 *baht* ($4,000 U.S.) and that was without an enclosed concrete ground floor that was to be completed later.

The most stylish homes in Baan Naa Sakae had all been built either with remittances from long-term (five years or more) overseas migration, or by families with access to the steady salaried income of a civil servant. For example the above-mentioned 100,000–*baht* home belonged to the family of a man who commuted to a government job in the provincial center some forty kilometers away. One family in Baan Naa Sakae managed to build the frame for a new house, only to leave it standing, unfinished and uninhabitable, when the money for labor and materials ran out. Yet even this partial achievement, as well as the efforts of many other families who were stockpiling construction materials beneath their old—and in their words "ugly," "falling apart"—houses, served as a sign to themselves and to others of their readiness to lay claim to *thansamay* standards of success and social prestige, if only in installments.

More than a statement about purely material assets, the construction of a new house was a claim to a particular identity, one which emphasized a knowledge and practice of up-to-date Thai ways. An important aspect of this identity was the possession of large commodity items. Many of these items, including electric fans, radios, and even small televisions, could be found in many households in Baan Naa Sakae, not solely those with "urban" style homes. But other, more expensive commodities, such as refrigerators, motorcycles and color televisions, were owned by only a few households.

In many ways, the value of these large commodities almost necessitated a modern house for their storage and display. First, the closed style of the new houses, with four finished walls and locking doors and windows, made it possible to keep these items safe from both the weather and potential theft. Second, the ideal of a finished ground floor allowed the household to keep their possessions safe and also display them to friends and neighbors. The open area underneath older houses was a relatively public space. Few people, including close neighbors, would enter the living area above unless invited for a meal or as guests at a ceremony, but the area below was more or less freely accessible. This was where people gathered in the hot afternoons or early evenings to talk and gossip while doing small chores, weaving cloth, or just relaxing. The finished ground floors of newer houses usually included a wide entryway, which often took up most of the front wall. Large wooden doors were folded back during the day, maintaining a sense of open space available to public observation. At the same time, the finished walls marked off the boundaries of household privacy more sharply. In general, visitors were hesitant to enter the walled-off ground floor areas of these homes, in sharp contrast to the easier movement of neighbors and friends in the space beneath older-style homes.

The display function of some newer homes was facilitated by the frequent decision to utilize the enclosed ground floor as a small store.[14] Food and sundry items, purchased on regular trips to the nearby market town and brought back to sell in the village, were arranged in glass cases and on wooden benches and tables. In addition to the goods offered for sale, however, the shop served as a display case for the household's most modern and expensive belongings. A refrigerator was often in plain view and also allowed the shop to stock small portions of fresh meat and other perishable items.[15] Large pieces of wooden furniture, cabinets with glass doors, plastic-covered armchairs and other evidence of material wealth would commonly be kept in this part of the house.

Most important, however, was the central placement of a color television. Although televisions were increasingly common in Baan Naa Sakae, they were by no means a universal feature, especially not color screens. The color televisions made village stores centers for public gathering (no doubt boosting sales). Usually the television was raised on a stand or small table and placed a meter or two inside the door of the shop; household members, close relatives, and small children would often sit on the floor immediately in front of the set while neighbors and other frequent customers generally watched from a wide bench or platform placed just outside the door in the yard. Small groups gathered in front of these stores every evening to watch the 8:00 P.M. national news, followed by the latest installments of nightly serial dramas.

The popularity of televisions in Baan Naa Sakae was no coincidence. Owning a television was desirable in part because, with market prices beginning at several thousand *baht*, the technology itself represented a significant investment of cash resources. But beyond signaling their owners' wealth and status, televisions were equally important avenues of cultural access for all viewers. News broadcasts, serial dramas, sporting events, advertising segments—all offered varied but largely celebratory images of the nation, especially centered on the consumption-oriented lives of the urban (Bangkok) elite and middle class. Television connected people in Baan Naa Sakae to dominant visions of the Thai nation and *thansamay* society, in which urban progress and commodified style often contrasted sharply with images of rural life that ranged from nostalgia for a simpler past to outright ridicule of backward and superstitious peasants.

More than just observers, however, television viewers in Baan Naa Sakae also engaged the images and ideas they encountered. The content of television broadcasts formed the subjects of casual conversation, as when, for example, neighbors recounted the latest plot twists in nightly serial dramas to those who had missed an episode. Television advertising frequently provoked commentaries in my presence. In particular, the lavish wealth and luxurious amenities depicted in many ads (such as cellular telephones, automated bathroom plumbing, palatial homes) prompted remarks about the presumed quality of life I had left behind in the United States and the comparative impoverishment of residence in Baan Naa Sakae. Such comments reflected, in part, people's unresolved curiosity about me and my reasons for wanting to live in their community. But accompanying these remarks was an awareness among most community residents that, regardless of the increasing convenience and progress that they might achieve in Baan Naa Sakae, their efforts inevitably fell short of the urban images of *thansamay* life beamed nightly into their homes and those of their neighbors.

Commodification and Migration Decisions

The commodification of production and consumption in Baan Naa Sakae and communities like it across Thailand reveal at one level the economic demands placed on small-scale agriculturists in a capitalist economy. At the same time, it is important to recognize how practices in Baan Naa Sakae reflected an ongoing redefinition of both basic subsistence needs and local understandings of what constituted a desired quality of life (see Turton, 1984:34). The central value of "updated" community infrastructure, new technologies, urban housing styles, and commodified practices—all point to what Maeyaay Sii implied in her comments on modern convenience, that is, a shift in community needs and aesthetic standards.

Urban-associated styles and commodities were popular in Baan Naa Sakae because they evoked images of wealth, comfort, and beauty; these, in turn, enhanced the standing of those villagers who could afford them. Similarly, improvements in community services (such as electricity and running water) bolstered local claims to standards of progress and development set by the dominant national society.[16] At the same time, however, access to markets and consumer commodities, electricity and piped water, and other such modern conveniences entailed regular and sometimes large amounts of cash expenditures to maintain even a minimal level of conformity to these new standards of community existence. The movement of local women and men into urban wage employment must be assessed in relation not only to the commodification of local subsistence needs but also to the parallel intensification of consumption desires more generally.

These aspirations for *thansamay* consumption intersect with household responsibilities to shape migration decisions. As I explain in the next chapter, rural-urban migration involves much more than household calculations of economic need. Labor mobility from Baan Naa Sakae cut across the community, involving almost every household from the wealthiest to the poorest. And in many cases the decision to leave for Bangkok had relatively little to do with the immediate economic needs of local households. In particular, young women and men, the most mobile segment of the community, viewed Bangkok employment as a chance to experience the dynamic core of the *thansamay* Thai nation, including the pleasures of mass-market commodity consumption. For many migrants, going to the city was an opportunity not only to see the economic and political center of the country but also to pursue a more sophisticated sense of personal modernity.

CHAPTER 4

Parents, Children, and Migration Decisions

══╪══

"Nowadays we must follow our children's hearts."
—Phôyaay Daeng

*I*n 1967 or perhaps in 1968—she could not remember precisely—Mae Kaew became the very first person to leave Baan Naa Sakae for Bangkok. She was then in her late teens. The second of eleven girls in one of the village's poorest families, she remembered well her decision to go with the agent who was recruiting women to work in the capital as domestic servants. "I got 150 *baht* per month. That was a lot in those days and we needed the money." A lot of young women from villages in the area went with the agent at the same time, Kaew recalled, although she was the only one from Baan Naa Sakae. She stayed in Bangkok for only a few months that first trip, but returned to the city many more times in the following years. "It was hard at first, especially being the only one going [to the city]. People in the village would gossip, saying I was working as a prostitute. But they stopped saying that when a lot of others started going [to Bangkok] too."

In 1971 recruiters came to Baan Naa Sakae looking for people to work in a burlap sack factory near Bang-pha-in, an industrial center fifty kilometers to the north of Bangkok. Nearly thirty women and two men, most in their late teens, agreed to go; the company provided a bus that brought them directly to the factory site. One woman, Yao, who was eighteen at the time, remembered that her parents were reluctant to let her go with the others: "But I asked them to agree, so that I could earn some money. It was a *very* dry year." Workers lived six to a room at the factory, women in one dormitory, men in another. Like factory workers a generation later, they worked shifts of eight hours and rotated shifts once a week. They earned sixteen *baht* per day ($0.64 U.S.). Yao left after just two months; some others stayed longer but, within a year or two, "Everyone came home again." Almost twenty years later, in 1990, Yao's memories of her time in the factory were still vivid. "[The work] was hard, long hours and the dormitory wasn't very clean. In the factory it was always hot and the air so dusty—and the noise! Also the money was not really enough and I missed home. But we had fun too. We would go around (*pay thiaw*) on Sunday, our day off, and buy things in the market."

Throughout the 1970s Baan Naa Sakae youth continued moving into Bangkok jobs in increasing numbers. Some found work as domestic servants, like Kaew, while others took on factory employment, most often in the city's growing textiles industry. Some left for the city as young as age thirteen or fourteen, almost as soon as they had finished their primary education. Others waited until their late teens or early twenties, sometimes after continuing their studies for several years at the district high school or a provincial college. This movement, particularly by unmarried sons and daughters, is generally understood both by migrants and those left behind as an important way for village youth to help their families. However, as Yao's comments suggest, the responsibilities young people feel toward parents and siblings are not the only concerns underlying the search for urban employment. Migration is also a chance for adventure, a means to acquire new experiences and to exercise a degree of personal independence that few would otherwise enjoy until much later in life as parents and householders in their own right. Parents and children alike identify migration to Bangkok as an encounter with *chiiwit thansamay*, "modern life."

Although framed by general conditions within the Thai economy and society, particular migration decisions are made in the context of rural households and respond to the needs, obligations, and aspirations of individual family members. For youthful migrants in particular, these decisions mark the intersection of two different sets of social relations and identities: first, their junior position and gendered obligations within parental households and, second, their own aspirations to participate in the *thansamay* excitement and adventure of urban modernity. Both help to propel the out-migration of Baan Naa Sakae youth while also shaping local expectations of the benefits to be derived from urban wage work as well as the dangers to beware. In the process, however, migration decisions and experiences often exacerbate conflicts in household relations, especially between parents and children. These tensions are usually strongest for parents of young women working in Bangkok, for whom the advantages of a daughter's urban wage earnings may clash with their loss of authority over her labor and sexuality.

Age, Merit, and the Authority of Parents

Ties binding parents and children in Baan Naa Sakae are informed by the asymmetrical reciprocity and deep-rooted morality of *bun khun*, the Buddhist concept of obligations based on "debts of merit." According to this powerful set of social and cultural ideals, parents bestow their *bun khun* (meritorious acts of compassion, sacrifice, and beneficence) upon children by giving them life, loving and caring for them as they grow. In return, children owe their parents not only life-long gratitude and respect but also—and increasingly as they mature—their active assistance, including labor and income, in the material and spiritual support of the parental household. Mothers and fathers, because of their greater age, knowledge, and experience of the world, have resources which they willingly employ to feed, clothe, and teach their children so that they can grow and mature into strong adults. As parents age and can no longer work to support themselves, it becomes the adult children's responsibility to see to their parents' material needs and comforts. Even after a parent's death, the child must continue to honor and care for the parent's spirit by performing periodic merit-making ceremonies. In accordance with Buddhist belief, such continuing acts of respect and gratitude help to speed the deceased on to the next rebirth and may turn aside possible misfortunes that neglected souls may visit upon the living.

Ideals of *bun khun* reciprocity place all children in a position of life-long obligation to their parents. Young people, as they reach adolescence and throughout their adult lives, owe their parents and elders not only obedience and respect but also material support. As soon as young children are physically able, Baan Naa Sakae parents begin to enlist their help with household and farm chores. Among the most important tasks assigned from a relatively early age is the care of young infants and toddlers by their elder siblings, thereby freeing the parents for other tasks. Parents entrust both daughters and sons with these and many other chores as they grow up. Boys and girls both learn a wide range of household skills; frequently I observed children age ten or younger doing their own laundry, tending chickens and ducks, helping in the household garden or with the evening meal. And as they get older, children take on more and more household chores. When the elementary school is in session, children between the ages of seven and twelve have considerably less time and energy for these activities. Nonetheless, by the time most children have completed their six years of mandatory primary education, they are already contributing to the household economy.

While many chores—hauling water from nearby ponds, laundry, gardening, helping in the family fields—can be performed by boys and girls alike, parents commonly teach their sons and daughters more gender-specific skills as well. Most children learn the rudiments of cooking, but daughters usually receive more extensive instruction in creating varied dishes and special confections. Many Baan Naa Sakae mothers also teach their daughters how to produce hand-woven cloth, especially simple patterns made with store-bought cotton or synthetic yarns. If their mothers or grandmothers raise silk, girls may also learn how to feed and tend the delicate worms and to spin their cocoons into long, even skeins of silk thread. However, when I lived in the community, only a few girls and young women were learning the most difficult skills of silk dyeing and weaving. Many in their mothers' generation no longer performed these tasks themselves; instead, they contracted with others to do dyeing and weaving for a fee or a share of the final cloth.

Sons, for their part, spend more effort learning the "heavy" tasks of farming—plowing, threshing, wood felling, house-building and repairs—as well as the tending of household livestock. Although I never encountered boys learning to weave or girls learning skills of carpentry, knowledge of most other household tasks is acquired to some degree by children of both sexes. This reflects the relatively fluid division of labor by gender in most rural households. In Baan Naa Sakae, as in most parts of Thailand, men and women share much of the agricultural work: harvesting, transplanting, weeding. Although men more often perform the most strenuous jobs, such as plowing, if no men are available then many women are quite capable of filling in. Similarly, even if domestic tasks such as cooking and cleaning are more often done by women, village men can and do take over when necessary. Nevertheless, this flexibility does not mean that Baan Naa Sakae parents look upon daughters and sons as interchangeable nor that adolescent boys and girls view their responsibilities to parents in identical terms. In fact, village parents tend to rely more heavily on the daily labor of daughters than that of sons, a pattern linked to the different paths young men and women are expected to take as they approach marriageable age.

Before marriage, a son's most important obligation to his parents is (if possible) to take up the yellow robes and ascetic vows of the Buddhist monastic order, the Sangha. The conventional ideal is for the young man to be ordained and reside in a temple community of monks throughout a single Buddhist Lenten season (the rainy months between July and October), but he may also observe the vows for a much shorter period, perhaps a few weeks, or for much longer. There is no required period of time. This act, which earns religious merit for his parents and anyone else who sponsors him, is seen as the primary duty a young man owes his parents. The link between a son's ordination and the *bun khun* received from his father and mother was made explicit by Baan Naa Sakae's ritual expert (*môô sut*) as he performed soul-tying ceremonies (*baay sii suu khwan*) for the young men who had decided (or agreed to their parents' suggestions) to take their vows the year I lived in the community. In each case, the ordinand was urged to think of his father and mother and their many sacrifices to feed and care for him, dwelling in particular on his mother's suffering during the long months of pregnancy and the pain of childbirth (see also Keyes, 1986:76). This segment of the ceremony never failed to move the young men to tears.

By entering the monastic order (whether he remains a monk only a short time or for many years), a son generates a store of merit for his parents, especially his mother, who have given him up to the higher authority and sacred power of the Sangha. The tremendous value attached to this act shapes parental expectations that sons will "leave" their care and authority when they mature. This belief is only strengthened when a son marries and, following the preference common in most of rural Thailand, he moves into his wife's household.[1] As a result, when young men marry they are often "lost" to their parents' household as a source of productive labor. In Baan Naa Sakae this was most obvious in cases where a man married into a different village from the one of his birth, but even when men married within Baan Naa Sakae, their primary household responsibilities shifted from working in their parents' fields to those of their in-laws.

The expectation that sons will leave the parental household—both through ordination and at marriage—contrasts sharply with the future most parents envision for daughters. Ordination into the Sangha is not an option for women in Thailand. There is an intermediary category for women who may become *mae chii*, "nuns," a ritual status greatly inferior to that of monks. Even the oldest nun ranks below the most recently ordained monk. Men are encouraged to spend some time as members of the Sangha, especially during their twenties, and thereafter are referred to by honorific titles marking this status. By contrast, women who become *mae chii* are often viewed as trying to escape from something in their lives such as an illness or a failed romance, rather than pursuing a positive route to spiritual development (Van Esterik, 1982b). Moreover, by taking on the status of *mae chii* a daughter does not earn a large store of merit for her parents. Rather, a daughter can uphold her *bun khun* obligations to parents only through her respectful obedience to their authority and by her contributions toward the physical and material well-being of the household. Furthermore, when Baan Naa Sakae

FIGURE 8. Returning from Bangkok, a young migrant prepares for his ordination as a Buddhist monk in his home village.

women married, they usually continued to reside at home; in such cases, parents not only did not lose their daughter's labor, they gained that of her new husband. Once a child was born or another sister was ready to marry, most couples moved out to set up a separate household. However, they might not move very far, often building a new house in Baan Naa Sakae, sometimes within the same residential compound as the wife's parents.[2]

These widely held beliefs concerning ordination and marriage patterns, shape not only the expectations that parents and children have of their reciprocal obligations and future relationships; they also encourage different patterns of gender socialization. In particular, sons are allowed more independence in their daily activities than daughters. By the time they reach their late teens, most young men in Baan Naa Sakae spend considerable portions of their time (if they are not in school) roaming about the village and local area in the company of friends. Young women, on the other hand, generally stay closer to home and, as far as I could observe, spend much more of their time performing household tasks. However, the new geographic and social mobility of Baan Naa Sakae's young women and men means that the understandings and desires of many village parents and children concerning their appropriate roles and relations do not always mesh smoothly. As I argue below and in the following chapter, these tensions are especially sharp in the case of young women's labor mobility.

Migration and Filial Obligation

As the demand for cheap labor in Bangkok's manufacturing and service industries began to expand in the 1960s and 1970s, urban wage employment presented new options for rural men and women. Farming families throughout the Northeast confronted unpredictable crop markets, a growing scarcity of new land to clear, and an increasing dependence on purchased commodities for every aspect of household and community life. When the first labor recruiters began to appear in the Baan Naa Sakae area toward the end of the 1960s, they found a receptive population. However, the new experiences and economic resources of Baan Naa Sakae's youthful migrants have also introduced alternative sources of authority into their relations with parents at home. At the time of my research, while economic and moral obligations to assist rural kin continued to legitimize the mobility of sons and daughters both in their own and their parents' eyes, most Baan Naa Sakae youth valued the move to Bangkok as an opportunity to be in the city and therefore at the heart of *thansamay* Thai society. Working in Bangkok offered young migrants a means to acquire prestigious commodity items and to engage in new, more "up-to-date" and sophisticated activities than were available at home. Migrants in Bangkok could accumulate both money and a store of *thansamay* knowledge and experience beyond the reach of their peers left behind in Baan Naa Sakae.

Young men's and women's keen desires for *thansamay* styles and practices were recognized by most village residents; indeed, the effects of such attractions on local youth were a common source of complaint among the community's elders. In 1990, Phôyaay Daeng, aged sixty-four, had two unmarried daughters and a son working in the capital city. Young people nowadays, he argued, behaved very differently than in his youth:

> In my youth we wanted to go work in the fields, to help our parents. All our friends did the same. Now children go to school for so many years and they don't want to do farm work. Especially boys. They would rather *pay thiaw*, drink liquor and smoke cigarettes, and their parents let them. Parents don't make their children do a lot of work because they want them to finish school. Boys, in particular, these days do not listen to or obey their elders. Girls do more at home and work harder, but they too are less well supervised than before. Before, if a young girl wanted to go to another village to a festival or to see a troupe of *môô lam* singers, then her mother would go along as well. Now they just go off with the boys and who knows what goes on?

Maeyaay Lin, age seventy-seven, echoed Phôyaay Daeng's assessment:

> Children today are irresponsible, especially the boys. They only drink, smoke cigarettes, and go around looking for fun. They don't know how to work in the fields, not like when I was young. Now they only play. Girls are better and help their parents more, but still they don't want to do work like weaving or transplanting the way they should. It began when the children started to study [past the mandatory primary level]. Those who did not study further stayed home and worked hard in the fields, looking after cattle and buffalo; but those going on in school wouldn't do these things as much. Now, though, the ones who study and the ones who don't, they are all the same. They just want to play.

No doubt part of the dissatisfaction of elders like Phôyaay Daeng and Maeyaay Lin may be traced to a feeling among members of most generations who, as they age, find that their juniors are not as obedient and respectful as they would like. The young people whom I observed in Baan Naa Sakae appeared to perform many household tasks: driving cattle and buffalo to pasture, helping to raise silk worms and spin their cocoons into thread, hauling water from nearby ponds, washing clothes, tending gardens, and more. At peak agricultural seasons, young people worked in the fields alongside their parents, transplanting, harvesting, threshing. Nevertheless, the possibility of migration to the city meant that young people in the village, with or without higher education, had other options.

Not surprisingly, household needs and parental authority were more likely to determine a child's departure for Bangkok when the child was younger. This was particularly true among those migrants who left Baan Naa Sakae soon after finishing their primary education, often at the age of thirteen or fourteen. In most cases these youngsters came from the poorest families in Baan Naa Sakae; their parents could not afford to send them on to the high school in the district center, and the added income of even a young teenager might be essential to keeping the family afloat. As Mae Kaew admitted, "Children of thirteen or fourteen can't earn very much. But Phô Tum and I have decided that Aen [their daughter] will have to go to work in Bangkok next year, as soon as she finishes her sixth year certificate [at the village elementary school]." Although Aen had good grades and there was a chance that she might earn a tuition scholarship to continue her studies at the district high school, Mae Kaew was firm in her plans to send Aen to stay with a relative who ran a small sewing shop in Bangkok. "My sisters in the city [both working as domestic servants] send money so our son can continue his studies a little longer, but there isn't enough for both and it's better that Aen work. Even if she got a scholarship, that wouldn't cover everything. There are the daily bus fares and the spending money she would need; we would not be able [to pay it all]."

Although such young migrants commonly worked in the lowest-waged positions—domestic service, small sewing or food shops—they at least might earn enough to support themselves and not be a drain on the family income. Somthop, a classmate of Kaew's daughter and the youngest child of Phô Lum and Mae Phim, faced a similar prospect as the son of another poor household. When asked about his own preferences, Somthop answered, "It would be good to study further, but my parents need me to work." He thought he would "probably like" working in the city. "He'll have to help out once he's done with school," Mae Phim commented. "I just hope he doesn't forget about us." Mae Phim's fear was expressed somewhat jokingly but it reflected the recognition among many in Baan Naa Sakae that parental authority over sons and daughters in the city was sharply diminished. In particular, parents' desires to ensure regular remittances of a child's urban wages had to compete with the more immediate pressures young migrants felt to spend their earnings on desired forms of *thansamay* style and urban entertainment.

Youth and *Thansamay* Autonomy

Baan Naa Sakae residents of all ages acknowledged that beyond the hard work and insecurity of farming, village life could seem boring when compared to the variety of entertaining sights and activities available in the city. These opinions received constant reinforcement from villagers' consumption of daily television broadcasts. News shows, dramatic and comic series, as well as the ever-present and highly sophisticated advertising segments drew rural viewers into the seductive symbolism, images, and meanings of Thailand's national (i.e., Bangkok-based) culture. Village youth were particularly avid television fans, perhaps because many media productions employ themes and images clearly directed toward a younger audience. The faces and fashions of youth are prevalent in advertising selling everything from cold medicine to soft drinks and cellular telephones. Popular serial dramas frequently focus on the romantic trials and tribulations of one or more pairs of youthful heroes and heroines. This is a formula also common to traditional folk tales and operas, but the plots of contemporary broadcasts almost always place the story and its protagonists in identifiably up-to-date settings, where the architecture, landscapes, and the characters' activities emphasize associations between youth, romance, and *thansamay* style. Luxurious urban homes, resort hotels and tourist beaches, discotheques and flashy nightclubs, shopping malls, university campuses, dance studios, martial arts classes, and automobile dealerships—these were the kinds of venues featured on television serials that aired in 1990 and that many Baan Naa Sakae viewers followed faithfully.

Many young people in Baan Naa Sakae were especially eager to watch the weekly broadcasts of popular music concerts. These include "traditional" *môô lam* performances of songs with Lao-Isan lyrics as well as *luuk thung* "country-style" soloists and duets; however, most popular among rural viewers were the shows featuring Thai pop-rock bands. For example, every Sunday afternoon, concerts featuring a famous pop music performer were broadcast nationally from an outdoor stage at the Crocodile Farm, one of several large amusement parks in the Bangkok area. Week after week, young Baan Naa

Sakae viewers watched this parade of stars whose hit songs they already knew from repetition on village transistor radios. They also saw the excited members of the audience, young men and women like themselves. Moreover, many looked forward to the day when, like others from Baan Naa Sakae already working in Bangkok, they could attend these concerts from time to time on their days off (see Chapter 7).

Such images of urban modernity combine with the real obligations young women and men feel to assist rural family to heighten the desires of adolescent sons and daughters to leave Baan Naa Sakae and find a job in Bangkok. Many discussed their wish to spend time in the city as though urban employment were almost an essential rite of passage through which they would gain an enhanced sense of personal autonomy and *thansamay* cultural authority. Even the children of Baan Naa Sakae's poorest families, for whom economic reasons to migrate were especially pressing, usually told me that they wanted to work in Bangkok, at least in part, "because I want to have the experience."

Nim's story reveals some of the appeal that Bangkok holds for village youth. When I met her she was twenty-eight years old and the mother of two young children, but she recalled how she had yearned to go to Bangkok as a girl. Like many poorer village residents, her parents could not afford to pay for her schooling beyond the primary level, then four years. Instead, they sent her to the regional town of Khon Kaen to live with an aunt and to learn to sew. In Khon Kaen, the aunt put Nim to work doing most of the housework, including the care of her young nieces and nephews; she attended sewing classes in her free time. "But what I really wanted was to see Bangkok. I wanted to be beautiful. I wanted to have white (skin)." As more and more of her peers from Baan Naa Sakae began to leave for the city, Nim's desire to join them only increased. Finally her chance came in the form of a truck driver from the Central region; she eloped and went to live with him in the capital.

During the four years she lived with her husband in Bangkok, Nim worked at a variety of odd jobs and eventually began selling noodle dishes on the street from a small, mobile vending cart. However, the marriage was troubled; her husband drank, gambled, and ran after other women. Still, they remained together in the city until one day he was involved in a serious traffic accident as a result of which he lost his trucking job. With no job and no money, Nim and her husband had to leave Bangkok; they returned to Baan Naa Sakae to live with her parents. "My luck has not been good. My marriage is not happy. It was a bad decision then [to marry him]. I'm tired of my husband and his drinking. If it weren't for my sons, I'd like to end [the marriage]. If I had stayed single, I could have done better." Nevertheless, Nim worked hard in Baan Naa Sakae to preserve aspects of a self-image that reflected her claims to urban experience in contrast to her present circumstances. Unlike other married women in the community, she wore stylish slacks rather than the more common sarong wrap (*phaa sin*); she also preferred a pair of higher-priced sandals with elevated heels to the cheaper rubber thongs worn by most of her neighbors.

Nim maintained her aspirations for urban status well beyond her actual migration career. Her actions reflect powerful meanings that dominate Thai society, and assert the primacy of urban *thansamay* styles and practices over those of rural communities. In Baan Naa Sakae it is not only migrants from poorer families like Nim who make connections between social status or achievement and city-bound mobility. Such concerns exercised an equally if not more powerful influence over the members of Baan Naa Sakae's wealthier households. This was especially clear in the cases of those village youth who had studied several years past the primary level, often completing high school, technical college, or even a bachelor's degree. Almost universally, these daughters and sons felt that the status they had already attained through higher education could not be sustained if they simply returned home to take up farming alongside their parents. Entering the civil service was the goal for most of these educated youth; government work was sufficiently prestigious in itself and need not involve an urban posting. But government positions were not always available nor quickly attained; as a result, some recent graduates from Baan Naa Sakae felt compelled to leave the village for Bangkok, at least in part, to uphold the new social standing they had acquired through education.

If the family was better off, a period of "rest" at home might be acceptable. This was the case for two sisters who remained in Baan Naa Sakae for over a year after graduating from the provincial teacher's college; during this time, they took periodic civil service exams and waited to test into a coveted teaching position. Just as I was leaving the village, the elder of the two received notification that she would start work the following term at a village primary school. The job required that she move to a distant province, albeit one still in Isan. In some cases, however, the stiff competition for government posts—as well as the potential for under-the-table payments to advance wealthier or better-connected candidates over others—meant that a graduate might have to wait indefinitely. This was the conclusion that Pui reached after graduating with a degree in agricultural sciences from a vocational college in Loey province. She had come home to Baan Naa Sakae to await her civil service exam results. When it appeared that a government appointment would be unlikely without an expensive gift to officials, Pui made up her mind to head for Bangkok. She had already worked there for a few years prior to her college studies; she had been a receptionist at a private job agency. The city no longer held any excitement for her: "I got bored after a few years." Nevertheless, returning to Bangkok would be better than remaining in Baan Naa Sakae with nothing to do: "I left home for higher studies. If I had to come back and live here . . . ?—I'd be ashamed. What would people think?"

Parental Dilemmas

Like their children, many parents viewed young migrants' search for urban employment both as a way to help the village family and as a way for children to build a better life. Ideally, they hoped that children would find a job that was at once higher in status and more secure than rice farming. These wishes, however, were tempered by concerns for the safety and moral development of offspring far from home. In particular, many parents feared their loss of authority to control the behavior and income of children.

Fathers and mothers in Baan Naa Sakae voiced mixed feelings about their sons' and daughters' migration to Bangkok. Like any parents, they wished their children to be happy and to have as comfortable a life as possible; yet, as they grew older, parents began to look to their offspring for material support. Labor migration offered an important means for children to pursue these goals both for themselves and for their parents. Yet men and women in Baan Naa Sake also worried about their children's safety living in the distant capital. For example, in mid-1990 a gasoline truck, rear-ended in a traffic accident, exploded on a crowded Bangkok street, causing a spectacular fire and the destruction of a major city block. News reports of the accident and its fiery aftermath were broadcast around the country. Baan Naa Sakae men and women watched in fear and horror. Could their son or daughter be one of the hundreds killed or maimed in the raging inferno? A few days later, an anxious father described his response: "I watched the television constantly until I could figure out where [in Bangkok] it happened. If it had been anywhere near the area where my children are working, I would have been on a bus [to the city] that night."

Nevertheless, most parents could put these fears aside; when a son or daughter wished to leave home for Bangkok, they usually gave their permission and as much money for the trip as they could afford. If the family were well off, this might be as much as 1,000 *baht* ($40 U.S.). Most hoped that the child would soon be able to assist the family, perhaps by making regular monthly wage contributions or, as was more common among Baan Naa Sakae migrants, through periodic remittances of larger sums. Still, the departure of a son provoked considerably less parental anxiety than that of a daughter. "Young men can take care of themselves," said Mae Sahn, whose son was working in a Bangkok bicycle factory. "I worry much more about my daughter, Phan." She was employed in a textile factory. Other mothers and fathers had similar responses.

But if sons were deemed more capable of coping with the uncertainties of urban life, parents also had fewer expectations that they would receive any direct material benefit from a son's urban employment. As noted above, by their early teens young men spent much of their time hanging about with friends, sometimes in Baan Naa Sakae and sometimes in neighboring communities where they might go seeking entertainment (*pay thiaw*). Consequently, their daily economic contributions to the parental household were often quite irregular, although at times of peak labor demand, these young men worked long hours in the fields alongside other family members. In this context, some parents reasoned that a son who was away working in Bangkok would at least be supporting himself. Any more than this was not to be expected.

Migrant sons who failed to send money home rarely faced parental censure, even in poorer households. I asked Phô Lum if he had received anything from his nineteen-year-old son, Beh, who had been working in Bangkok for several months. He laughed and said, "There's no point even asking that about a son [in Bangkok]. Now if it were one of my daughters, then you could ask that question." Of course, some young men in the city did bring or send money to their parents. This was most often the case if the migrants came from families with only sons or whose sisters were not yet of an age to find urban employment themselves. But a more common scenario was that recounted by Phôyaay Phum. When his son, Kiat, came home from Bangkok for a visit, he brought 1,000 *baht* for the family; however, by the time Kiat was ready to go back to his job in the city, he had no money of his own left. Phôyaay Phum had to give Kiat 1,100 *baht* for the return journey. "That's just the way sons are," he said.

Migrant daughters were usually considered "more responsible" with money and, therefore, a more reliable source of financial assistance to parents and kin in the village. "With daughters," one father argued, "parents will get something in return [*day phon*]." While fathers and mothers were proud of daughters working in the city who sent home regular earnings, their pride was tempered by fears for the young women's safety in the city. A daughter's absence in Bangkok could also mean a greater workload for her mother. By her mid-teens, a young woman often had responsibility for many of the most onerous household chores (cleaning, cooking, hauling water), easing much of the burden her mother had carried in earlier years. Furthermore, a daughter's early marriage could bring the benefit of an energetic son-in-law to boost the household labor supply. Unless another sister was available to help at home, Baan Naa Sakae parents might be reluctant to support a daughter's move to Bangkok.

However, such concerns had to compete not only with young people's wishes to see the big city but also with parents' own appreciation for the opportunities and benefits of urban employment. In at least one Baan Naa Sakae household, this led the parents to clash with their daughters over where the latter might go to work. Phô Som and Mae Nuu were extremely poor. They had lost all they owned—land, house, and livestock—to pay off debts that Phô Som acquired when he was cheated trying to find overseas contract employment. Soon after their two daughters finished primary school, the girls went to work in Bangkok: one in a candy factory, the other waiting tables at a sidewalk food shop. At first the teenagers sent money back every month, but after a while their remittances became more and more irregular. "They are young girls," admitted Mae Nuu. "They want to spend money on new clothes, luxuries like an iron, a cassette player, and going on outings (*pay thiaw*)." In early 1990, she and her husband persuaded their daughters to look for jobs closer to home. The two found positions as serving help for a food shop in the nearby district town. "The wages are less than in the city, but this way it is easier for us to get some money from them each month," Mae Nuu explained. But she and her husband feared that it would not be long before their daughters would leave again for Bangkok. "There's no progress here, not like in the city, and that's what young people want." A few months later, the two young women quit their local jobs and returned to work in Bangkok.

Like Mae Nuu and Phô Som, many Baan Naa Sakae parents acknowledged that their interests in a child's income and labor could not always compete with the desires of the younger generation for *thansamay* urban experience and excitement. In more than half a dozen Baan Naa Sakae households, parents lived all alone in the village while every one of their children had departed for employment elsewhere. I found similar patterns in almost every rural community that I visited in 1990, both in the area surrounding Baan Naa Sakae and in other Isan provinces. Over and over, rural residents pointed to a general exodus: "The youngsters all flee to the city. There's only old folks and the little children left at home." Most elders cited the potential for urban wage labor to serve as an appropriate way for youth to assist rural kin. Some parents, especially if money was short, strongly encouraged able children to try to find a city job. The consequence, however, for the parents of many of Baan Naa Sakae's mobile daughters and sons was a sharply diminished sense of their own authority. As more than one village parent told me, "These days we must follow our children's hearts."

Families in Baan Naa Sakae, both richer and poorer, viewed rural-urban migration, and especially the movement of young women, as a mixed blessing. Parents were as well aware as their children that village life held few chances for socioeconomic advancement. Desires for children to build a more secure future than that promised by the uncertainties of agricultural production alone were even sharper imperatives for those families that had been able to educate their children well beyond the primary level. Nevertheless, migration to the city was risky on many counts. Parents stood to gain both economically and in community standing from the successful urban career of a son or daughter. They did not do so, however, without cost—in particular, a distressing reduction in parental authority, both moral and economic—over unmarried children's lives.

Although in 1990 only a few Baan Naa Sakae households, like that of Mae Nuu and Phô Som, relied on migrant wage remittances for day-to-day subsistence needs, most parents of migrants called on their children to contribute wages toward major household expenses. These might include school fees and other costs at the beginning of each term (June and November), or harvest and transplanting labor costs (roughly November and December and July through September)—or whenever costly needs arose, such as medical expenses in the case of an accident or a sudden illness. The prospect of these benefits served to promote villagers' acceptance of their children's mobility; yet, unable to supervise the labor and leisure activities of absent children, Baan Naa Sakae parents could not enforce the economic contributions of migrant sons and daughters. Thus, a common complaint about village youth working in the city was that they sent money home to their parents only when specifically requested. Many villagers therefore faced an uncomfortable situation in which the cultural logic of parent-child *bun khun* relationships was reversed: Elders could no longer count on their ability to direct or even influence the actions of juniors. Parents were now in the unusual position of asking for a child's assistance and waiting for a share of their child's resources, rather than the other way around.

Such shifts were particularly dramatic when young women migrated for urban employment, for in these cases parents tended to expect more significant economic contributions than they did from migrant sons. When children were away working, parents missed and worried about them but, in the words of one father, "We worry more about our daughters, even if they have worked in the city for many years." As the next chapter examines in greater detail, these fears fed on the very images of urban sophistication, *thansamay* mobility, and autonomy that fueled their children's desires to leave home. Anxieties about migrant daughters often centered not only on parents' sense of diminished authority and control over the young women's labor and earnings but also on their sexual behavior: Many parents feared that absent daughters might become involved in romantic (and, therefore, potentially sexual) attachments. In particular, unmarried women's absence from the village raised questions back home about how (and with whom) they were spending their time. Village gossip often included speculation about the possible or actual sexual experience of young women working away from home.

Critical remarks about female migrants who were known to have had sexual relations before marriage exacerbated parents' concerns about their inability to control the sexual behavior of distant daughters. With no chance to supervise a daughter's contacts with young men (opportunities for which expand greatly in the city), parents feared not only for her physical safety but also that she might rush into an unsuitable romance.[3] If it became known (or reliably suspected) that their daughter was sexually experienced, parents worried that this loss of reputation might prevent her from making a suitable match. It could also make it difficult or impossible for parents to negotiate a respectable marriage payment. Just as worrisome were the experiences of several village households, where grandparents were raising grandchildren while their daughter, the mother, worked in Bangkok. Maeyaay Khan described her daughter's situation: "She met the father while she was working in the city; they came back here to live with us but he wasn't interested and left just after the baby was born. My daughter stayed on until the baby was weaned but then she went back to the city. She needs the money for the child now."

This case and others like it in Baan Naa Sakae and neighboring communities stood as sharp cautionary tales for many parents; village youth, although they often admitted that there were risks involved in labor migration, were sanguine. Young women as well as young men were more eager to emphasize the opportunities for excitement and personal growth. At the same time, the greater strength of daughters' household obligations meant that, much more than their brothers, young women had to reconcile their desires for the commodified forms and experiences of *thansamay* Thai society with the need to send money home to parents and siblings in order to maintain their standing as good women and dutiful daughters. In the next chapter I examine how these tensions converge to promote young women's labor migration. In the process, migrants' actions not only reflect conventional beliefs about their gender roles as rural daughters but also lead to startling reformulations of feminine identity that draw on dominant images of Thai modernity and mobility.

CHAPTER 5

Gender and Mobility

⇌

A friend who had been working in Bangkok came back to visit [our village]. She wore beautiful clothes. When she saw me, her greeting was, "Oh ho! How did you get so rundown looking? Want to come work with me?" . . . [That night] I lay thinking, "I ought to go give it a try." I dreamed that I would go [to the city], work really hard, and save money to help my family. I lay unable to stop thinking about this until I slept. I got up early in the morning and at once rushed to find my friend. I was so happy that I could go with her. I got my clothes ready and said good-bye to my brothers, sisters, father, and mother.
—Khem, Bangkok textile worker, age twenty-one[1]

*I*n this brief passage, a young Thai labor migrant gives an account of how she left home to begin urban employment at the age of sixteen. Central to this narrative is the moral impetus of a daughter's obligation— "I would work really hard and save money to help my family"—which anchors Khem's story in the affective world of village kin and agricultural poverty. But this projection of virtue and self-sacrifice parallels an alternate vision of the confident returning migrant with her "beautiful clothes" and teasing disdain for the sorry existence of her rural friend. It is as much the allure of urban sophistication and accumulation as her concern for the household economy that animates Khem's waking thoughts before sleep and propels her departure the next morning.

In these few sentences, Khem constructs two potential selves: the "good daughter," motivated by emotional ties and a deep sense of responsibility to rural family, and the "modern woman," whose independence and mobility are tied to her experience in urban society. Although Khem was not a native of Baan Naa Sakae—she grew up in a village in Central Thailand—her sense of obligation to rural kin and desire for *thansamay* status and commodified style were shared by almost all the women I knew in Bangkok. This was the case no matter what their regional origins, whether they came from Baan Naa

Sakae or elsewhere. Khem's brief narrative highlights some of the complex and conflicting motivations that push young rural women into urban labor. The labor mobility of rural youth is embedded in social and cultural tensions both within households (see Chapter 4) and within the individual herself. Khem's migration was prompted not just by dominant ideals of filial obligation (to "save money to help my family") but also by her desire to achieve the *thansamay* status enjoyed by already mobile peers, and by her longing for the "beautiful clothes" and other commodities that link their owners to valued standards of urban wealth and sophistication. This chapter explores how the movement of young rural women into Bangkok reflects these aspirations for distinct and at times competing forms of identity, the hope of most young migrants that they can be both good daughters and modern Thai women.

The Bangkok-bound mobility of Baan Naa Sakae and other village youth is a gendered process in part, then, because of the way Thai and Isan household relations shape the different expectations that parents have of daughters and sons. Migration to Bangkok represents an opportunity for Baan Naa Sakae's daughters and sons to fulfill household obligations by making money to send home. However, Buddhist ordination remains the most valued expression of a young man's gratitude to and respect for parents, an act in which daughters can never share. Instead, young women can only be judged on the basis of their obedience and industry, their attention to household chores and to the needs of parents and other family members. At the same time, these different standards for assessing young men's and women's household obligations incorporate contrasting beliefs about the appropriateness of their spatial mobility. The labor migration of sons is consistent with parental expectations that boys will eventually leave the home, first, ideally, to enter the Buddhist order of monks for a time, and, finally, moving into his wife's household at marriage. In the past, daughters have been much more likely to stay close to their parents, often living nearby throughout their lifetimes. Consequently, young women's participation in urban employment and rural-urban migration carries a different moral and cultural significance than the mobility of young rural men. In particular, women's labor migration departs sharply from established gender norms of spatial mobility.[2]

Gender distinctions can be subtle in Thailand. As in many parts of Southeast Asia, relations between men and women are not marked by a rigid patriarchal hierarchy. Buddhist conceptions privilege men over women, ascribing greater spiritual merit to men; however, in everyday interactions gender is only one factor influencing relative status and appropriate behavior between individuals. Women have access to important sources of authority and autonomy—through respected age or property ownership. Parental lands and assets, for example, are divided equally among heirs, daughters as well as sons. Other differences, such as education, occupation, a history of debts owed or favors given—which are not directly associated with gender—can mediate against the effects of female symbolic subordination in everyday practice. Distinctions of age, wealth, and other marks of status may have more bearing on the tone and character of social relations than the gender of specific actors.

Throughout Thailand, including the Northeast region and communities like Baan Naa Sakae, gender is neither a uniform nor a universal measure of status hierarchy. This does not mean, however, that Thai or Isan understandings either of how men and women differ or of their proper relationships are not deeply rooted or readily reproduced. Gender differences have important effects on the lives of people both in Baan Naa Sakae and throughout Thai society; they are embedded in the everyday patterns of social life, which are taken for granted. Gender distinctions are manifested subtly, but directly, in a gendered body language, which stresses limitation of contact between men and women, and the special necessity of controlling the movement of female bodies. These gendered body codes, in turn, have important effects on the meanings and contradictions that underlie the labor migration of rural women.

Central to these understandings of gendered bodies are Thai and Isan beliefs about sexuality, specifically the largely positive status attributed to masculine sexual activity in contrast to more negative assessments of feminine sexuality. Men's sexual behavior, unless constrained by a monk's vows of celibacy, has conventionally raised few moral questions in Thai society; indeed, sexual experience is generally considered a positive aspect of masculine identity, whether within or outside of a marital relationship.[3] By contrast, female sexuality carries a more ambivalent moral charge. Unless it is contained within a clear conjugal bond, women's sexual activity risks association with the stigma of prostitutes as women "with many husbands." Moreover, female sexuality and bodily fluids carry an inherent, though intangible, power that, if improperly directed, may have dangerous effects, particularly for men (see Mills, 1995). Masculine and feminine body codes link these gendered meanings of sexuality to appropriate styles and patterns of spatial mobility: Mobility in space is perceived as a natural and valued characteristic for men, while women's bodies and their movement are subject to far greater restrictions. As later chapters note, women's experiences of vulnerability in the course of rural-urban migration are linked to the way that geographic mobility challenges these conventional understandings of female bodies, their appropriate places, and sexual control.

First, however, it is important to look more closely at how people in Thai society, and specifically residents of Baan Naa Sakae, make connections between gender identity, spatial mobility, and sexual morality. Most scholarship has defined gender distinctions in Thai culture in relation to Theravada Buddhist concepts of women's greater attachment and men's relative detachment from worldly concerns, and related beliefs in the innate spiritual superiority of men over women. Without denying the significance of Buddhist precepts and beliefs, this chapter explores more corporeal understandings of gender difference.[4] Differences between men and women in Thailand are shaped by pervasive, if often subtle, beliefs about male and female bodies, the need to discipline their movement and to control their contact. These ideas underlie the gendered dynamics of rural-urban migration: In particular, they shape the values and desires that propel young women's movement into urban employment, while also contributing to the tensions and contradictions that women experience during their time in the city.

Gendered Bodies

Lek sat on her heels, resting, as I walked over to join her under the shade of the spreading tree. She was there at the Baan Naa Sakae temple grounds, like myself and most of the forty or so villagers who had gathered, to watch and help with a community work party. The construction of a large water tank was under way as part of a project to install the village's first system of running water. However, Lek, a slight woman in her mid-twenties, was also trying to keep an eye on her two small children, a boy of five years and a girl of two. "Yes," she answered my question, "it is hard work to raise small children. Especially boys." Her young son was tearing up and down the dirt path between the gate and the main temple buildings, shouting and play-fighting with a couple of other boys his age. "Boys are disobedient and obstinate; you tell them one thing and they will do the opposite, they are hard to teach. Not like girls." She looked at her daughter playing in the sand at her feet. "Girls learn quickly, they listen well." As she spoke, Lek began to play a game with her daughter, wrapping her about with a towel as though in a *phaa sin*, the sarong-like skirt particular to women's clothing. The little girl thought this a wonderful game, wiggling about until the *phaa sin* came loose

and then turning to Lek who re-wrapped her and carefully demonstrated the proper way to tuck in the cloth ends. "Beautiful," (*ngaam*)
she praised the little girl. They continued to play this way while Lek
and I chatted about the water project and her son raced back and
forth with his friends. A sharp fall on some gravel brought him crying
back to his mother and sister. Lek gently brushed him off and scolded
his tears: "Men don't cry, men must be strong (*khem khaeng*)." The
boy soon recovered and rushed off once more to his buddies.

This incident typifies the different body codes that boys and girls learn
in Baan Naa Sakae and that continue to shape their images of self and of
social interaction as they mature into adult men and women. Masculine virtues of action and strength contrast with feminine ones of beauty and restraint.
Although these provide lifelong codes of gender-appropriate behavior and
sources of social prestige, the points at which one may best fulfill either
strength or beauty fall in different stages of one's biography. Feminine beauty
is closely identified with virginal purity; it is primarily the domain of youth.
Masculine strength grows with age and experience; in general, it cannot be
fully developed without the maturity and knowledge gained by spending a
period of time in the Buddhist Sangha, the community of monks.[5]

Male potency entails not simply muscular development but the outward,
purposeful expression of the body's energies in action—movement, mobility, speed, and, for adult men, sexual prowess. This may appear to contradict
the monkly virtues of ascetic detachment; however, both strength and detachment are achieved through discipline.[6] Movement for its own sake is not the
point here; rather, a degree of self-discipline is necessary to guide and direct
bodily expressions of male strength. The time a young man spends as a monk
is perceived as an important means for developing the discipline he needs
for true maturity; in this way, ordination functions much like a rite of passage (Keyes, 1986). It tempers the "hot heart" (*cay rôôn*) of youth into the
"cool heart" (*cay yen*) of patience and good judgment, imparting knowledge
of when and how to act. Outside the Sangha, masculine strength is enacted
and validated in social relationships, primarily in male peer groups, such as
the drinking circle that exists at all levels of Thai society and is differentiated between classes only by the quality and cost of the alcohol consumed
and the sites frequented. While the rural laboring poor generally drink the
cheapest liquor on village porches and tell bawdy jokes and stories, elite urban men consume bottles of imported scotch at nightclubs or massage parlors where their claims to sexual prowess can be acted on directly. For Thai

men of every social status, drinking alcohol and sexual activity mark them off most clearly from monks but also characterize them as strong, masculine men. Failure to participate in these masculine activities, unless it is couched in a commitment to Buddhist precepts, risks labeling a man as unsociable, unfriendly, and perhaps of ambiguous gender identity.

Masculine strength also implies a degree of active participation in the world, including experiences that may require geographical mobility. Villagers in Baan Naa Sakae give considerable respect to adult community members who had been to distant places, who know about strange customs and have therefore acquired unusual sources of knowledge. Historically, opportunities to travel had been the exclusive prerogative of men. Until the early twentieth century, the institution of corvée labor enjoined mobility for large segments of the adult male population subject to the expanding authority of the Thai state; in some periods corvée duty took peasant men away from their own farms to work as laborers or conscript soldiers for up to six months a year (Akin, 1969). Coercive and highly disliked—like its present-day counterpart, the military draft lottery—corvée was nonetheless a masculine experience.

A more positive historical form of men's spatial mobility was the Northeastern "traveling salesman" (usually of cattle), the *naay hôôy*. One of Baan Naa Sakae's most prominent citizens had, as a younger man, traveled extensively in Isan selling cattle. He not only made a prosperous living but he studied *môô lam* singing during his travels and developed a fine reputation for his artistry both in the districts surrounding Baan Naa Sakae and in the towns along his trade route. Similarly, men and boys, when ordained as monks and novices, may travel to distant temples to pursue religious studies and other forms of special training. A monk may also take up the meditative practice of "wandering" (*thuu dong*).

Besides these long-standing opportunities for masculine mobility, most of the adult men in Baan Naa Sakae had engaged at some point in their lives in more general forms of traveling (referred to as *pay thiaw*). This activity occurs throughout Thailand but it is most closely associated with rural Isan (see Kirsch, 1966). In the 1960s, Thomas Kirsch reported that a period of youthful *pay thiaw* travel had been a common practice among Northeastern village men for several generations. Youths left home to seek adventure and sometimes to find work in other villages or other regions of the country; they might be gone for several months or even a period of years. Although most eventually returned home, some married and settled in far-away communities. Courting might also be an important object in these travels and Baan Naa

Sakae men, old and young, spoke to me of "going traveling, going courting" (*pay thiaw, pay len saaw*) both in the past or present, although their destination might only have been a village two or three kilometers distant. These comments underscored a widespread belief that some of the experience a man gained when traveling, unless he was a monk, was likely to be sexual. Certainly, a young man's absence from the home made it difficult for neighbors and family to know for sure. Moreover, as noted in Chapter 4, cultural preferences for men to move into their wife's home, at least in the initial stages of a marriage, further supported this association between male spatial movement and sexual activity.

By contrast, long-distance travel, especially alone and prior to marriage, was much less common historically for women in Baan Naa Sakae. In the past, women traveled to market towns in the company of relatives and friends to sell household produce, or they might move longer distances as part of a household to pioneer new land. By the 1980s, however, with the explosion of job opportunities for women in urban Thailand, single women regularly traveled from communities like Baan Naa Sakae into Bangkok and often did so on their own. Young women's increased geographic mobility could be justified in terms of daughters' obligations to help their rural families. Nevertheless, their departure from older, gender-differentiated patterns of mobility raised more serious challenges to norms controlling women's sexual activity through bodily restraint and physical modesty.

Beauty of the body is the particular concern of women in Thai cultural belief. Facial attractiveness is valued in both sexes, as in the phrase commonly used to describe men and women: *naa taa dii*, "good[-looking] face and eyes." In general, however, women's bodies are considered beautiful and alluring (*suay* or *ngaam*), not men's.[7] Although concepts of beauty clearly emphasize physical attractiveness, this feminine virtue, like masculine strength, is also concerned with the body's movement and its action in social contexts. In this case, however, the body's energy focuses inward in a discipline of restraint and modesty. A crucial task of feminine restraint is to guard the body's virginity or sexual purity (*khwaam borisut*). As in Lek's game with her daughter, controlled and graceful movement, decorum of action and of dress were praised and encouraged in Baan Naa Sakae girls from an early age. A girl who failed to show sufficient physical modesty or one who acted heatedly without regard for consequences was chastised for behaving in ways her elders considered "not beautiful" (*bô ngaam* in Lao or *may suay* in Thai). A young woman's beauty was located not only in the physical body but also in its gestures and, by extension, in the acts and situations in which it became involved. For example, when a young teenager shouted angrily during a fight with her parents—this open conflict was itself a significant breach of *bun khun* etiquette on the daughter's part. A neighbor commented on the situation: "It's not attractive, not beautiful (*bô ngaam*) to behave that way. She should be more respectful." Any situation that arises out of thoughtless and undisciplined actions to the discomfort and embarrassment of others may be described as "not beautiful," but particularly so when it involves a possible breach of modest behavior by or toward young unmarried women.

Mobility and Sexual Morality

I was sitting with several villagers in the shade of a roughly thatched shelter in a neighbor's yard. The intense mid-afternoon sun made the house interiors unbearable under their corrugated tin roofs so we congregated in this shady spot to catch what small breezes might blow by and to while away the day's hottest hours. The talk turned from the difficulties of the current planting season and the year's erratic rainfall to the return of our host's nineteen-year-old son from Bangkok, where he had been working at a cloth-printing factory for the past few months. The youth, Beh, who was sitting with us, had come home for a visit and would return to the city in a couple of days. As Beh answered our questions about his time in Bangkok, the thirteen-year-old daughter from the house next door, Wi', came over to join us. She sat down between Mai, her aunt, and Beh. Beh began to tease Wi', and poke her, saying she was becoming a *phuu saaw*, "a young woman," growing breasts and so on. Wi' scowled and pushed Beh away several times but she did not leave. Finally, Mai said to her, "What are you sitting so close to him for? If a young man (*phuu baaw*) acts like that, you have to leave. What you are doing now is the way to get a husband fast." Immediately, Wi' jumped up and moved away. No one said a word to Beh and the conversation continued as before.

Young girls like Wi' learn that it is their responsibility to maintain sufficient distance between their own and (sexually mature) male bodies. Although friends of the same sex may freely touch or embrace each other, physical contact of almost any kind between the sexes is considered a sign of sexual intimacy or at least sexual interest. Indeed, one of the only traditionally sanctioned occasions for public contact between a man and a woman is during the marriage ceremony. Yet as young women move into urban employment, their opportunities to meet with members of the opposite sex increase at the same time that parents and elders lose their ability to supervise these interactions.

My own experiences as a young unmarried woman in Baan Naa Sakae made the significance of the physical boundary between men and women clear. Members of the community were quick to criticize my actions when, unthinkingly, I transgressed this restriction against contact. On several occasions while living in Baan Naa Sakae, I encountered government officials or other individuals who, out of familiarity with Western customs, insisted on shaking my hand. I thought little of these encounters; however, they carried much weightier implications for Baan Naa Sakae observers. I did not become aware of this until one day when a male school teacher, hoping to practice some English, greeted me with a handshake. I was in the company of some twenty people from Baan Naa Sakae. We had traveled to another village in Buriram province, over one hundred kilometers distant, to attend a merit-making ceremony, sponsored by a former Baan Naa Sakae resident now living in his wife's community. After I shook the young man's hand, I was roundly scolded and teased for my inappropriate behavior in allowing the contact. However, the seriousness of my lapse was later reinforced in the villagers' eyes, and in my own, when not long after our return to Baan Naa Sakae, the teacher I had greeted so casually paid a visit to our community. He was traveling with a small group who were on a similar trip of ceremonial obligation to another village in our area; one of his companions was the man who had sponsored the ceremony we had all attended in Buriram. The travelers decided to stop in Baan Naa Sakae to visit some relatives; however, my neighbors assumed that I was the real attraction. As the only *farang* living in the area, everyone expected strangers to be interested in my presence, but the dynamics of this situation led several women to take me aside and warn me explicitly about the danger of accepting this teacher as a potential suitor. To begin with, they told me, he already had two wives in Buriram, one of whom had accompanied him on this trip.[8]

The demands of beauty, and its association with virginal purity, impose an ethic of constraint on young women's bodies. It was Wi's responsibility to guard herself from Beh's teasing advances, as it was mine to avoid inappropriate handshakes. This task is not necessarily an onerous one. Much of the pleasure and fun of courtship in Baan Naa Sakae derives from playful attempts by *phuu baaw* to breach barriers of feminine modesty and the flirtatious responses of *phuu saaw* by way of preventing this. Nevertheless, the greater limits on young women's actions mark important differences in the movements of unmarried adolescents within and beyond Baan Naa Sakae village. Both sons and daughters in their teens commonly perform chores for their families beyond the bounds of family compound and village: fetching water from a nearby pond, taking buffalo and cattle out to pasture or working in the fields. However, when not performing household chores, young women rarely range far on their own. Their brothers, however, may roam the community and the surrounding area with much greater freedom.

This contrast between the mobility of men's bodies and the controlled restraint preferred of women is by no means visible in every interaction or situation. These body codes define ideal standards of politeness and respectful behavior. A degree of physical casualness—often extending between individuals of the same sex to holding and touching of hands, legs, arms—is an important way to express intimacy and trust, comfort and relaxation in any relationship, especially between close kin and friends. However, unless the age differences are extreme or the kinship tie exceptionally close, the boundary between the bodies of men and women was carefully guarded. Almost any touch between a man and a woman—and especially deliberate contact—may connote sexual intentions, as I learned after my unfortunate handshake. The actual desires (or lack thereof) of either party were not important—a message of sexual interest was immediately assumed. And in such cases it is the woman who bears the blame for any impropriety. She has allowed the contact and, with it, an implied access to her body. The man is rarely faulted, and, indeed, is likely to be cheered for his boldness, at least by his peers. He is expected to be sexually aggressive and to take advantage of whatever opportunities come his way.

A *phuu saaw*'s beauty and allure are important so that she can attract desirable suitors. But she must not directly encourage, much less pursue, men's attentions. To do so, to show sexual interest on her own part, especially before marriage (and to some extent even after marriage) is to open herself to charges of promiscuity and the stigma associated with prostitutes of "having many husbands." Young men, on the other hand, are more often encouraged to pursue sexual experience. Older siblings will tease younger, teenage brothers for being shy in the presence of young women. Although some Baan Naa Sakae men undoubtedly go to their weddings as virgins, paid sexual services are available in most district and provincial towns—sometimes for as little as 40 or 50 *baht* ($1.60 to $2.00 U.S.) or the approximate cost of a bottle of cheap liquor—putting them well within the reach of village men on an occasional trip to town.[9]

The promiscuity of prostitutes is stigmatized, but that of their clients is not. According to this double standard, men's sexual interest is viewed as a "mood," *arom*, an ordinary need for physical release and relaxation. Moreover, engaging in sexual activity is often associated with and serves to reinforce masculine peer-group sociality and status relationships; this is most often associated with urban groups, especially salaried private or public sector employees who may go to brothels or massage parlors with their friends or in groups from work, perhaps to entertain a supervisor or a visiting superior (Jackson, 1989).[10] By contrast, women who openly express sexual interest risk association with the immorality and shame of the promiscuous "bad woman" (*phuu ying may dii*).

It must be noted that these idealized forms of male and female mobility (and their links to sexuality) form only one dimension of the Thai gender system. In addition to cultivating a self-image of strength or beauty, both men and women have alternative means to achieve social renown and prestige. Men may elect to join the ascetic discipline of the Buddhist Sangha, for which they receive the reverence of the lay populace. Women gain respect and status as nurturing mothers whose sacrifices for their children bring rewards of respect, material support, and religious merit as offspring mature (see Van Esterik, 1982b; Keyes, 1984). However, men and women have access to these respected social roles along very different social timelines.

In practice, most Thai men ordain for only a few weeks or months prior to marriage, and those who enter the Sangha more permanently usually do so after already reaching old age; nevertheless, ordination is possible for a man at any point in adult life. Moreover, a man who has spent time in the Sangha or as a novice carries the resulting status throughout his life in the form of respected titles. In Baan Naa Sakae these were: *siang*, for a former novice; *thit*, former monk; and *caan*, from *acaan* ("learned teacher"), indicating someone who has spent several years in the order and has acquired greater religious learning. Masculine sources of prestige, either as monks or men of strength and potency, represent parallel statuses, and a man may move between one and the other at any stage in his life—although going back and forth too many times is considered a sign of weakness of character, as in the derogatory expression, "a man three times a monk, a woman three times married."

Feminine status, as a beautiful maiden (*saaw*) or honored mother (*mae baan*—literally "mother of the house"), like masculine roles, may, in part, be defined by the individual's sexual status—monks and maidens are chaste, men of strength and mothers are not. However, the implications of this for men and women are very different. Maidenly beauty is predicated on virginity, not just chastity, the loss of which is irretrievable. Beauty and motherhood, then, are not parallel statuses, but consecutive ones. A woman after marriage, and especially with the birth of children, enters into her full social maturity as a *mae baan*. With marriage and motherhood, however, a woman quickly leaves the physical standards of beauty (most especially her virginity) behind. Unlike male strength, including sexual energy (which is not expected to wane until a fairly advanced age), claims to feminine beauty fade quickly with the passage of youth. Age and beauty are largely incompatible. Older women do not always accept the waning of their physical attractions, as witnessed by the many customers in Baan Naa Sakae village of the one woman who did permanent hair styling. Nevertheless, these sun-browned, older matrons who attempt to "improve their beauty" (*soem suay*) remained *mae baan*, clearly distinct from their daughters or younger sisters who were still *saaw* and needed no artificial enhancement of their maidenly beauty.

Older and particularly post-menopausal women enjoy considerable license to speak and joke about sexual matters, often contributing equally with men in ribald exchanges. Some constraints on physical modesty relax after marriage and childbirth, and especially after menopause. In Baan Naa Sakae, elderly women very often moved about their compounds and occasionally the wider community clothed only from the waist down. Wives and mothers are also much freer than their unmarried sisters and daughters to move unaccompanied, whether in the village community or on trips farther afield to go to market, or to visit friends and relations in other villages. Still, women must abide by conventions of sexual fidelity. Overt sexuality in any woman is unbecoming (and as such is a popular topic for gossip).[11]

Young unmarried women's labor migration, leaving home to travel long distances to work for long periods (often several years) far from anxious parents and elders, directly challenges the standards of beauty and constraint that define their status as *phuu saaw*. In Baan Naa Sakae, parents worried most that their daughters would acquire the same sexual experience that many expected of their sons. These concerns were often heightened by the seductive images of mobile, *thansamay* women portrayed in the popular media. In Chapter 4 I noted that Baan Naa Sakae adolescents were particularly avid viewers of television broadcasts in which the excitement and adventure of urban life were central themes. For young women, in particular, these images suggested the special glamour and sophistication enjoyed by modern urban women.

Gender and Thai Modernity

A television commercial offers a striking example of modern womanhood:

Two young women in their early twenties face each other across a
cafe table in downtown Bangkok, casually sipping coffee and laughing at each other's stories. A soundtrack of lively pop music makes
their conversation inaudible, but these are carefree and sophisticated
women. Their clothing bears witness to this—one wears a sleeve-
less, front-buttoning chemise, the other a loose, draping blouse with
dangling decorative strings; both sport fashionable earrings and blue
jeans. Also the venue, an air-conditioned cafe, and their beverage,
hot coffee, are distinctive signs of urbanity and, at the very least,
middle-class wealth. A young, strikingly handsome man passes their
table but the two women do not return his interested glance—although they are clearly aware of it. The next moment the two women
have left the cafe and are dashing boldly across the mad traffic of a
Bangkok road, laughing and holding hands as close friends do. The
fast rhythm of the musical soundtrack seems to match the dynamic
pace of the women's motion—long hair flowing out behind them,
stylish leather shoulder bags bumping against their denimed hips.
Now the view cuts to a changing room, lined with lockers, where
the two women are breathlessly beginning to disrobe; neither has
sought the privacy of a separate cubicle or the more common tech-
nique of changing under a sarong wrap. Suddenly the pop-rock
soundtrack changes to the sedate, classical sounds of the *khim* (a
Chinese cembalo—a low, flat, stringed musical instrument played by
striking the strings with two delicate felt-covered mallets). Simultaneously, the visual image switches to the *khim* players: the same two
women, but now they are clad in demure, though no less stylish,
skirts and long-sleeved blouses. They sit formally on the floor behind their instruments, at slightly oblique angles to each other; they
are playing in what appears to be a spacious, modern performance
hall. The two smile knowingly at each other as the logo and picture
of a scented deodorant fades in on the lower half of the viewer's
screen.

The slick, sophisticated packaging of Thailand's media industries—from
television commercials and movies to printed posters and magazines—uses
women and women's bodies as a predominant source of visual imagery. Femi-

nine beauty is a powerful symbol of Thai progress and modernity. Advertising and the entertainment media celebrate and promote the beautiful Thai woman as an example of up-to-date style and independence. Fashionably dressed, stylishly coiffed, carefully made-up, the modern woman (*phuu ying thansamay*) parades her beauty at work and leisure amid attractively urban—especially Bangkok—settings. Moreover, these images and practices of *thansamay* beauty in Bangkok are not defined primarily with reference to standards of maidenly modesty and constraint, although, as in the final scene of the deodorant commercial, these qualities may be invoked to indicate that *thansamay* women are fundamentally "good girls." More often, the modern woman is identified instead by her sophisticated use of fashion and other market commodities of bodily display, and by the ease with which she negotiates the diverse scenes and dynamic pace of urban life. Like the young women laughing over their coffee or dashing across a busy street, the *thansamay* woman's beauty is linked to her active, mobile participation in urban society.[12]

Baan Naa Sakae youth absorb these messages about modern femininity and its commodified accessories from an early age. The effects of media images on the imagination of community children struck me most forcefully during the 1990 annual campfire meeting held for the village school's girl and boy scouts (*luuk süa*).[13] The main event of the evening was a competition for group performances. The children had worked on their skits and routines for several days beforehand. One winning entry was offered by a dozen girls, aged ten to twelve, who staged a vigorous chorus line, dancing to the music of a popular Thai singer. Their routine was directly modeled on the chorus dancers who accompany the televised performances of *môô lam* stars and other well-known singers. The girls were especially proud of their costumes—hiked-up skirts, coordinated T-shirts belted with a long scarf, and a single white glove bought (after persistent appeals to their mothers) especially for the campfire.[14] A few years later, when I returned for a short visit to Baan Naa Sakae, several of these girls had left the village to follow their older sisters and cousins to Bangkok.

Growing numbers of young women from Baan Naa Sakae and throughout rural Thailand decide to seek urban employment, at least in part, because of unspoken but powerful suggestions that in Bangkok they can be at once beautiful, modern, and mobile. With an urban income, they can enhance their own beauty and modernity by participating in the adventure, excitement, and independence of *thansamay* city life. Indeed, one of the most valued aspects of urban employment for most of the migrants I knew was that it allowed them to work indoors, away from the skin-darkening effects of the sun. White skin is a crucial marker of physical beauty in both urban Thai and rural Isan aesthetic systems. Villagers in Baan Naa Sakae and other Northeastern communities frequently described women and men moving into Bangkok as "going to get [white] skin" (*pay aw piw*). While some offered these comments as a disparagement of youthful vanity, migrants on return visits were frequently complimented on their relative pallor.

Thansamay beauty and urban consumerism present new models to young women who wish to retain and enhance their youthful beauty while exercising greater independence and mobility. Nevertheless, key aspects of *thansamay* womanhood contrast sharply with household-based values of maidenly modesty, virginal beauty, and constraints on female spatial mobility. The portrayal of women and women's bodies in the dominant urban-centered culture, linking beauty with modernity and active sexuality, flirts dangerously with equally powerful ideas about beauty predicated on women's sexual propriety and modesty. The deodorant commercial is a case in point. The loose abandon with which the two women begin to disrobe carries a strong suggestion of sexual freedom: Nudity is associated with sexual experience or availability, just as physical modesty is equated with virginity. Highly sexualized images of women's bodies, already familiar to villagers from television, movies, and other media are reinforced in urban settings by the proliferation of commercial enterprises—shopping malls, salons, nightclubs, discos, massage parlors, go-go bars, and more—many of which link the celebration of modern female beauty to the actual sale of women's sexual services (Van Esterik, 1988).

Prostitution is not itself of recent origin in Thailand; however, the country's present-day sex industry is connected to the more respectable marketing of modern female beauty in many ways and not only by a shared imagery of the commodified female body. For instance, popular beauty contests are commonly believed to be arenas for recruiting young women into high-class escort and call-girl services. Indeed, some researchers note that women in the sex industry may enter or continue in their work at least partly because of the opportunities for economic autonomy, including commodity display and accumulation (see, for example, Cohen, 1982; Lyttleton, 1994:267; Odzer, 1994).[15] Although the strength of such considerations for women directly employed in commercial sex work vary widely (Lyttleton, 1994:272–76), the linkage between prostitution and "modern" womanhood remains a point of real concern for migrants in other occupations. For the women from Baan Naa Sakae and other industrial laborers with whom I worked, the stigma associated with prostitution still carried considerable force. No migrants I met, who were not themselves sex workers, viewed that occupation as in any way a desirable option. Migrants' awareness of AIDS was limited at the time of my research but, as public education campaigns increasingly identify HIV transmission with prostitution, their assessments of the risks involved in sex work will only increase. These linkages between commercial sex work and popular images of contemporary femininity point to a darker side of modern Thai womanhood. The prostitute stands as a reminder of the disreputable consequences that too much modernity may entail for the unwary.

It is not that *thansamay* women are all prostitutes or even suspected of it—although village gossip about migrant women often includes speculation about their sexual experience—but neither are they all blushing innocents. Rather, the image of women and women's bodies in Thailand's *thansamay* urban culture links feminine beauty both to modernity and mobility in ways that also imply active sexuality. The more urban styles and images pervade the lives and imaginations of people in communities like Baan Naa Sakae, the greater the challenge that portraits of modern Thai womanhood present to conventional values of maidenly modesty, virginal beauty, and constraints on female spatial mobility. This tension heightened the ambivalence that Baan Naa Sakae's mothers and fathers expressed in response to their daughters' employment in Bangkok. But for many young women, images of *phuu ying thansamay* offer compelling new ways to think about the kind of experiences they might have and the kind of person they might become amid the sights and sounds of the capital city.

Ultimately, however, migration decisions involve a delicate balance between young women's sense of duty and their desires for adventure. Earning urban wages might make the commodity accessories of a *thansamay* identity accessible to young rural women, but most migrants also hoped that by sending money home to parents and siblings they could uphold their obligations as good women and good daughters. At the same time, urban employment promises distance from parental and community supervision and, therefore, the chance to exercise a degree of personal autonomy that they would not otherwise enjoy until much later in life as mothers, yet without the burdens and sacrifices that motherhood entails.[16]

Marriage and motherhood have long been the most important sources of status and decision-making authority for women in rural households. Labor migration offers unmarried women a degree of independence and physical mobility that few could experience in their parents' home. It makes possible the acquisition of new experiences, knowledge, and forms of autonomy historically available only to men. However, by leaving Baan Naa Sakae for urban jobs, young women pursue practices of spatial mobility that challenge familiar village standards of daughterly behavior and raise questions for people at home about young migrants' sexual morality. As a result, women's movement into Bangkok employment becomes a process of self-construction, as migrants lay claim to, negotiate, and at times contest these contradictory aspects of gender identity.

The next three chapters examine these urban struggles more closely. Although young women's obligations to parents and kin dovetail with desires for *thansamay* experience to promote city-bound migration, the harsh realities of urban wage work highlight the underlying contradictions between these divergent motives. As a result, the urban sojourns of young women I met, both from Baan Naa Sakae and elsewhere, were characterized by persistent emotional and material conflicts.

CHAPTER 6

Bangkok Wage Workers

≈

"Bangkok is a city of heaven and a city of hell."
—Mae Kaew, former labor migrant, age forty-one

*I*n Baan Naa Sakae, young women's responsibilities as members of rural households dovetailed with aspirations for urban adventure and modernity to propel their movement into Bangkok jobs. There they joined the thousands of other rural migrants as members of the cheap, flexible labor force that fueled Thailand's urban economic boom throughout the 1980s and '90s. Once in Bangkok, however, many young migrants found the initial convergence of household obligations with personal desires a difficult juggling act to sustain, a task that often became more troublesome the longer they lived and worked in the city. Their actual experiences of city life usually diverged sharply from Bangkok's glamorous depictions in the dominant culture. These disjunctures informed the struggles of the young workers I met in Bangkok, who sought to reconcile their personal aspirations and material goals as migrants with the constraints they faced as urban laborers. Low wages, harsh working conditions, and the unfamiliar stresses of industrial labor discipline limited the scope of action available to young women in the city and diminished the *thansamay* autonomy they hoped to gain through rural-urban mobility. These experiences of marginalization shaped the strategies rural youth devised to cope with the urban setting.

Arriving in the City

Bangkok itself comes as a near-physical shock to many newcomers: The size, the noise, the pace may be overwhelming to the uninitiated. Migrants' urban sojourns begin as a visceral encounter with a chaotic, sprawling urban giant. Founded two centuries earlier as the royal seat of the Chakri dynasty, by the time of my research Bangkok (or Krung Thep Mahanakhon, as it is called in Thai) had become one of the largest cities in Asia. Official statistics in 1987 placed Bangkok's population at more than 5.5 million; by 1995 this had risen to over 8 million (National Statistical Office, 1988a:4; Pasuk & Baker, 1996:9); yet these figures at best underestimated the city's actual population due, in part, to the presence of rural migrants whose temporary sojourns were more likely to be overlooked in the collection of formal census data.

In addition to this demographic explosion, Bangkok's geographic area has grown rapidly in recent years. Until the currency crisis of 1997 (a consequence, in part, of years of unchecked real estate and financial speculation), the city witnessed a huge construction boom. New roads and expressways, hotels and housing estates, shopping malls and industrial sites transformed the urban landscape, extending it well beyond the official city boundaries into the surrounding provinces to form a vast metropolis. Growth far outpaced any efforts at official planning and the city acquired a well-deserved reputation for endless traffic jams. Noise and air pollution reached unhealthy proportions and rainy-season flooding became a serious annual concern. These environmental problems were especially pronounced in the industrial zones that expanded rapidly on the city's outskirts and where many migrants from Baan Naa Sakae found employment.[1]

Few migrants arrived in Bangkok without some knowledge of the city's environmental difficulties. Television and especially newspapers often carried stories dealing with the hazards of pollution, overcrowding, and flooding in the capital as well as sensational accounts of violent crimes. The news media also conveyed images of the city's less attractive sights and scenes: traffic jams, accidents, fires, and re-enactments of high-profile murders. Returning migrants related stories of crimes and accidents witnessed or rumored, contributing to popular perceptions regarding "the city of cheats and trickery" (*müang lôôk luang*).[2] But no amount of village rumor or media reports really prepared young travelers for the immediate, highly sensual shock of arriving in Bangkok.

Many migrants described their first experiences of the city in blurred images of confusion and disorientation. One young woman from Baan Naa Sakae, Tiw, recounted her initial impressions of Bangkok as an almost physical assault.

> I could hardly think at all, there was so much noise and traffic. There were so many people. I wouldn't have known what to do or where to go without Phii Ut, my older sister [Ut was an experienced

FIGURE 9. Migrants arriving in the city must cope with Bangkok's intense traffic and pollution.

migrant]. We traveled all night to get to the city. When we arrived at the northern bus station, I was excited and scared. I was afraid I would get lost. I couldn't have found Phii Ut's place on my own, I didn't have a clue. We had to take another long bus ride to get here and I was so confused by everything. Phii Ut held on to me and I stayed close. Now I know my way and can get around, no problem, but that first time everything was strange.

When I met Ut and Tiw in 1990, Tiw had been living with her sister in Bangkok for three years. Ut herself had been in the city for six years. Like most young migrants, Tiw remembers her first days and weeks in the capital as a period of difficult adjustment. "But," she said, "I was with my sister and there were others from our village working nearby, so it wasn't so bad." Friends and relatives from home helped to ease the transition from rural to urban life for many of the women and men of Baan Naa Sakae and other communities whom I met in the capital. This continuity of familiar relationships assists migrants in negotiating the initial journey, demystifies travel within the vast and confusing labyrinth that Bangkok streets present to the newcomer, and provides a place to stay while looking for work. Connections with people from home are also a shield against the dangers and uncertainties of life alone (and with little money) in a huge and unfamiliar city.

Few of the migrants I met, and almost none of the women, made their first move to the city alone without the assistance of friends or kin. Frequently, young people used contacts with experienced migrants from Baan Naa Sakae to arrange a place to stay and to help them find a job; it was not at all uncommon for young women to have a job waiting for them in the city before they left the village. In 1983 and 1984, ten young women from Baan Naa Sakae left together to take jobs in a textile factory. They were recruited through the employment service at the provincial office of the government Labor Department. Later, Ut and others in this first group helped younger sisters, cousins, and others to find jobs either in their factory or in others nearby. In addition, migrants frequently found work through word of mouth: Many employers, including large factories, hired new employees by announcing openings to their current workers and encouraging them to spread the word among people from home. In this way, Tiw went to Bangkok to "visit" her sister but quickly found a job in a plastics assembly plant located a few hundred meters from her sister's textile company.

Other Baan Naa Sakae migrants have served as similar points of entry into Bangkok employment for their fellow villagers.[3] In 1990, Aed, a man in his mid-thirties, had worked at a Bangkok leather factory for nearly ten years. Over his many years in the city and using the influence of his current position as a foreman, Aed had sponsored more than a dozen people from Baan Naa Sakae for jobs at his factory. In the mid-1980s Pui, a young woman who went to Bangkok after completing high school, found a job as a clerk in a Bangkok employment agency; she worked there for two or three years and during that time she helped several Baan Naa Sakae youth find city jobs. But one need not be in a position of special influence in order to assist incoming migrants. Lan, one of Mae Kaew's younger sisters, began work as a domestic servant in Bangkok in 1975. Since then, she had hosted many other new arrivals, the children of neighbors and relatives in Baan Naa Sakae—"more than I can remember." They would stay with Lan at her employer's home while she helped them find work.

The personal and material support that fellow migrants provided both for recent arrivals and experienced urban workers offered rural youth some respite from the chaos and alienation of the huge metropolis. Yet these familiar ties did not alter the fact that as urban workers, the day-to-day experiences of rural migrants were more immediately shaped by the unfamiliar conditions of urban wage relations and capitalist labor discipline. Moreover, the kind of occasional day-wage work that Baan Naa Sakae youth might have performed at home was enmeshed in ties of patron-client relations, kinship, and other personal connections that could moderate (though not eliminate) the inequalities within the community. As Andrew Turton has noted, in many rural Thai settings the social positions of employer and employee are not always easily distinguished, when "[e]ven the individual producer may be simultaneously landowner, sharecropper/tenant, wage worker, hirer of labor, petty trader, etc." (Turton, 1989a:75; see also Anan, 1989). For example, in Baan Naa Sakae the person who one day hired several women to help weed her field of newly sprouted kenaf might be found the next morning working in the field of a woman she had hired the day before.[4] Such shifts in status do not occur in migrants' relations with those who hire them in the city.

Migrants' urban experiences were most immediately affected by the kinds of jobs they entered. Baan Naa Sakae youth found work primarily in domestic service and in manufacturing. While both forms of employment sharply limited avenues for autonomy in the city, they did so in very different ways. The following cases illustrate the range of opportunities and constraints young women encountered in urban jobs and their attempts to retain some measure of control over their labor conditions.

Domestic Service

Lan first went to Bangkok to work as a domestic servant at age fifteen. She was hired to cook and clean in the household of a "distant" relative (she herself was not sure of the exact relationship) who had come to visit Baan Naa Sakae looking for a servant. Her wages were very low, only 150 *baht* per month after room and board, but the family treated her well. They encouraged her to take sewing lessons and even to find supplementary work. Thus, for several years, Lan worked mornings in a small restaurant, which served coffee and snacks to government workers at a nearby Ministry office. When I met her, Lan was thirty years old, and was still working for the same family. Her wages were still low, embarrassingly so when she compared her monthly earnings of 1,000 *baht* ($40 U.S.) to the nearly 3,000 *baht* that she knew other women from Baan Naa Sakae were making at factory jobs. Still, Lan could ask things of her employer that would never be possible in a different situation. If she had a particularly urgent need, an illness or other emergency at home, Lan could ask for extra money. If she needed or wanted to go home for a week or more, she rarely had a problem getting the time off.

Her employer also participated in a merit-making ceremony (*thôôt phaa paa*) for the temple in Baan Naa Sakae, the donations for which Lan helped to organize. The long years of association, the flexibility and potential for extra help and support, provided in this case a foundation for a more diffuse reciprocity than is found in the straight exchange of labor for a wage.

Puu, a young woman from Nakhon Ratchasima province in the Northeast, had a similar experience in her relationship with a Bangkok employer. When Puu got her first job in Bangkok, it was as a domestic servant in the home of a former villager who had become an army officer and settled in the capital. Puu called her employers *naa* (maternal aunt/uncle). She worked for them faithfully for three years until a romantic disappointment sent her back home. But like a proper *bun khun* relationship, Puu's tie to her former employers was not severed by the cessation of her labor in their household; several years later and after several intervening jobs in the city, Puu and two village friends found themselves broke and stranded in Bangkok. "I went to *Naa* . . . and we stayed with her for a week, helping in the house while she looked for jobs for us."

The utility of developing this kind of patron-client relationship in the city is obvious to migrant workers; it offers a secure source of income and assistance as well as the promise of extra cash or gifts if illness, debt, or other troubles arise back in the village. But few if any young migrants have either the experience or resources to cultivate such urban *bun khun* relations on their own. Moreover, in the isolation of private households, migrants were aware of their vulnerability to abuse, including physical or sexual assault, withheld wages, inadequate food, or inhumane living conditions. The general dissatisfaction with which most rural women viewed domestic service was reflected to some degree in the frequent complaints of middle-class Bangkok households that "good help" was hard to find and even harder to keep. Moreover, most migrants were quite ready to reject or ignore an employer's claims on their personal loyalty. Most women, whether in domestic service or other occupations, judged their situation in terms of the wages they earned. If the money was not enough or if a better proposition came along, few migrants hesitated to break off ties, even when they felt their employers were kind and deserving people. *Ngoen may phôô* ("the money was not enough") was their most frequent explanation for switching jobs; *ngoen dii* ("the money is/was good") was their most common praise for a satisfactory job. Certainly, the employment histories of migrants from Baan Naa Sakae and elsewhere, who began work in the city as domestic servants, frequently revealed their continued efforts to move into more desirable (and better paid) occupations.

Maew, twenty-one, left Baan Naa Sakae to go work in Bangkok at age fifteen. A cousin from home recruited her to work in a small garment factory. After six months she had learned to sew but her wages of 1,000 *baht* a month did not go up, so Maew left. "The money was no good." She went to stay for a few days with a friend she had made, and soon found another job as a telephone operator and housekeeper in a small air conditioning company. Although she stayed there for over a year, living with the employer's family, she finally tired of the long hours and pay of just 2,200 *baht* per month. "The people were nice but it just wasn't worth it." For nearly two years Maew moved through a variety of jobs from manufacturing to waitressing, never staying anywhere very long, until she found her current position. The last three years she has worked in a sewing factory producing bags and purses, earning just over 3,000 *baht* a month with overtime. (interview: June 1990)

Tui, thirty-three, is from a village in the northeastern province of Udon Thani and has held a number of different jobs in Bangkok since she was in her early twenties. She now sews shoulder bags for an export company, but she used to work as a domestic servant. At one point, Tui worked keeping house for a taxi driver and his wife. They were "good people" but they did not have the money to pay her 700 *baht* (about $28 U.S.) monthly wage. When Tui realized this, she told the man she had to go home. That way, she said, "At least I got 400 *baht* for bus fare from them." She did not, however, go back to the village. Instead, Tui contacted a friend working elsewhere in the city, who helped her find another job. This time she was a servant for an East Indian family. She disliked the food and thought the people "smelled bad" but they were "good hearted." However, once again, the money was not enough; so, after a couple of months, Tui left. "But," she said, "I felt sorry for them and looked for a friend to replace me." (interview: February 1988)

Wan is from Khon Kaen province in the Northeast, and has worked in a large textile factory for the last twelve years. She described her experience while working as a domestic servant just after her arrival in the city. Her employer was a soldier, the friend of a cousin-by-marriage who had helped Wan when she first got to Bangkok. The man treated her "like a family member, but the money just wasn't enough (*ngoen may phôô*)." She made 350 *baht* (about $15 U.S.) plus room and board each month. "I liked the job," she said, but after four months was ready to leave. When friends told her of the chance for factory work (at much better wages), she decided to go. Her employer wanted Wan to stay. "He brought me sweets and other presents." When Wan said she was going home to her village, he promised her a raise in pay if she would come back; it was still not enough. She left and started work at the textile factory. (interview: February 1988)

Migrants, even in the highly paternalistic context of domestic service, were clearly aware of the commercial basis of their relationship with employers. Like Tui and Wan, women might cloak their dissatisfaction with the job in the fiction of "going home," but the moral dimension of authority associated with *bun khun* only carried weight as long as the wage was acceptable. Whenever possible, most women from Baan Naa Sakae chose factory work over domestic service. They objected particularly to the latter's low status; service in a strange household represented a form of subordination uncomfortably similar to bonds of servitude and slavery—images that were reinforced by popular television historical dramas and by the obsequious or foolish personas ascribed to servant characters in advertising segments and other media productions. "I wouldn't work as a servant again," Maew stated. "Who wants to be a slave?"

For Maew and others who had worked as servants, the physical restrictions of living and working in the employer's home seriously limited their leisure time and opportunities to meet and spend time with friends or fellow migrants. Most importantly, however, servants' wages were generally much lower than those of any other job available to migrant women, even counting the free room and board. A 1980 survey of Northeastern women working in Bangkok found that domestic servants earned a mean monthly income, including payments in kind, of 800 *baht* or $32 (U.S.), while those with factory jobs averaged 1,200 *baht* ($48 U.S.) per month (Pawadee, 1982:103). While servants' earnings rose through the late 1980s and into the 1990s, they in no way kept pace with the wages available to migrants in most other occupations. Low wages were the rule for household service work and this, as much as the job's lack of *thansamay* glamour, prompted the near-universal disdain migrants expressed for this kind of work. Moreover, it was virtually impossible for women in domestic service to save and send money home, while at the same time participating in urban consumer lifestyles.

However, the ability of migrant women to leave domestic work and seek other employment was at least partly dependent on their contacts with friends or relatives in the city who could help them find another job. Migrants I met who remained in domestic service did so rarely out of obligation to their employers but rather because no immediate alternative was available. Even Lan, who appreciated the flexibility that she had been able to develop in her many years of employment with the same family, remained in the poorly paid position in part because of the periodically renewed suggestion that some time in the future her employer's adult daughter (who lived in Los Angeles and whom Lan had helped to raise) might take Lan back with her to work in the United States. Although no specific plans had ever been formulated to make this prospect a reality, the idea tantalized Lan. She feared, however, that the family in Bangkok would never let her go. "They are afraid they will have a hard time finding someone else as good as I am."

Manufacturing: Small Sweatshops

Migrants preferred industrial work to domestic service both because it was better paid and because they saw it as more "independent," at least during their leisure hours. Some people from Baan Naa Sakae found jobs in small family enterprises, where paternalistic relations continued to shape the day-to-day labor process. For example, Maem worked in a small garment-manufacturing shop that was run by a couple with kinship ties to Baan Naa Sakae. Maem was twenty-five when I met her in 1990, and had come to Bangkok after an early marriage broke up and she was left to support her infant son with the help of her widowed mother. When Maem heard through the shop owners' cousins in Baan Naa Sakae that they needed more help, Maem decided to try it. She left her son in her mother's care and headed to the city.

In a small, three-story row house facing a crowded back alley in one of Bangkok's main garment districts, Maem worked with more than a dozen young women, including several from Baan Naa Sakae. On the ground level, the main workshop was occupied by long tables with industrial sewing machines; Maem and the other seamstresses sat on small wooden stools in front of their machines for eight or twelve hours at a time. Wages, as in most small garment shops, were calculated by the piece, and when an order was due the women might sew from 7 in the morning until 2 A.M. "When there are orders, I can earn a lot—as much as 4,000 *baht* or more in a month ([$160 U.S.], nearly $50 more than the minimum wage for hourly workers at the time). It's hard, and we all suffer from back pain and are tired, but some months are slow and I might only make 1,200 or 1,500 *baht*. That's not enough to send money to my mother for my son because I still have to pay for food.

So when the work is there, I do it." The difficulties of the job were eased somewhat for Maem by the presence of others—everyone worked, ate, and slept in the shop, as did the owner, his wife, and family.

This kind of employment posed restrictions similar in some ways to those found in domestic service. Certainly the "family" context of the shop has many benefits for the employer. Owners are frequently migrants themselves and, in fact, commonly recruit from their own home regions and communities. Shop owners often claim that these personal ties are beneficial for all concerned: They help to reassure parents, who are more willing to let their children leave for the city if they know the employer; in addition, new arrivals adjust more easily and are happier in their jobs when working alongside cousins and friends from home (JPS, 1988).[5] While this may be true in some cases, the linkage of employee and employer through kinship and patronage connections in the village usually strengthens the owners' authority over new workers and helps slow down the often high rates of turnover in these sweatshop operations. Similarly, the erratic pay of piece-rate work and the stresses of working as many as twenty hours a day during peak periods pose real economic and health problems for the small shop employee. Meanwhile, the close quarters of sweatshop production subjects workers to the same round-the-clock surveillance with which domestic servants must also contend.

Maem felt "lucky" that her employer (*naay caang*) was "a good person"—he had never cheated on her wages or punished the workers unfairly. "But not all [shop house] employers are that way. And, of course, it's not like in the big factories, where my younger sister works. They have better standards (*mii rabob*), contracts, and shift work. If they work long hours, they get paid overtime." Maem felt her sister, Ning, had the "better" job, but though she might prefer to go to a "big factory," she was already too old—"I'm twenty-six. And my sister's company now only hires women who are twenty-five or younger."

Factories

Maem's sister Ning and ten other women from Baan Naa Sakae had come to Bangkok together, recruited in the mid-1980s by a large textile factory with the help of the Mahasarakham provincial labor department. Not everyone stayed: Two returned home within the year; three more had left a year or two later. But in 1990, half a dozen, most now in their early to mid-twenties, remained working in the city. This lengthy tenure with one company reflected the relative desirability of employment in larger factories for many young migrants, where the pay tends to be higher and workers' free time is less obviously supervised. This particular enterprise, which I will call "Sunrise Textiles," was Taiwanese owned and employed over a thousand workers in the highly mechanized process of spinning and weaving cotton cloth. Textile companies like this were the most common form of industrial employment for Baan Naa Sakae youth, accounting for nearly two-thirds of those who found factory jobs. Others worked in small-plastics assembly, rubber, leather, or food processing.

Work at companies like Sunrise Textiles was valued, in part, because large manufacturers were more likely to "follow the law" and uphold basic provisions of the Labor Act, such as paying the legal minimum wage. A minimum wage pay-scale was unheard of for domestic servants, and, like Maem, few piece-rate workers could count on a regular month-to-month income. But if many young migrants preferred higher-paying manufacturing jobs, this did not mean these were without their own drawbacks. In 1990, the minimum wage for Bangkok was set at just under $4.00 U.S. (97 *baht*) per day, allowing Ning and her friends a steady monthly pay rate of between 2,500 and 3,000 *baht* ($100–$120 U.S.), and perhaps more with regular overtime. However, few migrants could expect these wages to rise significantly, even after many years of service; most industrial workers saw their wages rise only when the legal minimum increased.[6] In addition, some factory workers toiled for much lower rates during an initial period of "probation." Fifty or sixty *baht* per day—$2.00–$2.50 U.S.—was a common wage for workers on temporary or probationary contracts throughout the late 1980s and, until the passage of new legislation in 1990, an employee's probationary status could easily be prolonged for months, even years. Sometimes legal loopholes allowed for the payment of lower wages; in other cases, wage laws were simply ignored.[7] Fines for lateness, failure to make production quotas, or minor infractions of shop floor regulations could also depress a worker's industrial wages.

To increase their base earnings, Ning and her friends, like most of their co-workers, often worked long hours. Overtime frequently increased their work days to twelve or sixteen hours. Most worked overtime willingly in order to be able to save more money. Many large factories operate twenty-four hours a day in three eight-hour shifts. Workers rotate into a new shift every week. This was a source of some complaint for many women. Even without the strains of overtime, this constant upheaval in work schedules frequently resulted in health complaints: disrupted menstruation, headaches and insomnia, intestinal problems and ulcers. Noi, another woman from Baan Naa Sakae employed at Sunrise Textiles, argued that she and many others in the factory suffered from insomnia and stomach complaints because of the changing shifts:

> I've been here a long time and so I'm used to it now, but still it can be difficult. Sometimes I get headaches and I can't sleep well, especially the first few days [of a shift], and often my stomach hurts from missed meals and having to eat at odd hours. The night shift is hardest because I get so sleepy, and if you don't pay attention it can be a problem—trying to keep track of several machines [industrial looms and spinners] and if the threads tangle and you miss it, the supervisor will really be mad. I know some people take medicine [amphetamines] to give them strength and energy, but that's dangerous too; you can get addicted pretty fast.

Noi and most of the other women from Baan Naa Sakae lived in the concrete block dormitory rooms provided on the factory grounds. This was considered a benefit of their employment; rent was free and the employer also provided rice in a factory canteen where workers could purchase their own accompanying dishes from company vendors. Unlike the sleeping quarters provided by some factories they knew about, these dorms were relatively good—at least the bathrooms were kept clean and there were only four or five women to a room. Still, regulations were fairly strict: For example, no fans or electrical appliances were allowed in the rooms, leaving residents to suffer the stuffy heat of the box-like concrete structures. The employer gave out room assignments and never allowed people from the same village to share a room. And visitors were forbidden, even relatives from home. If a worker were caught trying to bring in anyone from the outside, she risked instant dismissal. Ut, another Sunrise employee, and her sister, Tiw, rented a room nearby and often hosted the relatives of other Baan Naa Sakae workers in the area who had no place else to house visiting kin. More distressing on a daily basis, the rice provided in the factory canteen was not of good quality, and many workers preferred to eat outside the factory as often as possible. These meals, purchased at vending stalls outside the factory gates or at food shops located in a small commercial and residential area half a kilometer away, made steady inroads into some workers' monthly savings.

Beyond the daily stresses and discomforts that factory production and dormitory accommodations impose on workers, longer-term and more serious health threats exist as well: exposure to toxic chemicals and fumes (especially for those dealing with synthetic dyes) and excessive noise levels, accidents due to improperly maintained machinery or worker fatigue, or res-

FIGURE 10. On a quiet Sunday afternoon, a uniformed textile worker (center) walks to the market after finishing an overtime shift.

piratory infections from poorly ventilated work sites. Such physical hazards of the production process may be compounded by harsh supervisors, sexual harassment, fines for infractions, work speed-ups, and the arbitrary raising of production quotas, among other concerns.

Despite these drawbacks, industrial wage work remained the preferred occupation of most young migrants from Baan Naa Sakae. However, finding and then keeping such a job was not always a simple task, even in Bangkok's boom economy. In the late 1980s and early 1990s, the seemingly limitless pool of migrants and potential migrants meant few companies had trouble recruiting employees. Thus, many factories, like Sunrise, could restrict new hires to young women under age twenty-five; others only took on workers up to age twenty-one. Migrants themselves were well aware of these constraints and women who remained in the city past their mid-twenties were particularly cautious, often limiting their visits home at national holidays in order not to jeopardize their employment by missing too many days of work. Younger women might find another position without great effort, but many employers were not eager to protect the jobs of older and more senior workers. More confident than younger, newly arrived migrants, women with many years of experience may be more willing to protest treatment they perceive as unfair or in other ways contest the authority of supervisors and managers. Still, as with migrants in domestic service and small sweatshop work, industrial laborers have only limited resources with which to confront the power of employers and challenge experiences of exploitation.

Industrial Hegemony and Labor Control

Migrants' ability to express discontent or resist unfair treatment on the job is severely constrained. As low-status urban wage workers, they face many of the same inequitable structures of authority and power that their parents confront as peasants in rural communities like Baan Naa Sakae. On the one hand, the hierarchical power relations that characterize Thai society work to restrict workers' knowledge about the systems and structures that shape their lives while at the same time making open confrontations with authority a high-risk choice. While Thailand does offer more extensive legal protections for workers and a freer climate for labor organization than most other Southeast Asian countries, few workers have a solid grasp of their legal rights or the means to assert them. Furthermore, ideological constructs that depict wage employment as a form of patronage seek to define labor relations as bound by the moral obligations of *bun khun* reciprocity. Under these terms, employers occupy the same moral status as parents, to whom their employee-children owe the same kind of loyalty and obedience incurred by all recipients of *bun khun*. A state radio broadcast in May 1988 made these links explicit:

> An employer should show kindness and sympathy toward employees (*luuk caang*). He or she should welcome them at the office door and ask about their family "so that *luuk caang* feel at ease." But workers must "never strike, never stop work" because the "company brings [them] benefits . . . a regular salary to buy food, clothing, and to build a house." The employer is *phô liang mae liang* (foster father/mother) to workers. If conditions in the workplace are bad, it may cost a lot to make repairs. *Luuk caang* "must sympathize with the owner" and "work together so the company can move ahead"; they should "tolerate [the situation] so business can improve."[8]

Such statements by employers and state authorities mobilized the power of *bun khun* morality in the service of greater industrial discipline. In some

Figure 11. Bangkok factory workers form a cheering section at their company-sponsored Sports Day.

cases, employers sought to enhance their position as parent-benefactors of worker-clients by hosting periodic entertainment activities, from beauty contests and annual banquets to sports competitions. Frequently, these events attempted not only to cultivate workers' loyalty and gratitude for favors received but also to ensure employees' appreciation for such displays of employer generosity by surrounding these events with attractively *thansamay* forms and practices.

The employer-sponsored "Sports Days" that I attended at two Bangkok textile factories were good examples of the way companies used *thansamay* symbolism in their labor relations. While each aimed (in not very subtle ways) to promote worker identification—pitting groups from different production departments or different factories owned by the same parent company against each other—the events also incorporated a wide array of commodities and other "modern" symbolism. Players donned new shirts, hats, and other items printed in special team colors and marked with company insignia (in one case those who wished to participate in the day's activities were required to purchase these items out of their own wages). At the same time, workers sitting on the sidelines participated in animated chants and cheers modeled on the cheering songs of university and college students, an arena of *thansamay* prestige and status with which many migrants would otherwise have little contact. A sound system playing loud music, microphones for announcers and cheerleaders, and trophies or prizes for the winners of each contest added to an overall atmosphere of excitement and modern style.[9]

Despite employers' efforts to anchor labor relations in updated forms of *bun khun* generosity, neither Baan Naa Sakae migrants nor most other urban workers whom I met used the language of patron-client relations to describe their own experiences of urban wage work. Almost all migrants saw very clearly the difference between their ties to employers as *luuk caang* and their responsibilities to village kin. Nevertheless, the public construction of wage employment as a form of patronage, and the parallel expectations of loyalty and gratitude that this demands of workers, serves to weaken the moral legitimacy of labor protest.

Compounding these disciplinary pressures is the limited knowledge that most Thai workers and especially rural migrants have of their rights under the law. This is by no means due solely to low levels of formal education. Indeed, by the late 1980s it was not uncommon for Bangkok factories to hire women with three to six years of education beyond the mandatory primary level. Nevertheless, schooling did not necessarily impart a critical awareness of one's rights under the law. Not surprisingly, information regarding labor laws and workers' rights does not form part of the curriculum in Thai schools, even at the secondary level. In the words of one urban worker: "Schools don't teach about real life; they teach how to do certain things like how to *way* [a deferential greeting] but not the reason why things are [the way they are]." Many young migrants were keenly aware of their lack of knowledge and education, often describing themselves as "ignorant" and "stupid" (*may mii khwaam ruu, pen khon ngo*).[10] Workers readily admitted that conditions on the job were "difficult" (*yaak lambaak*) or "harsh" (*yae*), that supervisors were unfair or abusive, that employers were stingy or unfeeling, but translating these concerns into action was a much more difficult step.

Active protest may quickly undermine both workers' economic goals in the city and their ability to uphold obligations to rural families. Migrants observed the treatment meted out to co-workers identified as troublemakers, and many hesitated to follow their lead. Supervisors frequently watched such employees more closely than others, looking for infractions or minor mistakes that would otherwise go unremarked. These errors might be used to punish these workers, to dock their wages, or as a rationale for dismissal. For example, supervisors might deny or restrict workers' opportunities to work overtime, thereby sharply curtailing these disfavored employees' ability to earn enough money to save for remittances and other needs. Workers who lost jobs as a result of "making trouble" were likely to be blacklisted by nearby factories, and would have a considerably more difficult time finding a new position. In the face of such obstacles to open and collective protest, seriously discontented workers more often adopted individualized strategies of withdrawal, either by quitting to seek work with a different enterprise or by returning home to the countryside. As we will see in Chapter 8, migrants frequently postponed taking the latter option until they were ready to marry and begin a family of their own.

The young women I knew in Bangkok faced many difficulties as urban wage workers, which they had not envisioned before leaving home. Low wages, harsh and unhealthy working conditions, long hours, and constant supervision—many felt that as *workers* they enjoyed less "freedom" than they did at home. During one of my visits with the Sunrise factory workers, Ning remarked, "Living in the village, I feel freer. When I'm tired or hungry I can just stop what I'm doing. No supervisor to please, no bells [to signal shifts and breaks], no guards." The four or five others who had gathered in the privacy of Ut and Tiw's rented room, echoed Ning's thoughts in agreement. "It's true," said Tiw, "we are freer at home. But there's no money there and nothing to do either. Working in the city, at least there is money."

And money was what drew most migrants into the city, money as the means to fulfill not only obligations to family but also their own desires for excitement at the center of *thansamay* Thai society. Tiw, like Khem, and thousands of other young women working in Bangkok, desired to be both a "good daughter" and a "*thansamay* woman." Both self-images entered into young women's decisions to migrate to Bangkok, but in the city the harsh constraints of urban wage labor raised fundamental conflicts between them. Although many migrants I met felt constrained by the conditions of their urban employment or that their treatment as wage workers was to some degree "unjust" (*may yutthitham*), these were rarely matters young rural women felt empowered to challenge directly. Instead, most workers directed their energies elsewhere, viewing their places and conditions of employment as things to put up with in order to achieve other ends. In Tiw's words: "We have to endure (*tông thon*) for the money."

However, as we will see in the next chapter, migrants' focus on their earnings and what these could buy only shifted tensions from the realm of production to that of consumption. Migrants' urban sojourns were marked not only by the limitations they faced on the job but also by their attempts to balance conflicting consumption priorities off the job: saving money to assist family at home or spending it to acquire the commodity markers of urban status and modern style.

CHAPTER 7

Consumption, Desire, and Thansamay Selves

⇌

"I wanted to have lots of money, money to send home and to buy things for myself as well."
—Thip, cotton spinner, age nineteen

Consumption and Imagined Selves

Migrant workers, including those I knew from Baan Naa Sakae, viewed participation in Bangkok's mass-market commodity culture as one of the most valued features of their time in the city. In part, this reveals the power of new technologies of representation, such as television and other forms of mass media, over the popular imagination in Thailand; these pervasive forms of cultural production celebrated commodities, their accumulation and display, as signs of personal and social progress. Both rural migrants and their families acknowledged the desirability of *thansamay* styles and attitudes; both recognized commodity consumption as a primary vehicle for demonstrating *thansamay* status.

This chapter takes a closer look at the consumption practices of urban workers. The uses to which young women put their Bangkok earnings highlight the links between rural-urban labor migration and dominant cultural images of Thai modernity as newly imagined possibilities about the self. In particular, geographic mobility allowed young women to enact what Henrietta Moore has called "fantasies of identity," that is, "ideas about the kind of person one would like to be and the sort of person one would like to be seen to be by others" (1994:66).[1] For most migrants, the desire to be both good daughters and modern women coalesced in their decision to leave home, but their experiences in Bangkok made the fulfillment of either self-image a difficult task. Nevertheless, living and working in Bangkok rarely, if ever, prompted the young workers I met to choose explicitly between one or the other; rather, their time in the city involved an ongoing negotiation of the varied and often conflicting meanings that constituted their own and others' understandings of daughterly duty and *thansamay* self-expression.

Young women in Baan Naa Sakae who contemplated leaving for Bangkok employment were attracted by the prospect of adventure and *thansamay* style associated with urban life. City jobs also promised a level of independence that was not available to women in Baan Naa Sakae, especially not to unmarried daughters subordinate to parents and other elders. As we saw in Chapter 5, rural women expect their autonomy and authority as household decision makers to increase following marriage and motherhood; however, these gains come only with advancing age and the added responsibilities of raising a family. This was small consolation to the young woman whose peers had already left for Bangkok. Her friends might bring back cash and other gifts on their visits home, and tell tales of urban life that evoke images of glamour and style she might otherwise see only on television broadcasts. But while these cultural constructions of urban modernity help to shape migration aspirations, they do not correspond to the lived realities and hardships of Bangkok wage labor. Nevertheless, few migrants have the resources, abilities, or opportunities to challenge their experiences as workers. By contrast, commodity consumption (both of material goods and of commodified images and events) offers many young women more accessible means to confront the tensions and contradictions they face as urban wage laborers. Migrants' actions as consumers—not only as producers—reveal the complex dilemmas of women's urban employment and highlight a powerful avenue by which many labor migrants hope to express their new sense of autonomy and agency, and to construct socially satisfying and valued identities.

Being *Thansamay*

The young women I knew both in Bangkok and in Baan Naa Sakae found urban images of *thansamay* identity compelling, and the prospect of remaining at home dull by comparison. When describing their experiences before coming to the city, many migrants alluded to feelings of boredom: "In the village there's nothing to do." The Bangkok they saw on nightly television broadcasts and heard about from friends was, by contrast, a place of boundless novelty and excitement. Almost every migrant I met in the city acknowledged the effect of this urban mystique. As more than one young textile worker explained, "I wanted to go see for myself." Not incidentally,

Bangkok employment was also the only way these rural youth could hope to earn the money needed to acquire the style and amenities of a *thansamay* identity. This was the explicit goal of one young woman, Thip, who left her village home in a Central Thai province at age nineteen to take a job in a cotton spinning plant; she wanted to work in Bangkok because "at home there was no money and nothing to do. I wanted to have lots of money, money to send home and to buy things for myself as well."

Although many migrants spoke of their move to Bangkok in terms of seeking urban wages (and, more particularly, what those wages could buy), to some extent young women's desires to be up-to-date and modern could be addressed through the work experience itself. This was especially likely for migrants employed in Bangkok's booming manufacturing sector. In contrast to the undesirable and decidedly old-fashioned qualities of peasant production—hard, heavy, largely unmechanized work performed out-of-doors—the characteristics of urban factory work—lighter even if highly repetitive tasks, involving impressive new technologies, performed indoors out of the sun and rain—could at least initially project an attractive aura of participation in *thansamay* Thai society. Many young migrants expressed pride in their acquisition of technical skills as industrial wage earners, such as the ability to run complex textile machinery. Other aspects of the work process could also evoke a positive sense of *thansamay* style, such as special uniforms, or, as discussed in Chapter 6, management-sponsored sports competitions, beauty contests, or annual banquets.

Nonetheless, the endless routine of industrial assembly work, the strains of long hours and unpleasant, often unsafe, working conditions, soon overshadowed the attractively *thansamay* character of most jobs. Many of the migrants I interviewed contrasted the drudgery and stress of shift work with their relative freedom after working hours. This time was really what made their city jobs tolerable. Living conditions in company dormitories or rented rooms in the slums were commonly crowded, hot, and dirty, but they offered the chance to escape from direct supervision on the shop floor. It was then, at the end of the shift and outside the factory gates, that migrants were best able to explore and absorb images of sophisticated urban lifestyles by watching television and popular movies, going to department stores or entertainment parks. For many young women, these ventures into urban consumer culture were especially valued aspects of their time in the city; planning for and pursuing opportunities to engage in these new consumption practices were as likely to engage their attention on a day-to-day basis as were concerns over difficulties on the job.

The young women to whom I spoke were often reluctant to reveal exactly how much of their wages they spent in the city, especially on nonessential items; yet every visit I made to the rooms of urban workers highlighted the important place that commodity purchases and display had in their lives. Ut and Tiw's small lodging was a case in point. They lived in a small rented room, one of four tiny partitions crowded onto the second floor of an old wooden house. The building was located in a small slum area, occupying a poorly drained parcel of land squeezed between the much larger compounds of surrounding factories. Ut worked at the Sunrise Textiles Company, just across the road from their rooms; Tiw's job was in a factory a short bus ride away. Their room measured close to eight feet across by twelve feet long. One corner was walled off as a tiny bath and toilet area; another was used as a makeshift kitchen with a few pots and dishes, an electric rice cooker, and a small gas ring burner. The rest of the room was furnished with a few blankets and cushions, along with Ut and Tiw's prize possessions. An electric fan sat in one corner, usually idle unless the sisters were entertaining visitors. On a set of shelves by one wall, a small tape deck stood next to a row of cassettes. These included recordings by well-known Thai performers of popular "country" style vocal music,[2] as well as recent albums by Thai poprock groups. A half-dozen small photo albums and a camera occupied another shelf, while yet another held a haphazard collection of cosmetics, a bottle or two of deodorants, powders, and lotions, along with combs, brushes, and small novelty items, hair clips and ribbons. Not long after I first began to visit Ut and Tiw, I arrived one week to discover a small color television had been added to their belongings, the culmination of nearly three years' effort. The sisters had saved the 7,500–*baht* ($300 U.S.) purchase price out of their wages and by taking on occasional piece-rate assembly work given out by Tiw's company for those wanting to earn extra money on their own time.

In addition to the wish to acquire particular mass-market commodities, many rural-urban migrants prided themselves on their participation in new commodified patterns of sociality. At home, most young women were enmeshed in an intense web of social relations with parents and siblings, neighbors as well as friends, all of whom could observe, comment on, and potentially influence their behavior; as factory workers in the city, migrants' most immediate and intimate social interactions were almost exclusively with friends and co-workers, most of whom were of similar age and background. The expectations and interests of their peers played an important role in shaping the consumption behavior of many migrants.

Working side by side, sharing a rented room, or living in the common

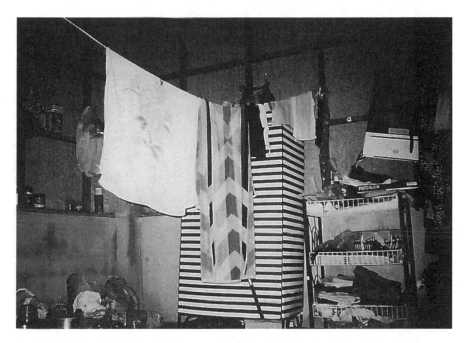

FIGURE 12. The rented room of migrant workers in Bangkok.

quarters of factory dormitories, young women found themselves in an intense world of peer-oriented companionship, far removed from the authority of parents and elders that would frame and intersect such ties in the village setting. Friendly pressures to participate in common activities—such as shared meals and outings—placed steady demands on the cash earnings of young workers. Many of the young women I knew in Bangkok described themselves as "great spenders" (*chaay ngoen keng*, literally "good at using money" [rather than saving it]). Money, they said, was hard to hang onto, not because of large or flamboyant purchases but because of the everyday demands of urban existence, including their desires to hang out and "have fun" with friends.

Some migrants relied on the consumption desires of their peers as a way to generate extra income for themselves through small-scale sales activities. In one example, a young woman took some savings and traveled on her day off to Bangkok's wholesale clothing district (Pratuunam). There she bought several dozen pairs of blue jeans that she resold for a small profit to friends and co-workers back in her factory on the city's outskirts. In some cases, migrants became agents for pyramid sales outfits (e.g., Avon and Amway, which were expanding rapidly in urban Thailand during the 1980s

FIGURE 13. In Bangkok young women and men from Baan Naa Sakae gather in the one-room flat of fellow villagers to relax on their day off and share a farewell meal with the author (at right, wearing glasses).

and early '90s), a fact several migrants I knew complained about, since sellers turned to their networks of friends in factory dormitories or rooming houses to "help them out" by buying their products. The high-pressure tactics of these sales companies provoked real irritation at times. Nevertheless, such retail ventures by friends and co-workers contributed to the importance that ongoing, if small-scale, commodity purchases had in the daily routines of many urban workers.

    In my experience, these interactions rarely took the form of competitive or conspicuous consumption—that is, the need to have better or more expensive items than others, or to treat groups of friends to meals or snacks. Instead, the factory workers I knew were generally quite careful to even out expenses, to pay their own share of meals eaten at streetside restaurants, to repay small debts to co-workers (such as money borrowed during a trip to the market), and so forth. The egalitarian emphasis of these interactions nevertheless did not mask a constant focus on consumption: whether gatherings revolved around purchased meals,[3] trips to local markets, or, more rarely, spending a day off at one of the city's commercial amusement parks (such as

"Happyland" or the part-zoo/part-rock concert venue, "The Crocodile Farm"). Participating in peer group activities also required investing in certain kinds of commodity display, such as urban styles of clothing—of which the most important component was the purchase of one or more pairs of blue jeans.

These peer group "outings" (*thiaw*) in search of fun and entertainment were, for many migrants, among the most satisfying experiences of life in Bangkok. Given migrants' limited leisure hours and low wages, a *thiaw* was usually brief—an afternoon's trip to the market, a shopping mall, or a park; but it might also be a much longer excursion, perhaps over a holiday weekend, to the beach or (more commonly) to a friend's home in a distant and unfamiliar province. Such outings offered a dramatic break from the tedium and exhaustion of factory shifts. They also provided the best opportunities for most migrants to incorporate dominant images of a truly "modern" lifestyle in their own lives. Women dressed carefully for these events, usually in blue jeans and colorful blouses or T-shirts. Other commodities like cameras were also in high demand, especially on longer trips.[4]

Even a small *thiaw* involved the mobilization of such commodity symbols of *thansamay* self-presentation. One Sunday afternoon (the day most factory workers have free), I was visiting Ut and several other women from Baan Naa Sakae who all worked at the same Bangkok textile factory. We had gathered in Ut's rented room but soon decided to go visit some young men, also from the same village, who were living in a one-room flat about thirty minutes away by bus. In preparation, two of the women had to go back to their dormitory rooms to change out of the casual shorts they had on; I stayed with Ut and her friend, Noi, who had suggested the outing. While we waited, Noi looked over Ut's small collection of cosmetics and began to try on two different colors of lipstick. When she turned back to us, Ut had finished changing into a pair of black stretch slacks. Noi scolded her, "Don't you want to wear something more *thansamay*? You look like a country hick [*duu baan nôôk loey*]." Ut quickly changed into a pair of blue jeans, even though they were not quite dry from the morning's laundry.

Ties to Home: Coping with Ambivalence

While the acquisition and display of commodities in these ways provided crucial demonstrations of *thansamay* identity and status among migrant peers, within the broader urban setting these claims received little recognition. Amid Bangkok's exploding consumerism, migrants' consumption patterns—restricted as they were by low wages and limited leisure time—offered only a weak approximation of truly up-to-date urban living. There were always more and newer commodities to acquire, more places to see, more outings to take. Wearing jeans and cosmetics, taking trips to the Crocodile Farm or an air-conditioned department store—these were pleasant and attractively *thansamay* activities, but surrounded by the city's hypermodernity and intense commercialization, rural women's access to and control over the extensive cultural repertoire of *thansamay* style remained partial at best.

Consequently, the women I knew in Bangkok, almost universally, expressed ambivalence about their experiences in the city. And their unease tended to increase over time. Mae Kaew's lament, following nearly twenty years' migration experience, echoed the sentiments of many younger women from Baan Naa Sakae and elsewhere: "Bangkok is a city of heaven and a city of hell." Many migrants acknowledged the "heavenly" aspects of urban life: The city was a place of progress, where people and society were sophisticated and modern. Living there had taught them a great deal; it had "opened the ears, opened the eyes." They appreciated the many comforts and conveniences of city life: easy access to running water, electricity, transportation, markets, and entertainment. And central to these advantages was the fact that, "In the city there's money; in the village there's none."

Just as recognizable, however, was Bangkok's "hellish" side: the pollution, noise, and congestion; crowded living spaces in which, nevertheless, it was very easy to feel alone and isolated; insecure, unhealthy, and often oppressive working conditions. Among the women I knew, whether they had worked in Bangkok for six months or sixteen years, enthusiasm for the *thansamay* qualities of city living was always tempered by unease over its alien and alienating aspects. In some cases, these tensions led to an explicit critique of their circumstances, including active participation in trade unions and labor protest (Mills, forthcoming); but labor organizing was a difficult and often risky venture. Only a tiny minority of migrant workers even have access to independent union institutions. The vast majority of migrants in Bangkok responded to the ambivalence engendered by their urban experiences with less radical actions, neither outright challenges nor passive acquiescence, but what might better be described as "coping strategies" (see Lamphere, 1987:30). A major focus of these was the maintenance of connections with rural kin and community. Ties to rural family and community remained crucial to most migrant women, no matter how long their stay in Bangkok.[5] Almost without exception, women spoke of plans to return to live in their village; periodic visits home were eagerly planned and awaited.

Young women working in Bangkok shared a common dilemma during their time in the city. Their attempts to pursue *thansamay* aspirations were fundamentally at odds with their obligations as young women to rural kin. Whatever the purpose of their urban expenditures (personal items, daily needs, entertainment with friends, education or vocational training) every *baht* spent in Bangkok was, at least in theory, one less available to assist family at home. New patterns of commodity consumption, while necessary for the pursuit of a *thansamay* sense of self, confronted migrants both with their own marginal status within the dominant, commodified culture of Bangkok and with their potential (or actual) failure to maintain the ideal image of a "good daughter." Although, among the women I interviewed, the economic hardships of rural households were rarely the primary motivating factor in their migration decisions, all recognized the moral force of family obligations. Women who described themselves as "good spenders" (*chaay ngoen keng*) often did so in the context of explaining their irregular remittances to village kin.[6] The amounts and frequency of migrants' contributions to rural households varied widely among the women I interviewed; self-reporting commonly elicited contributions totaling anywhere from 30 percent to 80 percent of monthly income, but these initial claims were usually revealed later on to represent much more occasional remittances. There were very few women who would admit to never having sent money, but most agreed that they would rather wait and save a particular sum (often 2,000 or 3,000 *baht*, $80–$120 U.S.) over several months, which they could then take home on a visit, instead of sending back smaller but more frequent contributions.[7]

In part, this allowed the women to exercise greater control over the use of their earnings by saving toward particular consumption projects, the most common being the purchase of materials to use in building their parents a new house. These goals were often supported by rural kin, but they could also be frustrated by periodic demands for increased or immediate contributions. Some of these requests tended to come at regular intervals: calls for help with harvest or transplanting expenses, or younger siblings' school costs at the beginning of term (e.g., uniforms, books, high school tuition, etc.). At other times, migrants were called on to help out in a household emergency, particularly when a sudden or severe illness struck. Although young women might complain among themselves that people in the village thought only about money, most migrants did their best to comply with requests from home. But sometimes daughters found themselves in the position of censoring the consumption demands of their own parents. For example, when Lan's mother asked for a color television to replace the black-and-white set that Lan and a sister (also working in the city) had bought a few years before, Lan responded with some exasperation: "I'm saving now for the cost of building her a new house. [My sister and I] bought the supporting posts last year. Mother will have to wait for the television."

Such feelings were only aggravated by a perceived (and often actual) difference in men's and women's consumption behavior. In the city as in the village, young Thai men enjoyed more freedom to dispose of their personal income. As I noted in Chapter 4, Baan Naa Sakae parents expected little direct financial gain from the migration of unmarried sons, although most did hope that young men's urban wages would at least cover their entertainment expenses: cigarettes, alcohol, gambling, women. While parents viewed a certain amount of personal expenditures as unavoidable for migrant daughters, these were not expected to be of the same type or on the same scale as young men's urban consumption practices. Similarly, many of the young women I knew in the city, including those from Baan Naa Sakae, asserted that parents and others at home were much more likely to criticize daughters who failed to send money home than sons. As Puu, a long-time domestic servant, claimed: "My brother has worked in Bangkok for years. He never sends anything home and my parents have never said anything about it. When they need money, they always ask me."

More often, however, migrants directed their critiques at the urban setting itself. The comments of Nimon, a twenty-one-year-old textile worker from a Central Thai village, represent sentiments that many others shared:

> In Thailand there are many "societies." People in the city and people in the village aren't the same. City people, Bangkok people, you can't trust them (*way cay may day*), they only think of themselves. In the city people don't know each other. I've lived in this room for many months now and I still don't know the neighbors. In the village I know everyone. We grew up together, we're all relatives and friends together. I know where they come from, their background. I can trust them (*way cay day*).

Nimon's explicit assertion of the moral and emotional superiority of rural life emphasized an attachment to the home village as a positive source of identity and sense of self-worth as well as a sense of dislocation and moral incoherence in the city. These feelings were shared by most of the migrant women I knew in Bangkok. While they enter urban employment as a way to acquire the cash and commodity signs of urban status and prestige, most young villagers distinguish clearly between their personal ambitions and what they see as the money-grubbing demeanor of the city's native inhabitants.

Migrants' desires for greater participation in the modern nation, to acquire and display the commodity symbols of progress and *thansamay* self-hood, clash with their lived experiences of urban wage labor. In response, many young migrants focus on the village home and community as an idealized site of moral order and compassion. Although Bangkok is a place of adventure, the glamorous and attractive center of *thansamay* Thai society, it is also a chaotic, impersonal, and alien environment. The bonds of compassion, trust, and mutual help that (ideally) link fellow villagers stand in opposition to the alienating quality of many women's (and men's) experiences as low-status laborers in Bangkok.[8]

Migrants' efforts here offer a sharp counterpoint to negative depictions of rural people as *khon baan nôôk*—rustic, unsophisticated, and outdated—within Thailand's dominant culture and mass media. In this imagery, "country folk" (*chaaw baan*) exist on the cultural and economic periphery of the Thai nation, out of step with the rapid pace, complex technology, and sophisticated, *thansamay* style of the urban center. In the media, and occasionally in urban interactions, Northeastern migrants to Bangkok encounter derisive images of their upcountry ways, strange food habits, "rough" and, to the Bangkok ear, largely incomprehensible Isan speech. Conscious of their continuing denigration within the national culture, including stereotypical images of the Isan country bumpkin depicted on television, in cartoons, and as the butt of popular jokes, the migrants I knew were adamant in their assertions of positive regional (non-Bangkok) identities. Even those who had worked in Bangkok for more than a decade assured me that their experiences had not made them "city people" (*khon müang*); Baan Naa Sakae migrants insisted that they would always be "100 percent *khon isaan.*"

In part, this pride and this sense of self-worth are nurtured through the urban use of ethnic and regional markers, especially language and food. Most migrants' daily interactions in the city—with employers, other workers, merchants, vendors—require the use of standard Thai. Nevertheless, migrants from Baan Naa Sakae continued to use their own Lao dialect both among themselves and with others from Isan. Moreover, their use of Lao speech forms was not limited to private conversations; I often heard migrants conversing in urban markets and other public spaces. In addition, most maintained their preference for Isan foods and, in particular, the staple grain, sticky rice. Northeastern dishes and sticky rice were felt to be more delicious and generally more substantial than Central Thai food. Although the latter was what migrants ate at most meals, special occasions and gatherings of friends almost always involved the preparation or purchase of Isan delicacies.

Celebration of these ethnic-regional markers, however, did not displace migrants' specific identification with their home village. When a dozen or so women and men from Baan Naa Sakae got together to host a good-bye party at the end of my fieldwork, the eruption of tempers between two young men who had had too much to drink was a source of serious embarrassment to a number of the others present. Despite the fact that our long acquaintance both in the village and in Bangkok meant that I had substantial knowledge of conflicts between community members in the countryside (some of which migrants themselves had discussed with me), this display of open tensions among fellow villagers in the city and in front of a guest was distressing. One apologized, almost in tears, saying, "It's embarrassing, people of the same village acting in this way. It shouldn't happen." Throughout their urban sojourns, migrants seek to uphold these attachments to communities of origin, despite the counter pressures of modernity aspirations and conflicts with parents or others back home.

Visits Home: Dramas of Duty and Modernity

If the demands of urban consumption styles jeopardize the fragile balance of migrants' desires to be both "modern women" and "good daughters," there are times when migrants can temporarily combine these desired identities into a more satisfying self-image. In particular, migrants' visits to their home villages present important opportunities to resolve the contradictions of their experiences as urban workers by linking their *thansamay* consumption to the maintenance of ties with rural kin. Traveling home, bringing money, wearing new clothes, and accompanied by new friends—this allows many young migrants to reconfigure, however briefly, the disjunctures of urban life and to project a solid identity incorporating both *thansamay* success and daughterly respect and gratitude. These desires inform not only the eagerness many urban workers expressed for periodic returns home but also their general reluctance to go even for a short time unless they had saved a sufficiently large sum of money (or purchased commodities) to take back with them. Such concerns play an even more obvious role in one of the most popular activities in which rural-urban migrants engage: the organization of (and participation in) elaborate ceremonial trips to make ritual donations to village temples. Although framed within the merit-making language of popular religious discourse, the enthusiasm with which migrants participate in these events often has less to do with desires to add to their store of karmic merit (although such goals are by no means irrelevant) than with the opportunities that these trips provide to resolve (if only temporarily) some of the tensions of their urban experiences. Specifically, these merit-making trips are occasions when migrants' *thansamay* consumption practices parallel and even complement their commitment to the village home.

Typically, several people, usually from the same village, will plan an excursion, renting a bus and recruiting friends in the city to come along. Passengers pay a fare for the bus trip and contribute to a merit fund, which is offered to the community temple. During my research, migrants invited me to join them on several such trips and I heard of many more. As merit-making occasions, they must be organized around significant Buddhist ceremonies: ordinations, commonly held at the beginning of the rainy season, prior to the three-month period of monastic retreat; *thôôt kathin*, the ritual presentation of new robes to monks that marks the end of this period; or, most often, *thôôt phaa paa* ("offerings of forest robes"), which may be held at almost any time of the year. All involve rituals during which significant offerings are made to the host temple, in addition to the presentation of robes and other items to resident monks. Frequently, migrants are able to collect donations of several thousand *baht*, usually with a particular purpose in mind, such as the construction of new temple buildings.

But organizing a merit-making trip, as the women I knew quickly pointed out, is a lot of work. A successful trip, that is, one that raises a substantial amount of money, depends on recruiting many participants. Organizers, usually migrants from the same village—both women and men—have to coordinate among themselves, not an easy task when they often live and work in distant parts of Bangkok and seldom have access to private telephone lines to facilitate contact. A rented bus has to be reserved for the occasion, invitations to participants and envelopes for their contributions printed, donors solicited.

This last task was often the most troublesome. One worker at the Sunrise Textiles factory complained that so many ceremonies took place every year that she was reluctant to ask her friends to contribute to yet another one. "If you ask them, they try to give something, but it may only be 10 *baht* [$0.40 U.S.]. And finding people to be *kamakaan* is really hard." A *kamakaan*, or organizing committee member, is a largely honorary position for which individuals get their names printed on the official invitations and on any other documents acknowledging key participants. However, in return for this privilege, a *kamakaan* is expected to contribute a significant sum of money. In 1990, migrants from Baan Naa Sakae calculated that a *kamakaan* ought to give at least 100 *baht* (about $4.00 U.S.), the equivalent at that time of a day's pay or more.[9] *Kamakaan* should also make an effort to attend the ceremony in person, although this was not considered essential.

If the trip's organizers could not recruit enough people to be *kamakaan,* then the chances of collecting a respectable donation would be seriously reduced. "If I helped organize a *thôôt phaa paa* and could not get enough people to be *kamakaan,* it would be terrible," Wan explained. "If the offering is not large enough, I would lose face (*sia naa*) and people at home would criticize." Consequently, when the Baan Naa Sakae headman and other community leaders approached Noi and Ut in the fall of 1990 about organizing a *thôôt phaa paa* from Bangkok, they were less than enthusiastic. The village was planning to build a new temple *saalaa* (meeting hall), the full cost of which was expected to be several hundred thousand *baht* or close to $10,000 U.S. Although no one expected the *thôôt phaa paa* to raise anywhere near the full amount, the women and their friends were clearly reluctant to take on the task: "We just did one last year," they told me, "and already they want another one!" They were not sure it would be worth all the time and effort. As this reaction suggests, ceremonial trips may, in fact, add to the pressures migrants experience in Bangkok, as they struggle to balance the demands of rural responsibilities with those of urban modernity. However, once organized, merit-making excursions allow migrants to synthesize temporarily their ongoing ties to kin and community with claims to *thansamay* autonomy and urban success.

On each of the several merit-making trips I attended, organizers chartered a large passenger bus, packed with people, and decorated on one side with a long banner proclaiming the destination and ceremonial objective of its purpose. Most excursions departed on a Saturday evening at the end of the main factory shift, because Sunday is the principal day off for most Bangkok workers. We traveled all night, arriving at the host community sometime in early to mid-morning.

The journey began in an atmosphere of celebration and revelry that continued throughout the night as we rode into the countryside, fueled in part by a steady flow of alcohol (consumed mostly, but not exclusively, by men), along with soft drinks and other treats purchased by passengers in anticipation of the evening's festivities. Those who tried to rest their heads against seat backs and windows, hoping to catch a little sleep, were loudly serenaded by their more energetic companions, usually with the aid of a microphone hooked into the bus's internal sound system and backed by drums and cymbals brought along by the celebrants. Sometime during the night, the organizers of the trip walked through the bus collecting envelopes they had

FIGURE 14. Migrant workers dance in the temple procession during a merit-making trip to the village of a friend and co-worker.

distributed earlier and that passengers had filled with cash contributions. The amounts would later be recorded, along with participants' names, for the final offering at the temple.

The ceremony itself generally took place soon after reaching the host community. On one *thôôt phaa paa* to a village in the central province of Ratburi, our departure was delayed until the early morning, which meant we arrived too late to complete the offering presentation before the monks' second (and last for the day) morning meal. The village residents had prepared food in large quantities and so, upon arriving, we immediately gathered in the temple hall to eat, making the ceremonial presentation after the meal. The offering included the central donation of money for the temple but also smaller offerings of commodity items for the personal use of resident monks: robes, bath and laundry soap, toilet paper, packaged drinks and drink mixes such as Ovaltine. These were presented in elaborate cellophane-wrapped bundles, a format that has been standardized by urban stores specializing in such ready-to-go merit packages. The ceremony concluded with speeches by community leaders and the most senior organizers of the *thôôt phaa paa*, as well as ritual chants and blessings led by the temple monks. Meanwhile, the final amount of money donated was tallied and announced for everyone to hear. The main organizers received specially blessed amulets from the temple's abbot in recognition of their hard work and larger contributions to the merit fund.

Following the ceremony, there was time to relax. On this occasion, participants had only a few hours before returning to Bangkok in which to visit with family and to introduce merit-makers from other communities or regions of origin who had come along. On other trips, planned to coincide with a long-weekend holiday, merit-makers might stay in the host village overnight. These longer trips allowed migrants from the host community to enjoy fully their display of devotion to temple and community concerns, emphasizing that their achievements as good daughters (and sons) derived from successful sojourns as modern wage workers. The presence of friends and co-workers, who had joined the group from the nation's capital, also emphasized that the connections these culturally sophisticated young women and men had established through geographic mobility were making possible their contributions to the prosperity of the village temple and, by extension, to the well-being of the community as a whole. Although most of the participants were themselves from rural backgrounds, many came from different regions of the country.

For those not from the host village, part of the attraction of participating in a *thôôt phaa paa* was the touristic experience of seeing new places and traveling to different parts of the country. Many participants were often keen to establish a record of the event and their own participation in it; thus, merit-makers, hosts and guests alike, took photos throughout these excursions.[10] Many trips also involved a variety of sightseeing components, increasing the consumption pleasures of these events for many participants.

During one such longer *thôôt phaa paa* to a village in the northeastern province of Khon Kaen, organizers and their guests spent the hours following the ritual presentation in a variety of casual sightseeing activities and other entertainments. Several other workers and I had joined the trip at the invitation of Wan, a textile worker and one of the organizers. From the temple, Wan took us to her mother's house, where we could bathe and rest before she led several of us on a tour of the village. Later Wan took us out to view several local points of interest, particularly a large lake just a short walk from the village center. The viewing and consuming excitement of the trip was heightened that evening by the staging of a Northeastern regional folk-opera (*môô lam*). The host community had hired a professional troupe for the occasion.

The next morning we watched local celebrations of the best-known and most exciting of the ceremonies in the Isan annual ritual cycle: the rocket festival (*bun bang fay*), held each year to welcome the first rains after the dry season. Participants in the *thôôt phaa paa* gathered with local residents to watch the firing of the first few homemade rockets (long bamboo or, increasingly, plastic cylinders, three to five meters in length, loaded with gunpowder and set off straight up into the sky). Before all the rockets could be fired, however, we were called to return to the bus for the trip back to Bangkok. On this occasion, as on all other ceremonial excursions I attended, the return journey included additional sightseeing attractions. When recruiting among friends and co-workers, organizers frequently emphasized the opportunities participants would have to visit such sites as famous temples, caves, waterfalls, national parks, dams, or archaeological ruins.

Returning from the *thôôt phaa paa* ceremony in Khon Kaen, for example, we detoured nearly two hours to visit the site of a major hydroelectric-power dam. Built in the 1960s, this was one of the major public works projects in Northeast Thailand following World War II, and a key source of energy, underlying (a largely successful) government campaign promoting rural electrification in the region. The dam itself has become a popular tourist site, with extensive landscaped grounds, parking lots, shaded walking paths upstream, concession stands and restaurant facilities, in addition to public access to the dam itself, which stands as an impressive monument to Thailand's *thansamay* technology and engineering abilities. Passengers on the *thôôt phaa paa* bus alighted eagerly and fanned out to take in the sights of the area. For an hour or more, groups of friends clustered on the dam's top rim, then moved on to purchase small souvenirs and samples of local foods at the concession stands. In this way, for a short whirlwind period, the excursion's passengers appropriated an urban, middle-class style of up-to-date tourism before reboarding the bus and turning once again toward Bangkok.

Thôôt phaa paa trips like this allow migrant youth an opportunity to exercise the *thansamay* identities and the associated consumption practices many hoped to achieve through Bangkok employment, and to do so in a way and within a cultural idiom (Buddhist merit-making) that also affirms their attachments to rural kin and communities of origin. This combination of spiritual and worldly purposes is central to the power of these events to help defuse ongoing conflicts, at least temporarily, between migrants' aspirations for achievement within the dominant culture of urban modernity and their continuing attachments to village family and community. *Thôôt phaa paa* and other ceremonial trips provide an opportunity to display success and to show off urban friends to people back home, as well as to renew and affirm solidarity with the rural community and its moral focus, the Buddhist temple. They constitute some of the few moments when fulfilling one's obligations as a good village daughter (or son) and the pursuit of *thansamay* identity appear to coincide.

Moreover, migrants achieve this balance by acting in the most prestigious arena of the Thai social and moral order: Buddhist merit-making. Offerings of money, robes, and other items earn spiritual merit for all participants, especially the organizers. In addition, the money raised by a *thôôt phaa paa* is often earmarked for new temple construction or renovation, among the most meritorious acts to which any Buddhist can contribute. The value of earning merit in this way is acknowledged by organizers and participants alike, even as they appreciate the opportunities for worldly entertainment that the trips offer. In addition, merit-making trips require (and demonstrate for all to see) a level of organizational skills and material sacrifice that would not usually be expected of young people who remained in the village, as dependents in their parents' households. For example, rural youth earn merit by attending temple festivals and other ritual events, but religious duties and daily support for the monks are tasks supervised and organized by community elders. Young women and men living in Baan Naa Sakae often help with preparations for major rituals, give food offerings to monks, and attend temple ceremonies, but they are not usually involved in the organization and planning of these events.[11] These decisions are made by members of their parents' and grandparents' generations (see Tambiah, 1970; Lefferts, 1980). Consequently, young people in Bangkok who organize *thôôt phaa paa* or other ceremonies, and make sizable contributions out of their own pockets, display a degree of responsibility and control over material resources that is quite unusual for their age and social status within most village settings.

Furthermore, the number of participants from outside the home village and the amount of monetary offerings are features not common to most rural ceremonies. Many aspects of these excursions from Bangkok—the long distance traveled, the participants from many different parts of the country, the drama and (at least potentially) large sums of money donated—recall the prestigious ritual offerings that wealthy patrons and ambitious politicians sponsor, usually at famous temples in Bangkok and provincial towns. Although none of my informants made this connection explicit, it seems likely that part of the attraction that merit-making trips had for young villagers lay in this vicarious association with the elaborate style of merit offerings practiced by the powerful and wealthy, groups to whom migrants and their families must defer in everyday life.

Thôôt phaa paa trips celebrate participants' *thansamay* knowledge and sophistication in other ways as well. In particular, migrants' enthusiastic sightseeing draws on urban, middle-class forms of domestic tourism. Especially popular among domestic Thai travelers are those destinations that represent or sacralize Thai identity and national heritage—including national parks, historical capitals, ancient monuments, as well as sites more emblematic of present-day, modern Thai ingenuity and material progress (such as the Khon Kaen hydroelectric dam). Usually, however, it is members of the urban middle and upper classes who have the resources to visit these disparate and distant sights of national pride and identity, to be tourist-consumers of the Thai nation. Migrant youth, in leaving their homes for urban employment, are at least partly motivated by a similar desire to be viewer-consumers of the wider Thai society, specifically its most prestigious and modern core, located in the capital city of Bangkok. Living and working in Bangkok, however, as low-wage, low-status proletarian laborers provides only limited opportunities to establish claims to the commodified signs of Thai modernity. *Thôôt phaa paa* trips allow migrant workers access to some of the signs and practices of *thansamay* Thai society as tourists in their own right.

As proletarian wage earners, migrants' desires for *thansamay* identity and self-expression receive little recognition within Bangkok's media- and consumption-dominated setting. Moreover, by pursuing styles and standards of urban commodity consumption, young women run the risk of failing to make the economic contributions expected of them by people at home and that they themselves feel obligated to make. Merit-making trips offer a compelling—if temporary—resolution of these conflicts. By organizing and participating in ceremonial offerings, young rural women affirm their connections with kin and community while at the same time demonstrating their claims to personal autonomy and material success. Merit makers mobilize the signs and symbols of a *thansamay* identity within the conventions of Buddhist rituals. Consequently, merit-making trips allow rural youth to assert (if only temporarily) some of the social authority and prestige that they had hoped to gain through migration to Bangkok, challenging everyday experiences of marginalization and subordination as proletarian wage earners. And they do so before their most appreciative audience, rural family and friends.

Nevertheless, these claims to *thansamay* success and autonomy are fleeting and difficult to sustain. In this chapter I have argued that commodity consumption (including ceremonial trips) represents an especially meaningful way that migrants can maneuver between the competing demands of being good daughters and modern women. But choosing between money spent in the city to acquire the commodity emblems of a *thansamay* identity and money saved or remitted home involves most migrant women in a series of fragile compromises. This fragility is nowhere more evident than when women must decide whether or not to remain in the city, a choice that most often revolves around questions of marriage and sexuality. As we shall see in the next chapter, contemplating who, when, where, and even whether to marry forces young migrants to confront fundamental contradictions between the material conditions of their urban experiences and the images, desires, and identities that propelled their move to the city in the first place.

CHAPTER 8

Courtship, Marriage, and Contested Selves

⇉

"We are not like our mothers."
—Ut, textile worker, age twenty-five

Noi's Dilemma

When I said good-bye to Noi at the end of my fieldwork in late 1990, she was in a drunken stupor. We had gathered at the rented room of some fellow villagers, along with more than a dozen other Baan Naa Sakae migrants, for an afternoon of food and drink in honor of my impending departure for the United States. To no one's surprise, several of the men got quite drunk, but Noi was the only one of the women to imbibe so heavily. However, this had recently become a pattern for Noi; she had begun drinking regularly and to excess during the weeks preceding the farewell party. By drinking, several of her friends told me, Noi was trying "to cure her worried heart."

Noi's difficulties had begun a few months earlier when her parents started to pressure her to accept an arranged marriage. The groom was the son of rather distant cousins living in another village; Noi had heard of him but they had never met before. His family was poorer than her own relatively prosperous household; his parents owned less land than Noi's, and they had offered a marriage payment of only 15,000 *baht* ($600 U.S.). While on a visit home, Noi had acquiesced to her parents' will and agreed to the formal engagement. Afterwards, however, she felt trapped and was unsure about what to do. "How can I live with someone I don't like? If I don't like him now, I'm not going to like him later." Furthermore, Noi objected to her fiancé's lack of migration experience. "He's never even been to Bangkok!" How could he understand what she had seen and learned during her years in the city? How could he appreciate how she had changed as a result of her time away?

Village elders have long urged reluctant brides to remember that "love comes later," but Noi and her friends, who had spent more than five years working at textile factories in Bangkok, saw themselves as part of a different generation. As Noi's cousin, Ut, explained: "We are not like our mothers. Our mothers stayed home, they never went anywhere, never saw anything. But we have not lived that way. We have not stayed at home, we have lived on our own here in the city." Their experiences in Bangkok had affirmed in them a new, specifically *thansamay* sense of identity.

In the context of an unwanted marriage, this *thansamay* self-image clashed with Noi's continuing emotional attachment and moral obligation to her home and family. Several months before, Noi had already decided to work for just one more year in the city before returning home to care for her aging parents. The third of six children, Noi was the eldest unmarried daughter and all her younger siblings were also working in the city. None were left at home to help with farm and household chores. Her parents had never relied on their children's urban wages for day-to-day subsistence needs, so neither Noi nor her other siblings had ever sent money home on a regular basis. However, when particular needs arose, she had always responded to requests for help—such as money to defray planting or harvest costs—often contributing two to three thousand *baht* ($80–120 U.S.) or more at a time. And more than once, Noi had taken time off from work (using her limited sick leave) in order to spend a few days at home working in the fields during peak labor periods.

This decision to return home after one more year was not based solely on Noi's sense of responsibility toward her parents. She herself was getting older. At age twenty-seven, Noi's options for Bangkok wage work were narrowing. She considered her present job a "good" one: she was a permanent contract employee at the Sunrise Textiles factory and earned the minimum wage (just under 100 *baht* per day in 1990). Nonetheless, her company only hired new workers of age twenty-five or less. If Noi lost this job, then finding another position, especially in a "good" factory, would not be easy. Returning to Baan Naa Sakae was a more realistic long-term goal, she felt. Still, this was a decision she planned to make on her own. Confronted with an arranged marriage proposal and a prospective husband she neither liked nor respected, Noi felt somewhat betrayed. For the past five years, Noi had exercised a degree of power over her own actions and income in Bangkok unlike anything she might have enjoyed in the village as a dependent unmarried daughter. Noi's urban autonomy and the personal independence it had fostered were not taken into account at all in the match her parents now urged upon her.

Noi and Ut, like many migrants I met, felt that their time in the city had resulted in profound personal changes, despite the constraints they faced as low-wage, low-status industrial laborers. Encounters with new forms of authority and labor discipline, long hours and overtime shifts, difficult—even dangerous—working conditions are all aspects of urban modernity very different from popular images of *thansamay* sophistication and commodified style. Outside the workplace, young women must also struggle—rarely with more than partial success—to fulfill both household expectations of economic assistance and their own aspirations for urban entertainment and up-to-date self-presentation. Amid the stresses of urban employment and consumption demands, Noi and her friends from Baan Naa Sakae agreed that, living in Bangkok, they often felt ill at ease (*may sabaay cay*): "Sometimes it is hard, we miss home (*khit thüng baan*) thinking about our families and those we love." These feelings of ambivalence persisted alongside their claims to personal transformation, reflecting the delicate compromises most women had to make between attachments to rural kin and their aspirations for *thansamay* autonomy.

Few women were willing to forgo entirely either goal for the sake of the other. None of the migrant women I knew in Bangkok arrived in the city with the intention of settling there permanently, and despite the appreciation most had for what they had learned and seen in the city, few were persuaded to change their mind. Most retained close ties with people in the countryside, visiting at least once a year or more. Almost all had plans to return home, sometimes after a specified period; more often at some more or less vague future date. But if ongoing ties to rural kin represented a bulwark against the hardships and marginality women experienced in Bangkok, control over their urban wages—including the often difficult decisions of how much to send home and how much to spend on themselves—provided unmarried women with a measure of autonomy largely unavailable to their peers in the village setting. Noi's case highlights the value many young women placed on their urban independence and their reluctance to give this up. At the same time, Noi's distress and self-destructive response reveal the precarious foundations of young migrants' claims to *thansamay* autonomy. Experienced migrants like Noi acknowledged their vulnerability as low-status, low-wage, and poorly protected workers, and recognized the long-term uncertainties of urban employment. But while migrants shared similar experiences of exploitation and subordination, few had the opportunities, knowledge, or resources to address these problems collectively. Instead, rural women's encounters with Thai modernity tended to provoke more individualized responses, a process that is perhaps most clearly reflected in migrants' concerns and decisions about courtship and marriage.

Courtship, Marriage, and Migration

In Northeast Thailand, as in other regions of the country, cultural convention allows children to play a role in selecting their spouse; moreover, parents cannot force a daughter (or son) into a marriage. However, historically, parents could and often did exert considerable pressure either for or against specific matches. The story of one Baan Naa Sakae widow—Mae Lin, one of Noi's maternal aunts—illustrates the constraints many young women faced in an earlier generation. As a young woman thirty years earlier, Mae Lin had a favored suitor. A young man from a neighboring village, the suitor had courted her at village festivals and they had fallen in love. However, he was from an undistinguished family; though Lin's own parents were dead, her uncles and aunts were not impressed with the match. The young man had few resources (he was orphaned as well) and could not afford to offer the marriage payment her kin were asking. Under such circumstances, the traditional option for young lovers was to run off together, returning later to offer a smaller payment to the woman's kin in reparation for the disrespect shown by eloping. When her suitor asked Lin to go away with him, she was afraid. "I loved him, but I didn't dare [go]."

Eventually, her relatives pressured her to accept an engagement with another man, one whose family could offer a respectable marriage price (*khaa sin sôôt*). They were married soon afterward. "But I didn't think about my husband. I still dreamed about the other one. Even when I was [lying] with my husband, it was not him I thought about. Even pregnant with my second child, I still hadn't forgotten." As a widow in her fifties with three grown children, Mae Lin said she was no longer troubled by the past, yet she and others in Baan Naa Sakae still remembered her youthful romance. One day a neighbor ran into Mae Lin's old suitor in the local market town (he had long since married and had a family himself). Back in the village, her report on the new physical attractions of Mae Lin's "boyfriend" (*faen*)—he was balding and had a bit of a belly—provided the main subject of conversation and much teasing of Mae Lin when she and her neighbors gathered to chat later that afternoon.

Mae Lin and her neighbors agreed that, in the past, parents and kin had more power to shape their children's choice of marriage partner, although this was not absolute. If a desired match did not meet parental approval, the young couple could always elope. This might, in fact, be encouraged either by the groom's parents if they were unable or unwilling to pay a high *khaa sin sôôt* or by the bride's parents if they could not afford to host a formal wedding feast. But where parental disapproval was strong, eloping was not necessarily an easy choice for many young women. Like the youthful Mae Lin, they could find it difficult to brave the anger and disappointment of their closest kin for the sake of a lover. To elope might also risk more than emotional relations; it could also undermine a woman's economic ties to kin and family resources. There was no guarantee that kin on either side would reconcile to the marriage, although if the couple returned to make an appropriate show of respect and to ask for forgiveness, most people felt that parents should relent.

A generation later, most people of Mae Lin's generation felt that the possibilities created by increased labor migration had transformed the marriage choices of village youth. Baan Naa Sakae parents were explicit about their sense of diminished authority—"Nowadays we have to follow the wishes of our children." Sometimes this meant that parents were asked to negotiate a formal engagement only after the couple had already made their choice and agreed on an appropriate marriage payment in advance. At other times, parents had to accept a child's selection after the fact. During my fieldwork in Baan Naa Sakae, at least three young women and one young man merely returned home after a period of urban employment accompanied by a new spouse, most often another migrant they had met through work. In addition, as one village mother argued, "Nowadays, if a young woman is unhappy with the man her parents wish her to marry, she can just leave for the city. In my time, we didn't think of such a thing; it wasn't possible."

Migrants themselves often spoke of postponing marriage "for another year or two" in order to stay longer in the city; many, like Noi, pursued this strategy until well into their twenties, an unusually late age for a first marriage in most rural settings. Sometimes parents might encourage this, at least for a time, in order to benefit from daughters' urban wages. Older women in Baan Naa Sakae also noted with some envy that urban employment allowed their own and their neighbors' daughters to prolong the pleasures of youth and courtship, as *saaw* (maidens), before taking up the burdens of marriage and motherhood. When the fifteen-year-old daughter of a Baan Naa Sakae family was married to a local young man, neighbors commented on her parents' hastiness in promoting the match: "She'd only just reached the age of courtship. She didn't have a chance to really enjoy being a *saaw*. Her father just wanted the extra help [of a son-in-law]."

Indeed concerns about household labor often prompted parents to exert more pressure on an absent daughter to marry and return to settle at home. In Baan Naa Sakae, as in most of rural Thailand, the expectation is that the man will reside, at least initially, in his wife's home and work on her parents' land. Therefore, as parents age or as the out-migration of other children decreases the household labor supply, mothers and fathers are more likely to stress the marriage prospects of absent daughters than those of migrant sons. At age twenty-one, Phan, the daughter of Phô Lat and Mae Sahn (introduced in Chapter 3), became aware of her parents' growing concern that she leave her textile employment in Bangkok and return home to marry. She responded by reducing the frequency of her visits home because each time her father suggested potential matches and pressured her to quit her job in the city. "But I'm not ready yet. I want to work another year or two before going home [to stay]."

While most young women in Bangkok appreciated the greater leverage migration gave them over the timing of marriage, this did not mean that they viewed romance and courtship as unproblematic issues. Women in the city confronted conflicting messages about appropriate gender roles and sexual morality that sharply limited the kinds of choices regarding marriage that most migrants were prepared to make. Like their sisters in the village, migrant women in Bangkok face a barrage of messages that challenged familiar definitions of appropriate sexual behavior. In the urban consumer culture, highly commodified images of the *thansamay* woman compete with conventional standards of modesty and virginal purity (*khwaam borisut*) as models for female sexuality.

On the one hand, women are urged in a multitude of ways to be up-to-date: to enhance their personal beauty and attractiveness as well as material success through the purchase of market commodities. This commodification of women's bodies and sexual charms permeates media images, shopping malls, and market districts, and is often highlighted in popular forms of entertainment. The *phuu ying thansamay* is celebrated—and her desirability enhanced—through the production and sale of modern clothing fashions, hair styles, cosmetics, and other beauty products, as well as the display of beautiful bodies and faces in advertising, television, movies, and beauty contests (Van Esterik, 1988, 1996). On the other hand, they are expected to behave as dutiful, respectful daughters, both toward parents at home and in their actions as subordinate employees. Specifically, they must beware the fine line between glamorous, sexualized images of modern femininity and the stigma and degradation of the "bad woman," epitomized by the promiscuous sexuality of the prostitute.

Contradictory messages in urban constructions of the *thansamay* Thai woman complicate the choices of migrants like Noi and threaten to upset the balance between personal desires for autonomy and obligations to rural kin.[1] In particular, while living away from home and without supervision, young women's sexual propriety cannot be verified. Furthermore, the actions of some migrants—returning on visits to Baan Naa Sakae wearing new clothes and makeup, drinking whiskey or flirting openly with young men—do not reassure rural observers. Many young women who left Baan Naa Sakae for Bangkok found that their mobility raised questions at home; moreover, these suspicions are not always put to rest by daughters' economic contributions to kin and community and may affect their value as marriageable women.

These concerns played a role in one of Noi's major complaints about her engagement: the groom's kin had offered, to her mind, an insultingly low marriage payment. Marriage payments are usually based on the status of the bride and her family. Noi's family was well placed in her home community. Her parents owned nearly 100 *rai* or almost 40 acres of land (well above the average community holdings of 35 *rai*) and her elder brother had recently been elected village headman. Daughters in families of similar wealth and status married in 1990 for amounts of 20,000 *baht* and more. Some of these young women had urban migration experience, but they all had completed high school and several had finished college or university degrees. It was their education that usually compelled a high marriage price, marking the potential (if not always the fact) that the bride would find a salaried job, preferably within the civil service. Noi, however, had only completed primary school and although villagers spoke approvingly of the help she had given her parents over the years, she did not have the educational credentials that might counterbalance local concerns about the potential young women had to acquire sexual experience while away working in the city.

In addition, on trips home, Noi and others from the village had occasionally brought along friends, including among them some young men. And like many other migrants, it was rumored that Noi had a boyfriend in the city. In fact, Noi was interested in someone; he was also from Baan Naa Sakae and worked in Bangkok, having returned a few months before from an unsuccessful stint of contract labor in Israel. However, he was from a family that was not on good terms with Noi's parents, and he had no money to "ask" for her himself. Under these circumstances, village neighbors agreed that a marriage payment of 15,000 *baht* was reasonable, but to Noi it was a further blow to her self-esteem—an admission to the community at large that despite her family's high status in the village, she was not "worth" a significant bride price.

Risk and Urban Romance

In spite of concerns about their reputations at home, romance and flirtation were important preoccupations for most migrant women. Most young women from Baan Naa Sakae leave home for Bangkok at the age (mid- to late teens) when courtship begins to be a subject of intense concern, both for village youth and for their parents. In addition, many of the migrants I knew were avid viewers of the romantic fantasies featured on Thai television: formulaic storylines of youthful heartbreaks and eventual happiness, set amid palatial Bangkok homes and other glamorous scenes of elite Bangkok life. Not surprisingly, then, many migrant workers view romance and flirtation as appealing ways to express their newfound urban independence. Parents and elders who might discourage such behavior in the village are far away, while migrants (especially those who find factory jobs) spend their days both on and off the shop floor working and living in the company of peers who share similar interests. Co-workers and friends tease each other about real or imagined boyfriends. They may meet after work to try out new ways of styling hair, to model new clothes and cosmetics. Other forms of relaxation and entertainment—shared meals, outings to markets, shopping malls, movies, or urban parks—are popular, at least in part, because they allow young women and men workers to meet more openly than might be possible in a village setting.

Working in Bangkok offers young women the chance to pursue excitement and romance far from the watchful eyes of parents, neighbors, and other elders. One Sunday in mid-1990, a group of Baan Naa Sakae migrants invited me to meet them for an excursion to the Crocodile Farm, a popular theme park on the city's eastern outskirts. Our party comprised half a dozen young women, most of whom worked at the Sunrise Textiles factory, and two young men who worked in factories close by. Having known each other from childhood, everyone was friendly and the morning proceeded amid much laughter and teasing, especially between the men and the women. Although some of this teasing flirtation might easily have taken place in Baan Naa Sakae, the public anonymity of the Crocodile Farm gave the gathering a sense of daring that heightened everyone's enthusiasm for the occasion. By early afternoon, however, most of the group was ready to leave the park; we were hungry and the concession stands at the park were expensive. We decided to stop at a nearby market to purchase ingredients to cook a shared lunch on the way back. The two men chose to remain at the Farm; they wanted to attend the park's weekend rock concert, a nationally televised event that regularly featured rising Thai pop music stars. One woman, Pim, stayed with them. Pim's decision sparked little comment from the rest, as it was no secret to them that Pim and one of the young men were sweethearts (*faen*); the concert was an opportunity to spend time together. Migrant peers accepted unproblematically this kind of open dating, but it would have been highly suspect—if not prohibited outright—at home. In Bangkok, however, one could have a *faen* and date without a public commitment to marriage. For Pim, like many young women (and young men), this was part of the fun and excitement that urban employment made possible.

Although young women like Pim can pursue romantic relationships in the city, they do not do so without concerns for potential consequences. Many limit their actions to casual flirting and daydreaming. Others get involved in more serious, sexual relationships; yet the stakes are high in such a gamble. If it does not lead to a recognized marital relationship—including, at the very least, a trip by the couple to visit the woman's family and ask forgiveness for taking matters into their own hands—then the woman's reputation and future marriageability may be seriously undermined.[2]

If news about a young woman's indiscretion reaches people back home, the embarrassing gossip may prompt parental action. This is more likely when a migrant works with others from her home community or if her lover is a fellow migrant from the same or a neighboring village. In one case that I witnessed, an engagement was contracted between a Baan Naa Sakae woman and man, who had both been away working in Bangkok. One evening, friends and relatives gathered in the woman's home for the formal negotiations between the two families. Despite the close observation of ritual forms, several people insisted that the couple had already agreed on the amount of the *khaa sin sôôt*; as one participant later commented, the back and forth of offers and counter-offers was "the way we do it, to make it fun and entertaining." The ceremony ended with the presentation to the bride-to-be's parents of an initial payment of 3,000 *baht* ($120 U.S.) out of the agreed upon 19,000 *baht* bride price. The marriage, however, never took place. Not long afterward, the story circulated that a wedding might never have been intended at all: The two young people had been lovers while away in Bangkok and the engagement had provided the families with a way to save face.[3]

The stigma attached to women who are sexually active (or believed to be) outside of marriage remains a powerful concern for women and their families in Baan Naa Sakae and in other northeastern communities.[4] But if urban romances may damage migrants' reputations at home, they also pose a threat to women's economic security in the city. On the one hand, urban courtship usually involves forms of consumption—purchase of new items such as clothes and cosmetics, participating in commercial entertainment such as movies, theme parks, restaurants, and the like—that most young migrants are eager to adopt; however, these expenses can easily strain a worker's limited wages and threaten her ability to save money for rural families. These urban pleasures also carry other, potentially longer-term, costs. In particular, many migrants I knew feared what might happen later on if their lover left them, particularly once there were children.

These fears reflect many women's grim assessments of their long-term prospects for urban employment.[5] Migrants soon learn that few factories will hire "older" women, that is, those over the age of twenty-five and sometimes over age twenty-one or less. Women who stay in the city after their mid-twenties must be careful not to lose their current employment or they may have to choose between a premature return home or poorly paid informal sector work such as domestic service or sweatshop subcontracting labor. Similarly, the women I knew were reluctant to marry and start a family in the city. They knew well that urban employers usually preferred not only youthful but also single, unencumbered employees. Many migrants believed that a woman who married, and especially if she became pregnant, would risk being fired from her job.[6]

Moreover, workers who struggled to manage on their wages as single women did not view the added expense of supporting a family (even with two wages) as an easy task. Poor married women in Bangkok, if they are unable to secure a regular waged job, have to rely on a range of insecure, low-paying jobs such as scavenging, small-scale cottage industries, and vending (Thorbek, 1987). However, women who are lucky enough to keep a factory job after marriage often must endure long and distressing separations from children who have to be left back in the village to be raised by grandparents. The migrants I met readily acknowledged the insecurity and hardship of these options.

Women's experiences and expectations of exploitation as poorly paid and insecure urban laborers are intensified by their perceptions that men in the city are more likely to be unreliable providers. "Men are not responsible"; "men like to have lots of wives"; "men drink, gamble, and spend their money on their friends"—all were commonly expressed opinions. Almost universally, women told me that men in the city were more likely to run after other women and not contribute to the household budget. Many of the migrants I spoke to felt that if a woman settled in the city, there was a good chance that she would have to support herself and her children on her own. And most could point to a friend or acquaintance whose city romance had left her in difficult straits. On one occasion, I went with several textile workers to visit a former co-worker who had been abandoned by her husband. We spent an hour or two helping her to assemble small plastic holders for artificial flowers, for which she earned a small piece-rate wage—amounting to less than 30 *baht* ($1.20 U.S.) per day—to support herself and her infant son. On the return trip, my companions were quick to point out the cautionary effects of their friend's situation; as one said, "You see, Mary, marriage only means problems for women. A good man, one to trust, is hard to find. You've got to be careful."

Although abuse and neglect occur in village families, most women believed it was both less frequent and that the consequences for women were less severe because of their access to the moral and economic support of relatives and neighbors. In the city, a young woman may be freed from familial supervision, but she is also no longer within easy reach of family assistance. While the vast majority of migrant women I knew looked forward to having a family some day, the idea of doing so while remaining in the city was daunting. Consequently, as Phan said, "I'm not ready to marry yet, but when I do he must be a village person like me. I'd prefer to marry someone from Baan Naa Sakae, or at least someone from Isan. I don't want to be in Bangkok forever; when I'm ready to go back home, then I'll think about getting married."

Young women working in Bangkok recognize their vulnerability in the city, but this does not mean that the prospect of a return home is an easy choice. If the idea of settling in the city is fraught with difficulty, going home to a future of rice farming and motherhood raises a different set of concerns, ones linked to migrants' ongoing aspirations for *thansamay* forms of success and autonomy. The wages they can earn in Bangkok, limited though they may be, provide a steady and individualized source of cash income, unlike the more irregular, often unpredictable, and collective earnings that characterize household agricultural production in the village. The undesirable consequences of leaving city jobs behind worried Lian, a former textile worker whom I met during a visit to her home village in the northeastern province of Khon Kaen. Lian was in her mid-twenties and had just returned to her village in anticipation of her upcoming marriage to a local man. Although she was happy with her husband-to-be, their union would put an end to her time in Bangkok; soon she would be "only a *mae baan* (mother and housewife)." Lian viewed this change in status with ambivalence and even a sense of loss. Many other migrant women expressed similar sentiments as they contemplated when to exchange their urban employment for the burdens of raising their own family.

Some young women responded by planning for a return home, but in a way that would preserve some of their hard-won *thansamay* status and autonomy. A common ambition was to open a small shop or food vending enterprise. Others, who were able to marshal their resources and energies during their limited leisure hours, chose to invest in further education or vocational training. Maew left Baan Naa Sakae for Bangkok at age fifteen. Four years later, when she was working at a leather bag factory, she decided to reduce drastically both her expenditures in the city and her remittances home in order to pay for a high school education. When I met her, she had been taking adult education classes every Sunday for the past two years; she expected to complete her diploma in another two or three years. She was also saving money in a bank account so that when she left Bangkok to go home she would be able to continue her education at the provincial teacher's college. In a similar vein, Phan saved from her wages to pay the 7,000 *baht* ($280 U.S.) tuition at a Bangkok beauty school. On her days off from the factory, she attended classes and practiced the skills of hairdressing and cosmetic application. Although Phan did not think that she could use these skills to make a living in Baan Naa Sakae, she thought she might be able to find a job in a beauty salon in the nearby district town.

Phan and Maew were somewhat unusual in their ability to marshal their resources toward such specific long-term future goals. For Maew, this decision resulted in an ongoing conflict with family in the village, particularly her mother, who regularly requested that Maew send money home and periodically threatened to travel to Bangkok (and did so on at least one occasion) to get money from Maew herself. Most of the rural-urban migrants I knew either had less concrete plans for their future or were unable or unwilling to ignore parental expectations so consistently. Nevertheless, they too hoped to be more than just "rice and upland crop farmers" (*chaaw naa chaaw rai*) when they left the city. Achieving this goal was more difficult—and even Maew and Phan wondered if their educational investments would really pay off in the end. Moreover, young women who planned and worked toward a successful return to the village could find that circumstances intervened. A sudden illness, an accident on the job, factory layoffs, a family crisis, or, as in Noi's case, the competing demands and expectations of parents—any or all such events might force a woman into an agonizing decision.

Of course, some migrant women did marry and remain in the city and not all encountered hardship as a result. Two Baan Naa Sakae women were well known for their successful urban marriages. One had gone to the northern city of Chiang Mai as a teenager in the early 1970s, where she began working as a waitress. Nearly twenty years later, at the time of my fieldwork in Baan Naa Sakae, her success story had taken on an almost fairy tale aura in local recountings: She had been befriended by the wealthy woman who owned the restaurant where she worked, and taken on as a kind of adopted daughter. The owner took a keen interest in the young woman, even arranging for and sponsoring her marriage to an industrious young man, and then setting the two up in their own restaurant business with which they did extremely well. (In one version of this story, the Baan Naa Sakae woman and her husband inherited their patron's business upon her death—after having nursed her through her final days). Although I was unable to talk to this village daughter-made-good, she did maintain ties to Baan Naa Sakae, returning periodically to make offerings at the local temple (including the donation of a television for the monks to watch) and periodically sponsoring younger relatives from the community who would go to Chiang Mai to find work.

The second woman was somewhat less admired. After going to work in Bangkok, she became the minor wife of a mid-ranking army officer.[7] With his financial backing, she was able to start a small sewing shop in the city. Although her less respectable marriage status was the subject of some gossip in the village (most of which was prompted by complaints about her superior attitude toward rural family and friends), she was also envied for the relative comfort of her urban home and livelihood. In both cases, people in Baan Naa Sakae felt that the women's gambles had paid off. Nevertheless, their successes did little to alter more general perceptions among migrants and their families that women in urban marriages risked significant economic and emotional vulnerability.

The extent to which urban marriage choices entailed serious risks was highlighted by the stories several Baan Naa Sakae women told about a mail-order bride agency that came to their factory to recruit women as wives for foreign men. No one from Baan Naa Sakae volunteered but some of their co-workers did. A few of these women had found wealth and prosperity, at least as measured by the photos and news they sent back of their new homes. One woman they knew of returned with her foreign husband to have a Thai marriage ceremony, bringing with her money for her parents to build a new house. But others did not fare so well. One story was particularly alarming to the women I knew; the new bride had arrived to meet her husband only to learn that she was expected to be the "wife" of an entire household of men.

Marriage Choices

Migrants, eager for excitement and *thansamay* entertainment, might find the idea of urban romance compelling, but they also feared the dangers and difficulties that could follow. Indeed, a number of women in Bangkok, both from Baan Naa Sakae and elsewhere, told me that they "might not" or "probably won't" marry at all. Even those in the majority, who stated that they intended to marry "some day," had often consciously decided to postpone marriage in favor of wage earning. In some cases, they feared this choice might leave them too old to find a husband. Several were already in their late twenties and early thirties, a very late age for a first marriage, particularly in rural communities.[8] This choice was not an easy one. Young women are raised to expect to take on the responsibilities of marriage and children from early in their own youth. Just as important, for many in rural Thailand a family of one's own represents the only real security one can have against poverty and neglect in old age. Nevertheless, many women working in Bangkok expressed considerable caution, even reluctance, toward marriage and, in a few cases, rejected it outright.

Lan, who left Baan Naa Sakae at age fourteen to work in Bangkok, voiced the kinds of concerns that many migrants face in the city. Although Lan had worked primarily as a domestic servant, many of her complaints were echoed by factory workers as they contemplated when, or whether, to take up the responsibilities and potential uncertainties of married life.

At thirty years of age, Lan was still single. She did not think she would ever marry. "I'm a stubborn person, I only do what I want to do." Her "bad habits," she said, would make married life difficult, especially given that it's usually the woman who has to "sacrifice" and make compromises. She was wary of men and did not trust them. Her own father drank and gambled, losing much of the family's land to debts before he died. "My mother suffered a lot." Men in the city, she thought, are just as bad, worse even. "Most are *cao chuu* [adulterers, "playboys"], they like to have lots of women." Her employer was like that and his first marriage ended in divorce as a result.

Lan herself had had many romantic disappointments: "My heart's been broken so many times." A few years before, there was one man she liked a lot. He was a clerk in a bank near where Lan works. He would often come by to chat and visit. But when Lan discovered that he had a wife already, "I stopped everything. I cut him off. Even though I still liked him, I had to show him I wasn't interested. Men like that are no good. You'll only have worse problems if you keep on." Now, she said, she would rather stay single. "It's easiest to be on my own." Nor did she want to go back to the village. There was not enough land to divide among herself and her nine living sisters. Besides, after almost sixteen years in Bangkok, Lan would find it difficult to adjust to village life, especially the attitudes of neighbors whom she felt were condescending about her family's poverty and always looking for ways to spread bad gossip about them. "I'd rather stay in Bangkok and just send money home. I don't want anything for myself; I just want my mother to be comfortable." However, she did worry about the future. With no family of her own, who would take care of her in her old age? "Well," she laughed halfheartedly, "I think I'll just die when I'm fifty."

Compared with other migrants from Baan Naa Sakae, Lan's perspective was a little extreme. She was unusual not only for rejecting marriage but also for preferring to remain in Bangkok. Her bitterness was at least partly tied to the lack of respect she felt she received from migrants and other people in the village because of the low status and low pay of her work as a servant. Although I met a number of women in the city who, like Lan, felt themselves too old and therefore unlikely to marry, most still saw themselves returning to their home village at some time in the future. In this they were joined by the great majority of migrant women who expected and desired to marry but preferred to postpone it until they were ready to stop working in the city. A return to the village was almost always preferred, but arriving at this decision was rarely a simple process, in part because it usually meant relinquishing much of their cherished *thansamay* independence.

Questions about the future force rural women to confront their material and moral vulnerability as urban laborers. Women's decisions about marriage and courtship reveal varied strategies for retaining their newfound sense of *thansamay* autonomy as long as possible, to maneuver within, if not to resolve, the tensions and disappointments of their migration experiences. Nevertheless, as Lan's comments indicate, the conflicts, rivalries, and factions—which, in Baan Naa Sakae as elsewhere, divide rural communities and families—may have a strong impact on migrants' decisions, including when or even whether to return home. The contradictions between migrants' relations with rural family and competing desires for *thansamay* fulfillment are rarely far from the surface. In Noi's case, the strain and tension of juggling these divergent sources of value pushed her to a crisis point. Yet the outcome of Noi's dilemma points to her resourcefulness and to a strength of will that even her friends and co-migrants did not expect.

What was she to do? When I left Thailand in late 1990, Noi was still drowning her sorrows, avoiding a decision. At the time, her choices appeared quite limited; her friends confided to me that she would probably be married within a few months. And when I next saw Noi, in 1993, she was not only married but also pregnant with her first child. She was still living in Bangkok but was preparing to return to her home village "to become a *mae baan*" a few weeks before her delivery.[9] But, to my surprise, her husband was not the fiancé of three years earlier. Noi had evaded that match, although only by remaining in Bangkok without returning home for over a year, waiting for the young man and his family to tire and withdraw their offer. Nor had she married the young man she liked in 1990. Instead, her husband was an entirely different suitor, a successful overseas contract laborer and a Baan Naa Sakae native. Noi admitted that he wasn't her romantic ideal but she liked him well enough. "And anyway," she said, "it's better to marry the one who loves you [rather than the one you love]." Moreover, his past travels made him sympathetic to Noi's urban experiences. Indeed, following the wedding, Noi kept her Bangkok job and he found work in a nearby factory. After living together in the city for almost a year, Noi became pregnant. Meanwhile, her husband had made arrangements for a new overseas work contract in Taiwan. Finally, Noi was ready to return to Baan Naa Sakae, "for good this time," she claimed. "My mother, aunts, cousins are there. Like this [with the baby coming] it's better to be in the village now."

Noi's dilemma was shaped not only by the difficulties of reconciling dominant cultural discourses about gender and sexuality with the material exploitation of urban wage work, but also by economic and emotional pressures from home. The expectations of rural kin were sources of pressure that most migrants I knew found difficult to ignore, sharpening the tensions they felt when their efforts to be both *thansamay* women and good daughters began to unravel. But as in Noi's ultimate course of action, migrant women rarely attempted to resolve these dilemmas by abandoning their identification with the rural home. Noi's anguished conflict over the fiancé she felt pressured to accept, but whom she could not ultimately marry, challenged her ability to sustain the valued, but fragile, gendered aspirations and identity she had found as a mobile, urban wage earner. Her actions reflected not only the frustration and ambivalence of many rural-urban migrants but also a common determination to make their own decisions and pursue their own goals within, and even despite, difficult circumstances.

CHAPTER 9

Gender and Modernity, Local and Global Encounters

≒

$\mathcal{N}$oi's story brings into sharp relief the conflicts and contradictions with which the rural women of her generation must contend. As members of a cheap and highly flexible work force, young rural women have been essential factors of production for Thailand's recent pursuit of explosive industrial expansion and economic accumulation. Their movement into urban employment reflects profound structural disparities within the Thai political economy and a long history of rural subordination to urban centers of power and wealth. Women's participation in new patterns of mobility and wage labor is rooted in the structural inequalities of economic production under conditions of uneven development. However, young Thai women enter not only new relations of production and authority as urban proletarians, they also traverse critical arenas of cultural and ideological production. Specifically, young migrants engage powerful meanings about modernity and gender identity that both promote their entry into urban wage work and constrain their options within the urban setting.

Thailand's dominant forms of cultural production, including the popular media, celebrate women's mobile and commodified bodies as symbolic expressions of national progress and *thansamay* style; young migrants encounter these images as seductive but largely unattainable, potential selves. While their journey between village and city encourages the exploration and imagination of new forms of self-identity, the lived experience of urban employment compels women and their families to confront the contradictions contained within dominant constructions of gender roles as well as notions of Thai modernity. During their time in the city, the alternatives young women perceive and the choices they make are shaped as much by these cultural struggles as by the oppressive structures of wage labor.

For the people I knew in Baan Naa Sakae, local gender and household relations—as well as dominant images of Thai modernity and progress—were both important factors in explaining and legitimizing the movement of young women into Bangkok employment. When migrants themselves spoke of the decision to go to Bangkok, as in Khem's account (Chapter 5), their stories almost always invoked the gendered imagery of good daughters and modern women. When women's labor migration drew on obligations of respect and gratitude that all children owe to their parents, it represented an important means for youth to acknowledge their debts to parents by earning money to send home. But most rural youth also viewed the move to Bangkok as an opportunity to be at the center of contemporary Thai society—to open their ears and eyes (*poet huu poet taa*)—and to earn the necessary cash to purchase the commodity emblems of a *thansamay* identity. Young women from Baan Naa Sakae and other rural communities encountered these seductive attributes of *thansamay* selfhood in a strikingly gendered form. Throughout Thailand, images of the beautiful *thansamay* woman—on billboards, in television ads, serial dramas, and many other formats—set powerful standards for defining this status. Additionally, the urban setting itself provided a multitude of sites and social institutions—from beauty parlors and shopping malls to movie theaters and nightclubs—where migrants could observe and pursue these standards of "modern" womanhood.

Consequently, commodity consumption was a central goal in migration decisions and an important feature of the urban sojourn. Reflecting more than material interests or economic need, the acquisition and display of new technologies and consumer commodities served as symbolic (as well as material) measures of success and status in both urban and rural contexts. Migrants' consumption practices engaged powerful, if often conflicting, cultural discourses about family relations, gender roles, and Thai constructions of modernity. But while urban consumption practices helped to constitute young migrants' sense of self as *phuu ying thansamay*, these aspirations remained sharply constrained both by women's lived experiences of Bangkok employment and by cultural expectations and personal desires to assist rural kin and community. Nevertheless, commodity consumption offered individual migrants an accessible realm of social practice and cultural expression: As consumers, young women mobilized prestigious symbols and meanings to construct and contest identities and, at least momentarily, to assert their claims to a degree of status and autonomy from which they were more often excluded within the wider society.

Young women view these urban experiences as a source of deep personal transformation: "We are not like our mothers." Living on their own and earning their own money, female migrants to Bangkok face choices and make decisions about themselves and their futures in ways that no previous generation of women in Baan Naa Sakae or other rural communities have shared. Urban work and wages offer young women a level of autonomy and even, at times, authority with respect to their elders that has no precedent. In this context, rural-urban mobility is more than a strategy for economic survival or accumulation; it is also a vehicle through which migrants and their families struggle over what it means to be modern in contemporary Thai society and how to reconcile these aspirations and images with equally compelling concerns and moral commitments to rural kin and community. Young women in Bangkok and families in Baan Naa Sakae experience these conflicts as contests over appropriate gender identities, roles, and relations.

The tensions underlying women's labor migration prompt young workers to negotiate a series of fragile compromises: balancing personal consumption and entertainment with contributions to the village home; enjoying romantic experimentation while maintaining a wary view of men and urban marriage; asserting claims to urban independence and personal autonomy, yet retaining a fundamental attachment to rural identity and village-based morality. These strategies respond to but do not clearly articulate the structural conditions and inequities that restrict rural migrants' access to material resources and opportunities in the urban economy. Limited by low wages, insecure employment, and long-term vulnerability, young migrants experienced these constraints as challenges to valued personal goals and identities. As young women's aspirations to be both modern women and good daughters unravel in the course of their urban sojourns, they experience these disjunctures most sharply as matters of personal distress or misfortune. Consequently, dominant cultural discourses about gender, modernity, and sexuality that help to propel young women into Bangkok jobs also help to obscure how migrants' urban dilemmas are rooted in the exploitive conditions of urban wage labor.

Migrants' ambivalent compromises between valued identities as good daughters and *thansamay* women never completely resolve the tensions they experience as urban laborers; instead, they serve to reproduce the very conditions that sustain young rural women's presence at the core of Thailand's cheap migrant labor force. In particular, the marriage decisions and dilemmas, discussed in Chapter 8, highlight not only women's material and emotional vulnerability in the city but also how these general conditions of subordination are reproduced as migrants attempt to resolve their difficulties in the context of highly individual and intimate choices. As migrants struggle over questions of whether, who, and where to marry, their personal dilemmas reflect broadly based inequities within Thai society, but they themselves rarely trace their personal quandaries to the wider context of women's exploitation within the labor force. More often, migrants' actions pose little challenge to industrial discipline and related structures of power in Thailand, and (as discussed below) may even help to maintain the flow of new workers into urban factories by perpetuating circuits of labor migration.

Should they return to marry in the village, migrants take up roles of production and reproduction as farmers, mothers, and *mae baan* that remain embedded in national and transnational circuits of dependent capitalist production and commodity consumption. Some women in the city worked hard to acquire the educational or material resources that might allow them to forge a future as more than just peasant farmers. But limited rural employment opportunities meant that most migrants would have to return to the same small commodity and subsistence crop production that their parents practiced. And, most likely, in a few years, these former migrants would themselves become mothers of the next generation of city-bound laborers.

Nor do the options available to women who remain in Bangkok pose a serious challenge to the maintenance of a flexible urban work force. Migrants who reject the familiarity of the village community and marry in the city face the prospect of having to rely on precarious informal sector employment—such as small-scale vending or piece-rate cottage industry work—among the few income-earning options available to poor women with families in Bangkok. Alternatively, women may retain the relative security of jobs in urban factories or sweatshops, but only by shifting the responsibility of caring for young children back to their own parents in the countryside. Given these difficult choices, some women are willing to reject marriage altogether, preferring to remain single and childless, a status that carries its own long-term risks.

The range of these various and varied personal strategies illustrates the determination of young migrants to shape their own lives in ways that they find meaningful. However, whether they choose to remain in the city or return to the village, their actions tend to accommodate rather than challenge wider economic and social structures. Migrants' individualized marriage strategies—returning to the countryside, sending children to be cared for by rural parents, remaining single, or shifting to informal sector employment—have the collective effect of reducing wage pressures for urban employers who need not, therefore, pay the full cost of reproducing an urban labor force. Thus migrant women's own struggles to limit the constraints and long-term vulnerability they experience as urban wage workers help to sustain the very conditions that brought them into urban employment and that continue to encourage employers to view young rural women as an attractive pool of cheap and easily replaceable labor.

Powerful constructions of Thai modernity urge young migrants and their families to pursue commodified models of self-fulfillment and status display that focus their attention on individual, gendered dilemmas rather than the underlying conditions of their subordination as wage workers and members of agricultural communities. In other words, discourses of modernity and gender identity have important hegemonic effects; that is, they work to harness the energies of a subordinate social group (i.e., migrant workers) to act in ways that help to reproduce existing structures of power. Consequently, Thai women's own aspirations as labor migrants encourage them to define the limitations they encounter in the course of urban employment as obstacles they must resolve individually as *women* rather than collectively as *workers* (or *migrants*). In the course of young women's labor migration, valued forms of gendered identity intersect with desired images and standards of Thai modernity, channeling collective experiences of exploitation into more limited, temporary, or ambivalent expressions of critique or discontent.

Rural-urban mobility in Thailand is framed both by oppressive political and economic structures and by powerful ideologies of gender and modernity. The young women I knew responded to these conditions surrounding urban employment in highly ambivalent ways. Nevertheless, this ambivalence cannot be taken as passivity or a failure to recognize the inequities they encounter. Throughout their time in the city, migrant women made very real efforts to sustain a sense of meaning and purpose in their lives, despite the many difficulties they faced. Their experiences represent an important model for thinking about patterns of labor migration and industrialization in other parts of the globe. Women's rural-urban migration in Thailand highlights the importance of examining the specific and culturally contingent motivations— or to return to Cynthia Enloe's phrase, the "needs, values, and worries" (1989:16–17)—that shape local participation in and lived experiences of new relations of production and authority at different times and places.

As the rise of increasingly feminized work forces gains more and more attention worldwide, it is important to ask how young women's own desires and concerns may complement or conflict with the expectations and interests both of capitalist employers and of workers' own families and sending communities. For example, the consumption practices of Thai migrant workers described in this book may suggest alternative ways to approach the study of other newly proletarianized groups within the contemporary global economy. Greater attention to the forms and meanings of commodity consumption in such contexts may provide additional insight into contemporary cultural and economic change in societies around the world. It is important to assess local encounters with capitalism not just in terms of the imposition of new demands and power relations from the outside but also in light of how this process may be actively received and even appropriated by people on the ground. As Benjamin Orlove and Henry Rutz have argued, attention to the complex agency underlying consumption practices, beliefs, and motivations may help to avoid reductionist views of social and cultural transformation and provide a richer and more complete understanding of local experiences of change (1989:6, 14–15). In different parts of the world, popular confrontations and resistance to wage labor and commodity markets exist alongside the rapid and even enthusiastic incorporation of capitalist forms and relations into daily life. Examining specific consumption patterns may help to illuminate how and why local responses to global processes vary across time and space. In so doing, it becomes clear that "consumption . . . can powerfully affirm certain social orders and can be a key arena of contestation and change of others. . . . [C]onsumption is thus linked to the constitution and transformation of hegemony" (ibid.:39).

Furthermore, this study suggests the powerful role that local ideologies of modernity and commodified forms of femininity may play in maintaining and reproducing the cheap, flexible, and predominantly female labor forces so essential to contemporary global capital accumulation. Images and ideas of modernity represent powerful forces of popular imagination in the contemporary global context (Appadurai, 1990). To the extent that these locally constructed notions of modernity emphasize goals of *individual* fulfillment and self-expression, they shift attention away from *structural* limitations that constrain the opportunities people may have to assert with any degree of success these newly imagined "modern" selves. When these hegemonic effects of modernity combine with compelling notions of gendered identity, their power to sustain existing arrangements of power and authority may increase substantially. Exploring how gendered forms of identity intersect with local forms and ideologies of modernity to promote or restrict women's (and men's) entry into new forms of production and consumption may illuminate both the different obstacles neophyte wage laborers are likely to confront as

well as the spaces that may exist for negotiating and reworking their new circumstances.

Even in the absence of systematic opposition or self-conscious resistance to conditions of exploitation and subordination, we need to be atten-
tive to people's lived experiences of struggle and agency.[1] Hegemonic
discourses are never total and, as a result may accommodate a range of imagined and imaginable possibilities for action and identity. People continually
select between and maneuver within these potential selves or self-images in
the course of everyday life (Moore, 1994:58–60). For the young Thai women
I knew, the imagined possibilities of migration and urban employment were
intricately bound up in desires for enhanced personal autonomy and status
both as "daughters" *and* as *thansamay* women. In the choices they made and
the identities they pursued, migrants from Baan Naa Sakae and elsewhere
were neither passive receptors of dominant meanings nor simple victims of
structures and processes beyond their control. Rather, their experiences reflect the complex dynamics and often ambivalent results of cultural and symbolic struggle (Ong, 1991).

Although constrained in significant ways, these young women actively
attempted to maneuver within and at times against the obstacles they faced
as low-wage, low-status laborers. To the extent that their efforts were oriented
toward individual assertions of identity and personal autonomy, they tended
to obscure and even diminish avenues for collective or organized forms of
opposition and critique. Yet this does not make women's efforts to maintain
a sense of meaning and purpose any less important to acknowledge or understand. Their choices reflect not only the structural disparities that characterize the contemporary Thai and global political economy, but also the
cultural resources that were available to them and through which they sought
to understand who they were and who they wished to become.

Epilogue

The research for this study was conducted during the peak years of
Thailand's economic boom. An expanding urban economy and fluid urban
job market meant that many migrants found sufficient maneuvering room to
sustain their individualized strategies for urban autonomy and *thansamay* success. Despite significant emotional and material pressures, many women, like
Noi, could exert a measure of control over how long they would remain in
Bangkok and what conditions would shape their decision to return home or
to keep working in the city. In the summer of 1997, a severe financial crisis

struck not only Thailand but most other Asian economies as well. The sudden collapse of the Thai currency prompted an almost immediate drain of international capital out of the country and the onset of a sharp economic recession. The long-term consequences of these events are not yet clear, but urban unemployment has risen sharply. If the economic restructuring now under way does not reverse this trend quickly, a growing number of Thai women may no longer be able to achieve a sense of *thansamay* autonomy in even the limited ways available to them during the boom years. Amid the present economic downturn, migrants are likely to be thrown out of work long before they feel "ready" to return home or start a family. At the same time, rural communities and households may be strained to the breaking point if the flow of returning workers turns into a sudden flood.

Under these circumstances, migrant women's personal quests for *thansamay* autonomy may give rise to heightened concerns over their collective difficulties as workers. Of course, the obstacles to such actions have not disappeared. The Thai labor movement is weak; it is especially poorly developed in private sector industries where young rural migrants dominate the labor force.[2] At the same time, one cannot ignore the historical willingness of the Thai state to mobilize forces of repression or coercion against open expressions of discontent. Nevertheless, since the late 1980s, Bangkok has been the site of occasional but in some cases quite militant strikes and other labor protests, many involving textile (and predominantly migrant) workers. Faced with drastically reduced opportunities to achieve goals of *thansamay* self-fulfillment and increased economic strains at home, migrant women in the city may yet turn to these or other oppositional tactics in greater numbers. In the ongoing economic crisis of the late 1990s, the intense vulnerability of rural-urban migrants and their village families may well preclude any concerted efforts to promote collective solutions. However, as personal hopes recede in the face of the economic downturn, workers may begin to encounter failure both as dutiful daughters and as modern women. At that point, women may find that the narrowing range of choice they face as migrant workers may shift the focus of their cultural struggles from individualized concerns with consumption, courtship, and marriage, to more collective and potentially more confrontational directions of action.

NOTES

CHAPTER 1   *Women, Migration, and Thai Experiences of Modernity*

1. Nok and Baan Naa Sakae are pseudonyms, as are the names of all Thai informants and village communities cited in the text. I have taken some literary license in composing this passage. Although the thoughts that I have attributed to Nok are represented here in the form of an internal monologue, they are based on actual statements and concerns expressed during interviews and informal conversations. While this passage is based on the experiences of one young woman, the general circumstances and ideas it portrays are familiar to many of the labor migrants with whom I have worked.

2. The contributions of migrant labor in relation to Thailand's economic boom are widely noted. See, for example, Girling (1981:178–79); Porpora and Lim (1987); Anchalee and Nitaya (1992); Pasuk and Baker (1995:198–99,205).

3. Migration surveys for 1987 and 1989 found that women made up 62 percent of total migrants to Bangkok and just over 50 percent of migrants to several other major urban centers (cited in Anchalee and Nitaya, 1992:165). The Thai government (National Statistical Office, 1992:38) reported that between 1990 and 1992 more than 272,000 women and 281,000 men moved from rural to urban areas, while 1,149,000 people moved in the opposite direction (of whom 41 percent were women). [The excess of movers to rural areas is probably due to the timing of the survey; it was taken between September and November, the months just preceding the annual rice harvest.] Similar patterns were recorded in migration studies of the 1970s (Wilson, 1983:58; Aphichat et al., 1979). Given the difficulty of counting the variety of temporary and circulating moves that characterize most rural-urban mobility in Thailand, these figures probably underestimate the full extent of population movement.

4. I do not mean by this that rural-urban migration has had no transformative effects for Thai men; rather, these are less obvious and less socially disruptive than in the case of women. Men's mobility reflects long-standing cultural ideals concerning the acquisition of status and social influence through contact with institutions of power and knowledge located in urban centers (O'Connor, 1987, 1995). Such activities have historically been the prerogative of men rather than women.

5. A parallel and not unrelated process is the importation of cheap "Third World"

labor into the "First World." Revelations about sweated (and even slave) labor practices in segments of the U.S. garment industry periodically capture North American headlines, focusing public attention, if only briefly, on the miserable conditions endured by a largely immigrant work force.

6. An early analysis of these patterns can be found in Elson and Pierson (1981). For a recent review of the literature on this topic see Ong (1991). Case studies from around the world include those found in Fernandez-Kelly (1982); Kung (1983); Nash and Fernandez-Kelly (1983); Ong (1987); Benería and Feldman (1992); and Safa (1995).

7. Assumptions concerning the docility of a female work force are frequently challenged by actual events. At different times and places, and depending on the opportunities and resources available to them, women industrial workers, both past and present, have resisted exploitation and protested intolerable working conditions in a variety of ways—from foot dragging or withdrawal from the shopfloor, to songs and petitions, to more militant strikes and organized protests. See, for example, Lamphere (1987); Ong (1987); Tsurumi (1990); and Margold (1995), to name only a few.

8. Deere and de Janvry (1979) provide a theoretical framework for understanding these relations as a form of surplus extraction, one to which peasantries worldwide are increasingly subject. Colin Murray (1981) documents similar patterns that sustain Lesotho labor migration to South Africa.

9. Louise Lamphere (1987) details the different generational and ethnic experiences of women in New England textile mills from 1790 to 1980. American women's industrial labor during the 1800s is the subject of a substantial literature, including Wallace (1972); Foner (1977); Dublin (1979); and Peiss (1986), among others.

10. See Harvey (1989:140–72) for a more detailed analysis of these and other features of contemporary global economic transformation.

11. There is an extensive literature on rural-urban labor migration in Thailand. For the most part, this research has focused on demographic and economic policy–oriented questions of identifying population flows (and whether they can or cannot be redirected away from Bangkok), patterns of urban assimilation, or the economic impact of remittances on rural households (see, for example, Aphichat et al., 1979; Fuller et al., 1983; Lightfoot et al., 1983; Pawadee, 1984; Goldstein and Goldstein, 1986; Parnwell, 1986; Porpora and Lim, 1987). Relatively little of this work has taken an anthropological perspective, although notable exceptions include Hanks and Phillips (1961); Textor (1961); Anchalee (1981); Juree (1983); and Muecke (1984, 1992).

12. A full analysis of modernity, let alone its late twentieth-century transformations (what is widely termed "post-modernity"), is beyond the scope of this discussion. Analyzing modernity in one form or another, has been the central preoccupation of Western social theory for much of the last two centuries. My own understandings of modernity as they are developed here are particularly indebted to the work of Marshall Berman (1982), David Harvey (1989), Anthony Giddens (1990), Alan Pred and Michael Watts (1992), among others.

13. Although very often defined as "the ways in which signs, meanings and values help to reproduce a dominant power" (Eagleton, 1991:221), ideologies need not

always be hegemonic. An ideology does not simply represent or reflect a particular (existing or projected) organization of social power. It is one of the means by which such social interests are actively constituted. See Eagleton (1991:29, 221–23). Ideological modernity began in the West in the eighteenth century as a philosophical basis for bourgeois revolt against aristocratic rule. Notions of modernity helped to define the goals of an ascendant bourgeois "order" under early industrial capitalism, including: to consolidate political and economic power through national (as opposed to dynastic) state bureaucracies and to promote the expansion of industrial and commercial capitalism (see Bauman, 1991). However, by the nineteenth and twentieth centuries, ideas about modernity helped to legitimize the spread of European colonial rule as the necessary and desirable extension of modern "civilization" and "progress" to the rest of the world.

14. Recent studies of localized "modernities" and experiences of modernity include Donham (1992); Pred and Watts (1992); and Miller (1994). Chatterjee (1993) takes a similar approach to post-colonial nationalisms and states.

15. However, the ability to formulate or assert such disagreements varies significantly and in relation to one's access to or control over key material or social sources of power. The concept of discourse that I employ here is intricately connected to social relations and experiences of power. Andrew Turton's explication of the term is helpful here: "The notion of discourse refers to the way in which power intervenes to construct the agenda and rules of procedure for social debates, for the construction of knowledge" (1991:10). More than language and speech alone, discourse encompasses the broad range of "social intercourse" through which ideas and understandings may be reproduced and disseminated. This breadth, however, allows for the possibility of questioning or modifying relations of power, usually at the margins of a discursive arena but sometimes through more direct, counter-hegemonic challenges.

16. An interest in the constitution of Thai modernity is also an underlying theme in academic debates, especially those that address the social, political, and economic transformations involved in the construction of the modern Thai nation-state. See, for example, early "modernization" studies (Riggs, 1966, Jacobs, 1971) as well as more recent anthropological and historical analyses, such as Keyes (1989) and Thongchai (1994).

17. For a useful application of these ideas, see Steven Kemper's (1993) reading of Appadurai (1990) in relation to the social production of a national(ist) imagination in Sri Lanka through the practice of one new form of mass consumption—lotteries.

18. See, for example, London (1980), Demaine (1986), Turton (1987), and Hirsch (1990).

19. The variability and flexibility of gender categories and meanings in Southeast Asia are explored by the contributors to several recent edited collections: Eberhardt (1988), Atkinson and Errington (1990), Ong and Peletz (1995).

20. Fortunately, my research assistant was more closely attuned than I was initially to our political obligations as guests in the village. Her promptings guided me to make more appropriate responses to the requests of local patrons than I might have made on my own.

CHAPTER 2   *Village and Nation*

1. Baan Naa Sakae was one of nearly two dozen villages in Mahasarakham and neighboring Khon Kaen province that I visited over a period of three weeks searching for a research site. This task was made vastly easier by the generous assistance of faculty and research staff at Khon Kaen University and at Srinakharin Wiroj University (Mahasarakham) and by the staff members in both provinces of Plan International (an international, non-governmental community development organization).

2. Mon (Pranee Monthongdaeng) worked for me while she was a student in the Master's program in anthropology at a major university in Bangkok. In addition to her work as my assistant, she collected data that formed part of the basis for her master's thesis (Pranee, 1991).

3. The house was made available to us because none of the teachers at the village school wanted to live there. Most had more substantial homes in the village or else commuted to work from the district town.

4. Only a tiny fraction of arable land in Isan is irrigated; there is no dry-season irrigation in Baan Naa Sakae. All crops depend entirely on what rain falls in the wet season between June and October. This is especially important for the rice crop, which requires a sufficient amount of standing water in the paddies to attain full growth.

5. During my fieldwork, popular notions about Isan's poverty and isolation were only strengthened by the highly publicized "Green Isan" campaign. This was a Thai Army–sponsored (and ultimately unsuccessful) program to address regionwide environmental problems (such as deforestation) and underdevelopment. Special efforts to target the economic problems of the region, coordinated by prominent Army leaders, were promoted as bringing new "development" and "progress" to Isan, although the beneficiaries of these projects were more often commercial interests than small-scale farmers.

6. These two nineteenth-century Bangkok kings are widely credited with bringing Thailand (or Siam, as it was then known) into the modern era (Wyatt, 1982:181). King Mongkut and his successor, King Chulalongkorn, are better known to Western audiences as characters in the popular musical *The King and I.* Not surprisingly, this play—and the caricatures it makes of the nineteenth-century Thai monarchy—is deeply offensive to most Thai audiences. Reverence for the royal family in Thailand is remarkably high, an attitude that receives steady reinforcement from national religious and educational institutions.

7. The practice of slavery in Siam (and its tributaries) was a highly complex system, ranging from war captives to different types of debt bondage. For example, Thai commoners could sell themselves, their wives, or their children in exchange for debts. Depending on the price, some of these slaves were considered redeemable while others were not. The contemporary practice among many employment (and sex industry) recruiters, who give cash advances to parents in return for their child's labor service, has historical precedents in earlier patterns of debt slavery. See Turton (1980) for a detailed discussion of Thai institutions of slavery.

8. Isan is a Pali-derived word meaning "northeast." The language spoken by most Isan residents is variously termed Thai-Isan, Lao-Isan, or, more simply, Isan by

Thai linguists. It is more closely related to the language of lowland Laos than to the standard Thai of Bangkok and Central Thailand (although Lao, Thai, and Isan are all members of the same Tai family of languages).

9. Archaeological evidence of moated settlements and water reservoirs indicates that, in the first millennium A.D., the Khorat Plateau was home to a large number of small agricultural societies (Higham, 1989:218–19). Many of these were incorporated into the Angkor empire toward the end of this period, but as the latter's power waned in the thirteenth and fourteenth centuries, the population of the plateau declined dramatically. The earliest traces of human settlement in the Khorat Plateau stretch back as far as 3000 B.C. (ibid:80).

10. One of these was called *monthon isaan*, after the Pali-derived word for "northeast." The directional label "Isan" has since come to represent the entire Khorat Plateau and its population, as in *khon isaan* ("people of Isan").

11. An openness to democratic processes emerged briefly in the mid-1970s, and with renewed strength in the mid-1980s, as political authority in Thailand began to shift away from military leaders with the rising influence of business and financial power. Although this has brought greater opportunities for popular political action and debate, it remains primarily an urban, middle-class phenomenon. Nor has the shifting pattern of alliances within the Thai state done much to reduce political corruption. The national elections of 1996 were among the most violent of recent history and, according to many witnesses, involved widespread vote buying.

12. Tai refers to a large number of linguistically related peoples living throughout mainland Southeast Asia and into southern China. They include not only the large lowland, Theravada Buddhist, and wet-rice farming populations that dominate contemporary Thailand and Laos, but also smaller pockets of upland, often swidden farming minority groups scattered through northern Burma, Cambodia, Vietnam, and the Xipxong Panna region of southern China.

13. The title "*Maeyaay*" and its male equivalent "*Phôyaay*" (literally, "big mother," "big father") are respectful terms of address and reference in the Isan language for older men and women, usually those with children nearing marriageable age or older. In Isan, titles of "*Phô*" (father) and "*Mae*" (mother) are applied universally to the names of men and women in one's parents' generation; in Central Thai, the equivalent polite forms are "*Lung*" (uncle) and "*Paa*" (Aunt). The use of kinship terms as forms of polite address between people who are not directly related is common in both Isan and Central Thai. Same-generation friends, schoolmates, including new acquaintances, commonly address one another as older or younger sibling (*phii* or *nôông*) depending on relative age. Failure to use such kin terms, especially by the younger or socially inferior party and in the absence of even more formal titles—such as *khruu* (teacher), *naay* (mister), *huanaa* (leader or supervisor)—can be a serious insult.

14. For more detailed analysis of the ideological work performed by the Thai educational system, see Chayan (1991), Keyes (1991), and Uthai (1991).

15. People in Baan Naa Sakae identified themselves as Thai citizens: members of the Thai nation-state and subjects of the Thai King (see also Keyes, 1967). At the same time, however, they referred to their distinctive regional language and customs as "Lao." In my experience this ethnic self-designation was as, if not

more, common than assertions of their regional identity: "people of Isan." The use of these terms was partly situational. Baan Naa Sakae migrants in Bangkok tended to refer to themselves as *khon isaan* (people of Isan), avoiding the pejorative stereotypes often associated with the Lao in the dominant Thai culture. However, within the village community, a Lao cultural identity was proudly asserted and contrasted favorably with that of the Central Thai.

16. The United States also gave considerable support to Thailand's internal counterinsurgency programs (see Bowie, 1997).

17. In the late 1980s, over 70 percent of rural households had some access to television; by the early 1990s, more than 75 percent of rural households owned their own television set (Pasuk and Baker, 1995:315, 374).

CHAPTER 3   *Cash, Commodities, and Modernity*

1. These figures are based on a survey of 97 Baan Naa Sakae households (approximately one-half the village), conducted in January and February 1990. Only 5 percent of community households were entirely landless, and some of this group included young families that had not yet received their share of parental property. This was not unusual for the area; unlike the North and Central regions of Thailand, the vast majority of rural households in Isan own and work their own land (Tongroj, 1990:12; Turton, 1989b:60). In the 1970s and 1980s, holdings in the region averaged about 25 *rai* (approximately ten acres; one *rai* equals 0.4 acres), and although Isan land ownership was by no means equally distributed, neither large-scale absentee landlords nor landless and tenant farmers were dominant features of the regional class structure (National Statistical Office 1988b:410). However, as Mae Tan's case shows (below) the relative lack of landless households may be due, in part, to the irregularity of agricultural wage work, forcing the poorest of families out of the village altogether. It should also be noted that while a plot of 25 *rai* is substantially more land than average holdings in other regions, the lack of irrigation and generally poor quality of soil in Baan Naa Sakae significantly limit the productivity of local fields.

2. Cattle and water buffalo were the main income-earning livestock owned by Baan Naa Sakae households, although three families raised pigs for sale. Though water buffalo were valued as plow animals, they were rapidly losing out to mechanical plows (sometimes called "iron buffalo"). Cattle ownership was concentrated almost entirely among the one-quarter of village households owning more than 45 *rai* (18 acres) of agricultural land, allowing them to leave some land fallow for grazing the animals year-round. Local market prices for cattle in 1990 were approximately double that of water buffalo; cattle sold for 6,000–7,000 *baht* as calves and 10,000–12,000 *baht* as mature beasts, while parallel prices for water buffalo ranged from 3,000 *baht* to 7,000 or 8,000 *baht*.

3. Six years earlier, in 1983, the family had had some trouble when Phô Lat traveled to Singapore as a contract laborer. The agent Phô Lat contacted charged him 20,000 *baht*, but when he got to Singapore, Phô Lat learned that the agent had neither arranged a job for him nor provided him with the proper immigration papers. Phô Lat was deported a month after his arrival.

4. To the extent that the poorest and most desperate landless families in Isan may also be forced out of rural communities, Mae Tan's case may mean that the Northeast's consistent reports of low rates of rural landlessness obscure ongoing experiences of land loss rather than representing a more evenly "shared" rural poverty in comparison to other regions where substantial landless populations remain in many rural communities.

5. Entry into the civil service, however, is far from easy. Competitions at the provincial and national level are fierce; a high school or college education is required for most positions, while use of connections and bribery are commonplace (as they were for villagers' dealings with government officials in many other situations). Few in Baan Naa Sakae, who were not themselves already members of the civil service, had the necessary contacts, education, and wealth to snare a government job. Working in the civil service also meant that one might be transferred to a post in other parts of the region or country. In 1990, ten Baan Naa Sakae residents held positions in the civil service, mainly as teachers at the village elementary school and schools in nearby communities. However, during the preceding decade at least twice as many Baan Naa Sakae natives had left the village to take up government jobs in more distant parts of the Northeast, as well as a few in other regions of the country. By 1990 a small number of these had retired to the village, including a former police officer, but it was unclear from my discussions how common this was likely to be in the future.

6. Not long before I arrived in Baan Naa Sakae, the video player apparently broke down, but I was told that previously the owner had used it to show pornographic videos and charged a fee to the men who came to watch.

7. My discussion here is indebted to Penny Van Esterik's (1984) work on the meanings of rice in Thai culture. Although Van Esterik's research focused on Central Thailand, much of her analysis also holds true for the Lao inhabitants of the Northeast region.

8. I am indebted to Peter Vandergeest for his insight into the way rhetoric of "help" may obscure experiences of inequity and exploitation (personal communication; see also Vandergeest, 1989).

9. At the height of the transplanting and harvest season, it was common to see large and small groups of people from other villages in the area riding in trucks in search of wage labor in the rice fields. According to Baan Naa Sakae residents, these people were mainly those with small (or no) land holdings looking for work once their own fields had been planted or harvested, or else coming from communities where, for lack of rain or other reasons, their own crops were not ready. On at least one occasion in the 1990 transplanting season, a similar truckload of people left Baan Naa Sakae to look for work in neighboring villages.

10. By Lao identity I do not mean to suggest that Baan Naa Sakae villagers felt any nationalist loyalties to present-day Laos. A few men in their fifties or older spoke of having traveled to Vientiane to work for a few months or years in their youth, but this was the only direct link any in the community had to Laos. Like all Isan villagers I met, people in Baan Naa Sakae identified themselves as Thai citizens, members of the Thai nation-state and subjects of the Thai King (see also Keyes, 1967).

11. *Bun caek khaaw* is a ritual feast lasting one or two days. It is similar, at least in its religious purpose, to the Central Thai memorial ritual called *bun uthit suan kusol*. The feast is hosted by the immediate family in honor of a deceased relative and should be held between one and three years after the death. Through this event, survivors fulfill an important obligation to feed and clothe the spirits of the deceased, help to speed the dead on to their next rebirth, and seek to ensure that the dead will not trouble the living with illness or other misfortune. Relatives and friends, often from distant communities, are invited to attend and to help make merit for the deceased.

12. In many ways these events resemble what Arjun Appadurai has called "tournaments of value" (1986:21–22). These household ceremonies are complex ritual events "removed . . . from the routines of economic life" through which "what is at issue . . . is not just status, rank, fame, or reputation of actors, but the disposition of the central tokens of value in the society" (ibid:21). While commodity items were not exchanged on a large scale between hosts and guests, the "disposition" of commodities and cash donations did play a vital part in these rituals, either as gifts to a new ordinand or newlywed couple and/or as offerings presented to monks and the village temple.

13. These teams of house builders usually comprised men from Baan Naa Sakae and nearby villages, many of whom learned their skills as construction workers in Bangkok or as overseas contract laborers. They continued, however, to follow a number of customary rituals associated with the construction of new houses. For example, in order to ensure good luck, construction should only begin in an even-numbered month of the Buddhist lunar calendar. In addition, special packages were blessed by a ritual expert and suspended from two of the central house pillars, called "first" and "second," respectively; these were to appease any spirits attached to the house grounds and to ensure the health and good fortune of both the builders and those who would live there.

14. Owners of the handful of such houses that did not feature small stores explained their choices either by the competition from already existing stores or the lack of sufficient time and interest on the part of household members. None of these businesses provided enough income to support a household, and in every case store owners also farmed and/or derived income from a civil service job or from overseas-migrant remittances.

15. Refrigerators had a clear use function in the households that ran successful stores, but their display value was especially evident in households that did not have a store. These refrigerators were rarely used for more than making ice and chilling drinking water, both luxuries in the village context.

16. See Philip Hirsch (1990) for an insightful discussion of the Thai state's rhetorical (and often cosmetic) approach to rural development. Hirsch argues that through such mechanisms as village "development contests," criteria such as the number of houses with toilet facilities and fenced compounds or the tidiness of village lanes and yards are often given greater emphasis in state policy than measures of economic equity and productive capacity.

CHAPTER 4 *Parents, Children, and Migration Decisions*

1. This is a preference rather than a rule, as Keyes (1975), among other ethnographers of Thailand, has noted. There are a number of circumstances in which residence with the husband's family may be chosen. This is often the course selected if there are no daughters or other siblings to take care of the husband's parents, or if his family has more land or financial resources to support the new couple. Residence with the parents of either side is also a temporary stage in any marriage. Although one child, usually the youngest daughter, will remain with the parents until they die (for which she and her husband inherit the parental house and often an extra share of the family's fields), all the other married siblings will establish their own separate households.

2. At this point the parents often decided to give the daughter and her husband their share of the family land. Alternatively, many such divided households continued to farm land together and to "eat out of the same rice granary" for years. See Keyes (1975) for a discussion of the timing and manner of household inheritance divisions in a Northeastern village. He found that the decision of when to divide the family property depended on both the size of land holdings and the availability of sufficient labor to work them.

3. Although some young women from Northeast Thailand do become involved in Bangkok's commercial sex trade, this was not a part of the migration patterns in Baan Naa Sakae. Migrant networks channeled local residents into domestic service and factory work. Although I cannot say with absolute certainty that no women from Baan Naa Sakae became commercial sex workers, none of the migrants I knew were so employed and there was no hint of any others in local gossip, despite widespread speculation in the community about more informal dating practices and the possible sexual experience of migrants in general (see Chapter 8).

CHAPTER 5 *Gender and Mobility*

1. Khem's (a pseudonym) comments are excerpted (my translation) from a short autobiographical narrative written during the time I was interviewing her in 1987–88. Parts of it were also published in the monthly newsletter of Friends of Women Group (*klum phüan ying*), a Thai women's rights organization. See Friends of Women Group (1988).

2. This is not to say that young men's rural-urban migration raises no concerns for rural families; nor should it be understood that young men themselves experience no conflict as a result of their urban experiences. However, the difficulties involved in male youth migration are rarely viewed as challenging more broadly based cultural expectations concerning masculine gender roles and sexuality.

3. Male (particularly hetero-) sexual expression has rarely been a topic of ethnographic analysis. One exception is Christopher Lyttleton's (1994) work on men's use of commercial sex services in the rural Northeast. In general, studies that examine cultural understandings of sexuality in Thailand have focused on the "problem" of female prostitution and the moral stigma attached to female promiscuity, often linking this primarily to Buddhist teachings and beliefs (e.g.,

Thitsa, 1980; Pasuk, 1982; Siriporn, 1985; Muecke, 1992). Some preliminary work has begun on Thai understandings of male homosexuality, in particular its relation to an indigenous cross- or third-gender category, the "transvestite" *kathoey* (Jackson, 1989, 1997; Morris, 1994).

4. In this discussion, I am following the insight of Penny Van Esterik (1990) who has argued that any analysis of gender identity in Thailand must be "solidly body-based."

5. The concept of masculine potency or strength that I am using here is related to a concept of power that is widespread in Southeast Asia. Benedict Anderson (1972), in a classic statement of this conceptual complex as it occurs in Java, argued that power is not held to be a by-product of social position or office. In this view, power is not an external thing but an internal quality, a kind of divine energy or spiritual potency, the existence of which in any given individuals is demonstrated in the effective range of their personal authority. Thus, in Javanese society, as in Thailand, the most potent or powerful individual figure is the king. Yet the king does not have power because he is the ruler; rather, he rules because he has power.

6. In a discussion of Northern Thai society that could as easily apply to the Northeast, Charles Keyes (1986) has argued that male gender is constructed in terms of two opposing ideals: the monk who renounces worldly desire and the *nakleng*, an aggressive figure who pursues desires for power, wealth, and women (for himself and his followers) with all the resources at his disposal, including physical violence. Both monks and *nakleng* inspire respect, but the great majority of men achieve neither the transcendent morality of the one nor the amoral prowess of the other. Consequently, the dominant ideal of male gender identity takes an intermediate form, that of "a man who has morally tempered his desires through temporary submission to the discipline of the Sangha and has then returned to play an active role in society" (Keyes 1986:87–88).

7. Penny Van Esterik (1988) has suggested that a historically rooted "ideology of beauty" shapes key Thai cultural understandings. This draws, in part, on the popular belief that one's store of merit from past lives is reflected in the relative perfection of physical features both for women and men. But as Van Esterik notes, the adornment and enhancement of these features focuses primarily on women's faces and bodies, as in herbal cosmetic traditions and the colorful and elaborate patterns woven into women's (especially young women's) *phaa sin* skirts.

8. Their opinion that this woman was his sexual partner was reinforced by the fact that she was traveling with him; to go off with or "follow" a man (*taam pay*) is the expression for a couple eloping.

9. I am indebted to Pamela Dagrossi (personal communication) for her insights into the small-town sex industry in Thailand.

10. Frequenting brothels, massage parlors, and other sites of commercial sex services is extremely common among the urban male population. Students are also a significant clientele at such establishments (Pamela Dagrossi, personal communication). It is a common practice for older male students at universities and colleges to welcome the men of incoming classes with initiation trips to local

brothels. The educational object of this tradition is evident in the expression *khün khruu*, "mounting the teacher." At one regional university, the prevalence of attitudes encouraging men's sexual activity was implicit in a small AIDS awareness poster decorating many campus buses in 1989–90. It declared "*khün khruu, khün meen*," or "mounting the teacher [means or leads to] mounting the funeral pyre." The widespread use of commercial sex by Thai men (and not just foreign tourists) is increasingly recognized as a primary vehicle for the spread of HIV infection in Thailand.

11. Restrictions on women's sexual activity are also sustained by beliefs in the polluting power of women's genitals and bodily fluids, specifically menstrual blood, and, by association, women's lower garments (Thitsa, 1980; Terweil, 1975). Women's underwear and *phaa sin*, associated with the dirt of menstruation, must not come into contact with men's garments, nor most especially with men's heads, the most ritually pure or high (*suung*) part of the body. When washing or hanging up clothes to dry, women must be careful to keep their lower garments separate and at a lower level than men's; laundered underwear and *phaa sin* are generally hung at waist height or lower and in a spot slightly out of the way, where it is unlikely that a man would walk near enough to be offended by their sight or contact. These matters are part of the taken-for-granted patterns of daily life and hardly worth commenting on unless to a child (or an anthropologist) who does not yet know any better. Thus, when I asked why laundry had to be hung in this segregated manner I received no elaborate explanations but was told only that to do otherwise would be "ugly" (*may suay*), "inappropriate" (*may mô*), or "[morally and aesthetically] repulsive" (*naa kliat*).

12. Feminine beauty serves not only a symbol for Thai modernity; it has become itself a dynamic field of cultural and commercial production. Urban centers—and most prominently Bangkok— host a vast range beauty-oriented industries: the studio productions of popular movies and television serial dramas; the promotion of "star" (*daaraa*) singers, models, and actresses; the intricate network of local, regional, and national beauty contests; and all the sundry manufacturing and service industries, which produce the accessories of beauty—clothes, cosmetics and personal products, beauty parlors, skin and cosmetic-surgery clinics (Van Esterik, 1988; 1996).

13. Participation in Thai scouting (*luuk süa*) is mandatory for all primary school students as part of the nationally standardized curriculum.

14. Incorporating images of international origin is common in Thai constructions of *thansamay* style; at the time of my 1989–90 research, Michael Jackson's one-glove motif was a frequent part of the costumes of televised chorus line, although not all viewers were aware of its association with the American singer.

15. For analyses of the cultural contradictions that frame the experiences of some women sex workers in Thailand, see Muecke (1992) and Lyttleton (1994).

16. Marjorie Muecke (1984) found similar patterns at work among Northern Thai women involved in construction labor, for whom, she argued, cash earnings were replacing maternity as their main source of social value.

CHAPTER 6   *Bangkok Wage Workers*

1. Many of the women and men I knew from Baan Naa Sakae as well as other migrants I met in the city worked in these outlying industrial zones, located in provinces beyond the city proper. However, almost without exception (or unless specifying their address) these migrants spoke of themselves as living in "Bangkok" (Krung Thep), of leaving "Bangkok" for visits home, and of returning to "Bangkok" afterwards. This was true for migrants I knew working in industrial areas of Samut Prakan, Samut Sakhon, and Nakhon Pathom, provinces adjoining the metropolitan Bangkok area.

2. This phrase is a play on the common phrase, *müang luang,* meaning "capital city."

3. Virtually every rural community in Thailand has its own particular network of contacts in the city. These individuals often have an important influence on the range of urban occupations into which members from their home community will enter. In Baan Naa Sakae, this employment network funneled new migrants almost exclusively into factory work and domestic service. In other villages, connections may be more heavily weighted toward construction work, seasonal employment on Central Thai sugar cane plantations, restaurants, or the commercial sex industry.

4. Weeding upland crops like kenaf is a task that women perform almost exclusively; both men and women work at harvesting and transplanting rice. In Baan Naa Sakae, people occasionally hired work parties from outside the village but most labor needs throughout the agricultural cycle were filled by local residents.

5. These operations typically employ twenty-five to thirty people, often teenagers and usually women. Workers are paid on a piece-rate basis and work extremely long hours.

6. Bangkok minimum wage increased to 110 *baht* ($4.40 U.S.) per day in 1993 and by 1996 was nearly 150 *baht* daily; somewhat lower rates applied in other regions of the country.

7. Small-scale sweatshop operations and domestic service receive limited, if any, protection under Thai labor laws. For larger-scale operations, labor regulations on the books are not difficult to evade. Inspections by state labor officials are infrequent at best and, as in other branches of the Thai civil service, bribery is by no means unknown. Such conditions provide little incentive for the reform of employment practices in many industries.

8. This is a précis and excerpt of an official May Day program, broadcast on national radio, May 1, 1988. At the time, a bitter strike was under way, staged to protest unhealthy working conditions at a large Bangkok textile factory. Several comments during the broadcast clearly referred to this industrial conflict, reflecting the fact that *bun khun* interpretations by authorities or employers are not always shared by Thai workers.

9. It is important to note that workers' enjoyment of "up-to-date" styles and events associated with the workplace made these useful management strategies for structuring worker "morale," informal means of labor control. But these events occasionally had strikingly different effects on workers. The distribution of uniforms, hosting of competitions, and staging of banquets may be presented by manage-

ment as a "gift" or an act of patronage toward employees, but the same acts may be interpreted as rights or benefits owed to workers, and therefore become points for contestation. For example, in 1987 I met one young woman who had participated in a confrontation with her employer because she wanted the factory to institute a system of uniforms. In another example, one male worker was moved to consider union membership after he was reprimanded and fined for wearing a company soccer team shirt on the shop floor.

10. This negative self-image also parallels stereotypes and caricatures in the dominant culture of peasants and migrants as country bumpkins, idiots, and fools.

CHAPTER 7   *Consumption, Desire, and* Thansamay *Selves*

1. Moore argues that such "fantasies of identity" play a significant role in the way individuals confront and potentially transform existing social discourses about appropriate roles and (gendered) identities, because they are "linked to fantasies of power and agency in the world" (1994:66). However, these efforts at self-construction do not necessarily involve an explicit, self-conscious choice between clear and distinct identities. Rather, the experiences of young Thai migrants point to what Henrietta Moore has identified as the need in anthropology to theorize the "internally differentiated subject" (1994:58). In this sense, the lived experience of individual identity (including gender identity) always involves negotiation and conflict between and within available "subject positions" (such as "good daughter" and "modern woman" in the case at hand), themselves constituted by the multiple discourses that exist in any society.

2. These conventional "child of the fields" (*luuk thung*) and ethnic Lao-Northeast Thai (*môô lam*) singing styles have become major genres of popular entertainment in Thailand's highly commercialized media industries.

3. Food is, of course, a basic consumption need, and not all meals involve peer-based sociality. What is interesting is the extent to which migrants engage in these meals—often featuring special regional cuisines, seasonal fruits, ready-made sweets, and soft drinks consumed either in local food shops or purchased in the market and taken back to be served in workers' lodgings—even when living in factory dormitories where all or part of their daily meals are provided by the employer. This may reflect on the quality of food provided and the often limited hours of cafeterias, but group outings to markets and restaurants are also important and enjoyable social occasions.

4. Of course, not all leisure time is spent on such outings. Many migrants spend much of their time off doing laundry and other chores, and generally "resting." However, the latter often includes visiting with friends, chatting or watching television, and perhaps sharing a meal, activities that incorporate aspects of more elaborate, consumption-oriented *thiaws*.

5. This finding parallels that of Anchalee Singhanetra-Renard (Anchalee, 1981) with respect to out-migration from a Northern Thai community. She observed that villagers did not measure the strength of continuing community membership by the distance or time period of a move but by the degree to which mobile individuals maintained their economic and social ties through visits, remittances, and ceremonial donations.

6. Interestingly, very few migrant women I met participated in "share games," a kind of informal credit circle. These are prevalent in many parts of urban Thailand and are an important mechanism for saving among industrial workers in other parts of the region (see, e.g., Wolf, 1992:188–89). Several women mentioned fear of being cheated if the share game organizer could not keep control of the participants. Migrants were most likely to accumulate savings in the form of gold jewelry or bank accounts.

7. In fact, few of the migrants I knew made regular monthly remittances to village families. Those who did were usually working to support a child left at home in the care of grandparents.

8. In the late 1950s and 1960s, initial studies of rural-urban labor migration by Isan men reported similar effects of increased ethnic-regional identification. This migration to the nation's capital, usually by male heads of household, was predominantly economic in motivation, but it also brought many Northeastern men into direct contact with Thai national culture. In the process, migrants found themselves working and living alongside men from villages they had never seen or heard of in provinces all over Isan. Local differences in dialect, custom, or history—issues that can divide residents even between neighboring communities—lost much of their relevance in Bangkok, where migrants, as identifiable Northeasterners (*khon isaan*) encountered similar experiences of discrimination and even contempt from Central Thai, urban society. While urban sojourns strengthened ties of loyalty and friendship between members of the same village (with whom migrants were likely to work and live most closely), migrants also returned home with a heightened, and perhaps for some a new, sense of regional and ethnic identity (Keyes, 1966; Textor, 1961). Charles Keyes (1967) argued that this contributed to an emergent regional consciousness by which natives of the Northeast or Isan conceived of their place within the Thai nation (this was not, however, tied to nationalist sympathies for the newly independent state of Laos), as evidenced by rallies and other mass actions in support of Northeastern politicians by migrants in Bangkok during the 1950s and 1960s.

9. The Bangkok daily minimum wage rose to 110 *baht* ($4.40 U.S.) as of 1994; somewhat lower rates apply in different regions of the country.

10. John Urry discusses the significance of the "tourist gaze" as directed toward the consumption and collection of views, especially ones that can be "captured" for later reviewing and reproduction (as in photographs):

    Central to tourist consumption then is to look individually or collectively upon aspects of landscape or townscape which are distinctive, which signify an experience which contrasts with everyday experience. . . . People linger over such a gaze which is then visually objectified or captured through photographs, postcards, films, models, and so on. These enable the gaze to be endlessly reproduced and recaptured. (1995:132–33)

11. Rural youth often look forward to Buddhist ceremonies and festivals, though, like many migrants, this is frequently less out of religious devotion than because these have historically been occasions when young people could mingle, more or less freely, and perhaps meet a lover or potential suitor.

CHAPTER 8   *Courtship, Marriage, and Contested Selves*

1. Of course, these contradictions are even more complex for women whose work directly involves their sexuality—commercial sex workers. See Cohen (1982), Siriporn (1985), Muecke (1992), and Lyttleton (1994) for discussions of how some women in different sectors of the sex industry negotiate these dilemmas.

2. Legal marriage involves registration with the local district office but many couples, both in rural and urban Thailand, do not register their unions. Co-residence is sufficient to establish the relationship in most people's eyes, especially once a marriage payment (*khaa sin sôôt*) has been made by the groom's family to the woman's parents.

3. This episode mirrors what Christopher Lyttleton (1994) found in his work in another part of Northeast Thailand. In at least one community that he studied, negotiated "engagements" had become a mechanism for some rural families to redress instances of sexual misconduct among young people, without requiring that a marriage be formalized.

4. The moral discourse surrounding women's sexuality may take on different nuances in other parts of the country, specifically in the north of Thailand and in communities where employment in the sex trade is the dominant destination of female migrants. There, according to Marjorie Muecke (1992), the idiom of sacrifice and suffering for the benefit of others may provide a cultural model through which kin and community look on women's sexual experience as an expression of gratitude and obligation, at least for those daughters who remit sufficient sums of money to rural kin.

5. This echoes the survey finding of one study wherein 85 percent of industrial workers sampled responded that factory work "had no future" (Saowalak, 1992:65).

6. Although such actions are illegal under Thai labor laws, standards are not easily enforced in Bangkok's chaotic industrial sector. According to Thai labor rights activists, such violations are most likely in (but not limited to) smaller, domestically owned establishments than in larger and foreign owned factories.

7. She was a *mia nôôy*, the second, or "minor," wife in a nonlegal but common form of polygamous marriage practiced by some, most often urban, Thai men.

8. The actions and attitudes of these women, although not statistically representative, may reflect broader trends in the Thai population. Recent studies of marriage patterns in Thailand point to a slow but steady rise in the age of marriage, especially among urban populations, and to initial signs that the proportion of Thais who never marry is growing (Knodel et al., 1984:38–39).

9. By doing so, she aimed to take advantage of new labor legislation that mandated several weeks' paid maternity leave for women workers. Noi planned to take the leave owed her, after which she would remain in the village. However, keeping the option to return to work might be useful, especially if her husband's job in Taiwan proved less lucrative than hoped, a not uncommon occurrence for overseas laborers (Mills, 1995).

CHAPTER 9   *Gender and Modernity, Local and Global Encounters*

1. In fact, a small minority of migrant women do find urban employment an avenue to more sustained and critical opposition as participants in Thailand's fledg-
   ling labor movement. Although very few workers (even in the industrial sector)
   have access to independent labor organizations, some of the most militant strike
   actions in recent years have taken place among textile employees, most of whom
   are women and of rural origin.

2. The Thai labor movement encompasses only a small minority of the private sector industrial work force; most migrants in Bangkok have little or no access to
   organized labor institutions. Labor organizations, even when active, remain po-
   litically weak. Some migrants who participate in union organizations gain more
   sustained and critical understandings of their circumstances as a result; however,
   in recent fieldwork with migrant women active in labor unions, I found that their
   heightened consciousness of labor concerns did not necessarily alter their plans
   for the future. Most continued to view their time in the city as temporary and
   planned to return home, particularly at the point of marriage.

GLOSSARY OF THAI WORDS
AND PRONUNCIATION GUIDE

Unless otherwise noted, all words and phrases are transliterated from standard Thai. I have also included a number of Isan terms, as indicated by notes in square brackets. The system of transliteration that I use is based on that of Mary Haas (see, e.g., Haas, 1956) with some modifications. Although standard Thai distinguishes five tones, and Isan dialects may have six tones or more, for reasons of simplicity I have not included any tonal markings here. Thai and Isan speakers also recognize a number of vowel and consonant sounds not easily represented by the Roman alphabet. The following explains the most common of these sounds and the transliterations I have employed.

Pronunciation Guide

VOWELS

(Note: a doubled or "long" vowel differs from a single or "short" vowel only in the length of its duration, e.g., "a" and "aa" in "*acaan*.")

a, aa	pronounced as in "dram*a*"
ae	as in t*a*x
ai, ay	as in s*igh* or b*uy*
aw, ao	as in c*ow*
e, ee	as in l*a*ke
i, ii	as in s*ee*
o, oo	as in c*o*mb or l*o*am
ô, ôô	as in *fough*t or l*aw*
oe	as in l*oo*k
u, uu	as in s*oo*n
uay	as in K*uwai*t

ü, üü   this sound is not found in English; it is pronounced like the vowel in 'to*o*k' but with the mouth drawn back at both sides, as in a wide smile

CONSONANTS

Consonants are pronounced as in English with the following exceptions:

c   as 'j' in *j*uice
ch   always a "hard" pronunciation, as in *ch*eap
kh   an aspirated 'k' as in *k*ite
k   an unaspirated 'g' as in *g*ood
ng   always as in si*ng*
ph   an aspirated 'p' as in *p*ie
p   an unaspirated 'p' as in sto*p*
th   an aspirated 't' as in *t*able
t   an unaspirated 't' as sho*t*

Glossary

acaan	professor; honored teacher
amphoe	district
baht	the Thai currency, 1 *baht* = approximately $0.04 U.S. (1990 values)
baan	village; house, home
baan nôôk	rural or remote areas (often with pejorative connotations: isolated, "backwards")
baay sii suu khwan	soul-tying ceremony, traditional Lao/Isan rite of blessing
bô üt bô yaak	not going without; to have enough to live on [Isan idiom]
bun	Buddhist merit
bun khun	debt of merit, especially between parent and child or patron and client
cangwat	province
cao	lord, ruler
caroen	progress (see also *khwaam caroen*)
cay	heart
chaat, satsana, phra mahakasat	nation, religion, king (the symbolic triad of official Thai nationalism)

chaay ngoen	to use/spend money
chaaw baan	villagers, peasants (see also *khon baan nôôk*)
chaaw naa	
chaaw rai	rice and upland farmers
chiiwit thansamay	modern life
chuay	help
faen	boy- or girlfriend; husband or wife; lover
farang	foreigner
hua naa	leader, boss
isaan	northeast, northeast region, Isan (see also *phaak isaan*)
kamakaan	committee member, e.g., for organizing merit-making ceremonies
kan phatthana	development (as in "economic development")
keng	to be good at, skilled
khaa sin sôôt	marriage payment, bride price
khaaratchakan	civil servant
khaaw cao	rice (of the lords), the nonglutinous staple grain of the central Thai plains
khaaw niaw	glutinous or "sticky" rice, the staple grain of Isan
khon	person/people
khon baan hao	person/people of our community [Isan]
khon baan nôôk	country folk, villagers (often pejorative)
khon chaat thai	Thai citizen
khon isaan	person or people of Isan
khon lao	ethnic Lao person or people (often used as equivalent to *khon isaan*)
khon muang	city person, city people
khruu	teacher
khwaam borisut	purity; virginity
khwaam caroen	progress
khwaam pen thansamay	being up-to-date, being modern, modernity
long khaek, haa raeng	exchange labor, cooperative work parties
lung	uncle (literally, parent's older brother)
luuk	child
luuk caang	employee, wage worker
luuk thung	popular "country-folk" music
mae	mother

mae baan	housewife; female householder; matron
maeyaay	"great mother" [Isan, respectful title for older women]
may	not, no (negates phrases that follow—as in *may suay*, not beautiful)
may dii	not good; bad
mia nôôy	minor wife; mistress
mii ngoen	to have money
môô lam	singer or singing style traditional to Isan
müang	country, domain; city
müang luang	capital city
muubaan	village
naa	aunt/uncle (mother's younger sibling); also rice field or face (when spoken in different tones)
naay	mister; also master or lord
naay caang	employer
naay hôôy	itinerant cattle and buffalo traders of Isan
nakleng	bandit, tough, strongman
ngaam	beauty, beautiful [Isan]
ngaan bun	merit-making festival
ngoen	money; silver
ngoen may phôô	not enough money
nôông	younger sibling
paa	aunt (literally, parent's older sister)
pay	to go
pay thiaw	travel around; go out for fun (often in groups); also (for men) to go out for women/commercial sex
phaa sin	woman's sarong-like, wrapped skirt
phaak isaan	northeast, northeast region, Isan
phatthana	to develop (see also *kan phatthana*)
phii	older sibling
phô	father
phôyaay	"great father" [Isan, respectful title for older men]
phray	commoner
phuu baaw	young man; suitor
phuu saaw	young woman; maiden
phuuyaaybaan	village headman
phuu ying thansamay	modern woman
plaa raa	fish paste [*plaa taek* in Isan]

rai	a measure of land area equal to approximately four-tenths of an acre or 1,600 square meters
saaw	young unmarried woman, maiden
sabaay	comfortable, comfort (either physical or financial)
saduak	convenient
samay kôn	old times, the past
samay tae kii	old times, the past [Isan]
samay may	new times, modern times, the present
sia naa	lose face
songthaew	"two-bench" bus, often a converted truck or pick-up
sôôy	help [Isan]; see also *chuay*
suay	beauty, beautiful (see also *ngaam*)
tambon	subdistrict (administrative unit above the village level)
thansamay	up-to-date, in step with the times, modern
thiaw	outing, excursion, trip (usually in a group)
thôôt kathin	Buddhist merit-making ceremony held at the end of the rainy season retreat
thôôt phaa paa	Buddhist merit-making ceremony, "offering of forest robes"
wat	Buddhist temple (includes buildings and grounds)

REFERENCES

NOTE: Thai scholars are commonly known by their personal names rather than by surnames. In keeping with this convention, Thai authors are cited in the text and listed here by their first names.

Akin Rabibhadana. 1969. *The Organization of Thai Society in the Early Bangkok Period, 1782–1873*. Data Paper No. 74. Ithaca, NY: Cornell University, Southeast Asia Program.

———. 1984. "Kinship, Marriage, and the Thai Social Order." In Aphichat Chamratrithirong, ed., *Perspectives on the Thai Marriage*, pp. 1–27. Bangkok: Institute for Population and Social Research, Mahidol University.

Anan Ganjanapan. 1989. "Conflicts over the Deployment and Control of Labor in a Northern Thai Village." In Gillian Hart, Andrew Turton, and Benjamin White, eds., *Agrarian Transformations: Local Processes and the State in Southeast Asia*, pp. 98–122. Berkeley: University of California Press.

Anchalee Singhanetra-Renard. 1981. "Mobility in North Thailand: A View from 'Within.'" In Gavin W. Jones and Hazel Richter, eds., *Population Mobility and Development: Southeast Asia and the Pacific*, pp. 137–66. Canberra: Australian National University.

Anchalee Singhanetra-Renard and Nitaya Prabhudhanitisarn. 1992. "Changing Socioeconomic Roles of Thai Women and Their Migration." In Sylvia Chant, ed., *Gender and Migration in Developing Countries*, pp. 154–73. London and New York: Belhaven Press.

Anderson, Benedict. 1972. "The Idea of Power in Javanese Culture." In Claire Holt, ed., *Culture and Politics in Indonesia*, pp. 1–69. Ithaca, NY: Cornell University Press.

———. 1991. *Imagined Communities: Reflections on the Origin and Spread of Nationalism*. New York: Verso.

Aphichat Chamratrithirong, ed. 1984. *Perspectives on the Thai Marriage*. Bangkok: Institute for Population and Social Research, Mahidol University.

Aphichat Chamratrithirong, Krittaya Archavanitkul, and Uraiwan Kanungsukkasem. 1979. *Recent Migrants in Bangkok Metropolis: A Follow-up Study of Migrants, Adjustment, Assimilation, and Integration*. Bangkok: Institute for Population and Social Research, Mahidol University.

193

Appadurai, Arjun. 1986. "Introduction: Commodities and the Politics of Value." In Arjun Appadurai, ed., *The Social Life of Things: Commodities in Cultural Perspective*, pp. 3–63. Cambridge: Cambridge University Press.

———. 1990. "Disjuncture and Difference in the Global Cultural Economy." *Public Culture* 2(2):1–24.

Asia Watch and the Women's Rights Project. 1993. *A Modern Form of Slavery: Trafficking of Burmese Women and Girls into Brothels in Thailand*. New York: Human Rights Watch.

Atkinson, Jane M., and Shelly Errington, eds. 1990. *Power and Difference: Gender in Island Southeast Asia*. Stanford, CA: Stanford University Press.

Bauman, Zygmunt. 1991. *Modernity and Ambivalence*. Ithaca, NY: Cornell University Press.

Benería, Lourdes, and Shelley Feldman, eds. 1992. *Unequal Burden: Economic Crisis, Persistent Poverty, and Women's Work*. Boulder, CO: Westview Press.

Benería, Lourdes, and Martha Roldán. 1987. *The Crossroads of Class and Gender: Industrial Homework, Subcontracting, and Household Dynamics in Mexico City*. Chicago: University of Chicago Press.

Berman, Marshall. 1982. *All That Is Solid Melts into Air: The Experience of Modernity*. New York: Penguin Books.

Bonacich, Edna, Lucie Cheng, Norma Chinchilla, Nora Hamilton, and Paul Ong, eds. 1994. *Global Production: The Apparel Industry in the Pacific Rim*. Philadelphia: Temple University Press.

Bourdieu, Pierre. 1977. *Outline of a Theory of Practice*. Cambridge: Cambridge University Press.

———. 1984. *Distinction: A Social Critique of the Judgement of Taste*. Cambridge, MA: Harvard University Press.

Bowie, Katherine A. 1997. *Rituals of National Loyalty: An Anthropology of the State and the Village Scout Movement in Thailand*. New York: Columbia University Press.

Chatterjee, Partha. 1993. *The Nation and Its Fragments: Colonial and Postcolonial Histories*. Princeton, NJ: Princeton University Press.

Chattip Nartsupha. 1984. "The Ideology of Holy Men Revolts in North East Thailand." In Andrew Turton and Shigeharu Tanabe, eds., *History and Peasant Consciousness in Southeast Asia*, pp. 111–34. Osaka, Japan: National Museum of Ethnology. Senri Ethnological Series No. 13.

Chayan Vaddhanaphuti. 1991. "Social and Ideological Reproduction in Rural Northern Thai Schools." In Charles F. Keyes, ed., *Reshaping Local Worlds: Formal Education and Cultural Change in Rural Southeast Asia*, pp. 153–73. New Haven, CT: Yale University Southeast Asia Studies.

Cohen, Erik. 1982. "Thai Girls and Farang Men: The Edge of Ambiguity." *Annals of Tourism Research* 9:403–28.

Condominas, Georges. 1975. "Phiban Cults in Rural Laos." In G. William Skinner and A. Thomas Kirsch, eds., *Change and Persistence in Thai Society*, pp. 252–78. Ithaca, NY: Cornell University Press.

Deere, Carmen Diana, and Alain de Janvry. 1979. "A Conceptual Framework for the

Empirical Analysis of Peasants." *American Journal of Agricultural Economics* 61:601–11.

Demaine, Harvey. 1986. "Kanpatthana: Thai Views of Development." In Mark Hobart and Robert H. Taylor, eds., *Context, Meaning, and Power in Southeast Asia*, pp. 93–114. Ithaca, NY: Cornell University, Southeast Asia Program.

Donham, Donald. 1992. "Revolution and Modernity in Maale, Ethiopia, 1974 to 1987." *Comparative Studies in Society and History* 34(1):28–57.

Dublin, Thomas. 1979. *Women at Work: The Transformation of Work and Community in Lowell, Massachusetts, 1826–1860*. New York: Columbia University Press.

Eagleton, Terry. 1991. *Ideology: An Introduction*. London: Verso.

Eberhardt, Nancy. 1988. "Siren Song: Negotiating Gender Images in a Rural Shan Village." In Nancy Eberhardt, ed., *Gender, Power, and the Construction of the Moral Order*. Monograph 4, pp. 73–90. Madison: University of Wisconsin, Center for Southeast Asian Studies.

Elson, Diane, and Ruth Pierson. 1981. "The Subordination of Women and the Internationalisation of Factory Production." In Kate Young, Carol Wolkowitz, and Roslyn McCullagh, eds., *Of Marriage and the Market: Women's Subordination in International Perspective*, pp. 144–66. London: CSE Books.

Enloe, Cynthia. 1989. *Bananas, Beaches, and Bases: Making Feminist Sense of International Politics*. Berkeley: University of California Press.

Fernandez-Kelly, Maria Patricia. 1982. *For We Are Sold, I and My People: Women and Industry in Mexico's Frontier*. Albany, NY: SUNY Press.

Foner, Phillip S. 1977. *The Factory Girls*. Urbana: University of Illinois Press.

Foster, Robert J. 1991. "Making National Cultures in the Global Ecumene." *Annual Review of Anthropology* 20:235–60.

Foucault, Michel. 1977. *Discipline and Punish: The Birth of the Prison*. New York: Vintage.

———. 1980. *Power/Knowledge: Selected Interviews and Other Writings 1972–1977*. New York: Pantheon.

Friends of Women Group. 1988. *Cotmaay khaaw phüan ying [Friends of Women Newsletter]* (in Thai). February issue. Bangkok, Thailand: Friends of Women Group.

Fuller, Theodore, Peerasit Kamnuansilpa, Paul Lightfoot, and Sawaeng Rathanamongkolmas. 1983. *Migration and Development in Modern Thailand*. Bangkok: Social Science Association of Thailand.

Giddens, Anthony. 1990. *The Consequences of Modernity*. Stanford, CA: Stanford University Press.

Girling, John L. S. 1981. *Thailand: Society and Politics*. Ithaca, NY: Cornell University Press.

Goldstein, Sidney, and Alice Goldstein. 1986. "Migration in Thailand: A Twenty-five Year Review." Papers of the East-West Population Institute, No. 100. Honolulu: East-West Population Institute, East-West Center.

Haas, Mary. 1956. *The Thai System of Writing*. Washington, DC: American Council of Learned Societies.

Hanks, Lucien. 1962. "Merit and Power in the Thai Social Order." *American Anthropologist* 64(12):47–61.

_____. 1972. *Rice and Man: Agricultural Ecology in Southeast Asia*. Chicago: Aldine, Atherton.

Hanks, Lucien, and Jane Hanks. 1963. "Thailand: Equality Between the Sexes." In Barbara Ward, ed., *Women in the New Asia*, pp. 424–51. Paris: UNESCO.

Hanks, Lucien, and Herbert Phillips. 1961. "A Young Thai from the Countryside." In Bert Kaplan, ed., *Studying Personality Cross-Culturally*, pp. 637–56. New York: Harper and Row.

Harvey, David. 1989. *The Condition of Postmodernity*. Oxford: Blackwell.

Higham, Charles. 1989. *The Archeology of Mainland Southeast Asia*. Cambridge: Cambridge University Press.

Hirsch, Philip. 1990. *Development Dilemmas in Rural Thailand*. Singapore: Oxford University Press.

Hobsbawm, Eric. 1983. "Introduction: Inventing Traditions." In Eric Hobsbawm and Terence Ranger, eds., *The Invention of Tradition*, pp. 1–14. Cambridge: Cambridge University Press.

Hong, Lysa. 1984. *Thailand in the Nineteenth Century: Evolution of the Economy and Society*. Singapore: Institute of Southeast Asian Studies.

Jackson, Peter A. 1997. "Katoey><Gay><Man: The Historical Emergence of Gay Male Identity in Thailand." In Lenore Manderson and Margaret Jolly, eds., *Sites of Desire, Economies of Pleasure: Sexualities in Asia and the Pacific*, pp. 166–90. Chicago: University of Chicago Press.

_____. 1989. *Male Homosexuality in Thailand: An Interpretation of Contemporary Thai Sources*. Elmhurst, NY: Global Academic Publishers.

Jacobs, Norman. 1971. *Modernization Without Development: Thailand as an Asian Case Study*. New York: Praeger.

JPS (Justice and Peace Commission). 1988. *Report on a Case Study on Sewing Labour in Small-Scale Industry (Shophouses)* [in Thai]. Bangkok: Political Economy Program, Chulalongkorn University Social Research Institute, Bangkok.

Juree Vichit-Vadakan. 1983. "Small Towns and Regional Urban Centers: Reflections on Diverting Bangkok-Bound Migration." *Thai Journal of Development Administration* 23(1):79–99.

Kemper, Steven. 1993. "The Nation Consumed: Buying and Believing in Sri Lanka." *Public Culture* 5(3):377–93.

Keyes, Charles F. 1966. "Ethnic Identity and Loyalty of Villagers in Northeastern Thailand." *Asian Survey* 6:362–69.

_____. 1967. "Isan: Regionalism in Northeastern Thailand." Data Paper No. 65. Ithaca, NY: Cornell University, Southeast Asia Program.

_____. 1975. "Kin Groups in a Thai-Lao Community." In G. William Skinner and A. Thomas Kirsch, eds., *Change and Persistence in Thai Society*, pp. 275–97. Ithaca, NY: Cornell University Press.

_____. 1976. "In Search of Land: Village Formation in the Central Chi River Valley, Northeastern Thailand." *Contributions to Asian Studies* 9:45–63.

_____. 1984. "Mother or Mistress but Never a Monk: Buddhist Notions of Female Gender in Rural Thailand." *American Ethnologist* 11(2):223–41.

_____. 1986. "Ambiguous Gender: Male Initiation in a Northern Thai Buddhist Society." In Carolyn Walker Bynum, Stevan Harrell, and Paula Richman, eds., *Gen-*

der and Religion: On the Complexity of Symbols, pp. 66–96. Boston: Beacon Press.

_____. 1989. *Thailand: Buddhist Kingdom as Modern Nation-State*. Boulder, CO: Westview Press.

_____. 1991. "The Proposed World of the School: Thai Villager's Entry into a Bureaucratic State System." In Charles F. Keyes, ed., *Reshaping Local Worlds: Formal Education and Cultural Change in Rural Southeast Asia*, pp. 89–130. New Haven, CT: Yale University Southeast Asia Studies.

Kirsch, A. Thomas. 1966. "Development and Mobility Among the Phu Thai of Northeast Thailand." *Asian Survey* 6:370–78.

_____. 1975. "Economy, Polity, and Religion in Thailand." In G. William Skinner and A. Thomas Kirsch, eds., *Change and Persistence in Thai Society: Essays in Honor of Lauriston Sharp*, pp. 172–96. Ithaca, NY: Cornell University Press.

_____. 1982. "Buddhism, Sex-Roles and the Thai Economy." In Penny Van Esterik, ed., *Women of Southeast Asia*, pp. 16–41. DeKalb: Northern Illinois University, Center for Southeast Asian Studies.

_____. 1985. "Text and Context: Buddhist Sex Roles/Culture of Gender Revisited." *American Ethnologist* 12(2):302–20.

Knodel, John, Nibon Debavalya, Napaporn Chayoan, and Apichat Chamratrithirong. 1984. "Marriage Patterns in Thailand: A Review of Demographic Evidence." In Aphichat Chamratrithirong, ed., *Perspectives on Thai Marriage*, pp. 31–68. Bangkok: Institute for Population and Social Research, Mahidol University.

Kondo, Dorinne K. 1990. *Crafting Selves: Power, Gender, and Discourses of Identity in a Japanese Workplace*. Chicago: University of Chicago Press.

Kung, Lydia. 1983. *Factory Women in Taiwan*. Ann Arbor: University of Michigan Press.

Lamphere, Louise. 1987. *From Working Daughters to Working Mothers: Immigrant Women in a New England Industrial Community*. Ithaca, NY: Cornell University Press.

Lefferts, H. Leedom. 1980. "Women, Men and Merit: The Household in Rural Thai Buddhism." Unpublished paper, Department of Anthropology, Drew University, Madison, NJ.

Lightfoot, Paul, Theodore Fuller, and Peerasit Kamnuansilpa. 1983. "Circulation and Interpersonal Networks Linking Rural and Urban Areas: The Case of Roi-et, Northeastern Thailand." Paper No. 84. Honolulu: East-West Population Institute, East-West Center.

London, Bruce. 1980. *Metropolis and Nation in Thailand: The Political Economy of Uneven Development*. Boulder, CO: Westview Press.

Lyttleton, Chris. 1994. "The Good People of Isan: Commercial Sex in Northeast Thailand." *The Australian Journal of Anthropology* 5(3):257–79.

Margold, Jane A. 1995. "From the Assembly Line to the Front Lines: Filipina Workers in Multinational Factories." Working Paper No. 3. Department of Anthropology, Chinese University of Hong Kong.

Medhi Krongkaew. 1993. "Poverty and Income Distribution." In Peter G. Warr, ed., *The Thai Economy in Transition*, pp. 401–437. Melbourne, Australia, and Cambridge, UK: Cambridge University Press.

Miller, Daniel. 1994. *Modernity: An Ethnographic Approach*. Oxford: Berg.

———. 1995. "Consumption Studies as the Transformation of Anthropology." In Daniel Miller, ed., *Acknowledging Consumption: A Review of New Studies*, pp. 264–95. London and New York: Routledge.

Mills, Mary Beth. 1995. "Attack of the Widow Ghosts: Gender, Death, and Modernity in Northeast Thailand." In Aihwa Ong and Michael Peletz, eds., *Bewitching Women, Pious Men: Gender and Body Politics in Southeast Asia*, pp. 244–73. Berkeley: University of California Press.

———. 1997. "Contesting the Margins of Modernity: Women, Migration, and Consumption in Thailand." *American Ethnologist* 24(1):37–61.

———. (forthcoming). "Enacting Solidarity: Unions and Migrant Youth in Thailand." *Critique of Anthropology*.

Moore, Henrietta L. 1994. *A Passion for Difference: Essays in Anthropology and Gender*. Bloomington and Indianapolis: Indiana University Press.

Morris, Rosalind. 1994. "Three Sexes and Four Sexualities: Redressing the Discourses on Gender and Sexuality in Contemporary Thailand." *Positions: East Asia Cultures Critique* 2(1):15–43.

Muecke, Marjorie. 1981. "Changes in Women's Status Associated with Modernization in Northern Thailand." In Geoffrey B. Hainsworth, ed., *Southeast Asia: Women, Changing Social Structure, and Cultural Continuity*, pp. 53–65. Ottawa: University of Ottawa Press.

———. 1984. "Make Money Not Babies: Changing Status Markers of Northern Thai Women." *Asian Survey* 24(4):459–70.

———. 1992. "Mother Sold Food, Daughter Sells Her Body: The Cultural Continuity of Prostitution." *Social Science and Medicine* 35(7):891–901.

Murray, Colin. 1981. *Families Divided: The Impact of Migrant Labour in Lesotho*. Cambridge: Cambridge University Press.

Nash, June, and Maria Patricia Fernandez-Kelly, eds. 1983. *Women, Men, and the International Division of Labor*. Albany, NY: SUNY Press.

National Statistical Office. 1988a. *Key Statistics of Thailand 1988*. Bangkok: National Statistical Office, Office of the Prime Minister.

———. 1988b. *Statistical Reports of a Region: Northeastern Region*. Bangkok: National Statistical Office, Office of the Prime Minister.

———. 1992. *Report of the 1992 Migration Survey*. Bangkok: National Statistical Office, Office of the Prime Minister.

O'Connor, Richard A. 1987. "Mechanical and Organic Solidarity in Bangkok." *Contributions to Southeast Asian Ethnography* 6:13–26.

———. 1995. "Indigenous Urbanism: Class, City, and Society in Southeast Asia." *Journal of Southeast Asian Studies* 26(1):30–45.

Odzer, Cleo. 1994. *Patpong Sisters: An American Woman's View of the Bangkok Sex World*. New York: Arcade Publishing.

Ong, Aihwa. 1987. *Spirits of Resistance and Capitalist Discipline: Factory Women in Malaysia*. Albany, NY: SUNY Press.

———. 1991. "The Gender and Labor Politics of Postmodernity." *Annual Review of Anthropology* 20:279–309.

Ong, Aihwa, and Michael Peletz, eds. 1995. *Bewitching Women, Pious Men: Gender and Body Politics in Southeast Asia.* Berkeley: University of California Press.

Orlove, Benjamin S., and Henry J. Rutz. 1989. "Thinking about Consumption: A Social Economy Approach." In Henry J. Rutz and Benjamin S. Orlove, eds., *The Social Economy of Consumption.* Monographs in Economic Anthropology, No. 6, pp. 1–57. Lanham, MD: Society for Economic Anthropology and University Press of America.

Paitoon Mikusol. 1984. "Social and Cultural History of Northeastern Thailand from 1868 to 1910: A Case Study of the Huamuang Khamen Padong (Surin, Sangkha and Khukhan)." Ph.D. dissertation. University of Washington, Seattle.

Parnwell, Mike. 1986. "Migration and the Development of Agriculture: A Case Study of Northeast Thailand." Occasional Paper No. 12. Hull, UK: University of Hull, Center for Southeast Asian Studies.

Pasuk Phongpaichit. 1982. *From Peasant Girls to Bangkok Masseuses.* Geneva: International Labor Organization.

Pasuk Phongpaichit, and Chris Baker. 1995. *Thailand: Economy and Politics.* Kuala Lumpur, Oxford, and New York: Oxford University Press.

———. 1996. *Thailand's Boom!* Chiang Mai, Thailand: Silkworm Books.

Pawadee Tongudai. 1982. "Women, Migration and Employment: A Study of Migrant Workers in Bangkok." Ph.D. dissertation, New York University, New York.

———. 1984. "Women Migrants in Bangkok: An Economic Analysis of Their Employment and Earnings." In Gavin W. Jones, ed., *Women in the Urban and Industrial Workforce: Southeast and East Asia,* pp. 305–23. Canberra: Australian National University.

Peiss, Kathy Lee. 1986. *Cheap Amusements: Working Women and Leisure in Turn-of-the-Century New York.* Phildelphia: Temple University Press.

Porpora, Douglas, and Lim Mah Hui. 1987. "The Political Economic Factors of Migration to Bangkok." *Journal of Contemporary Asia* 17(1):76–89.

Pranee Monthongdaeng. 1991. "Thit thang kaan phüng ton eng nay sangkhom thii kamlang plianpay: süksaa chaphô koranii muu baan sôông haeng nay phaak tawan ôôk chiang nüa. [The Direction of Self-reliance in Changing Society: A Case Study of Two Northeastern Thai Villages]." M.A. Thesis (in Thai). Thammasat University, Bangkok, Thailand.

Pred, Allan, and Michael John Watts. 1992. *Reworking Modernity: Capitalisms and Symbolic Discontent.* New Brunswick, NJ: Rutgers University Press.

Riggs, Fred. 1966. *Thailand: The Modernization of a Bureaucratic Polity.* Honolulu: East-West Center Press.

Roseberry, William. 1989. *Anthropologies and Histories: Essays in Culture, History, and Political Economy.* New Brunswick, NJ: Rutgers University Press.

Safa, Helen I. 1995. *The Myth of the Male Breadwinner: Women and Industrialization in the Caribbean.* Boulder, CO: Westview Press.

Saowalak Chaytaweep. 1992. *Chiwit thang sangkhom khong khon ngaan nay phaak utsaahakam kaan phalit (Social Life of Manufacturing Workers)* [in Thai]. Bangkok: Institute of Social Technology (Krirk) and Arom Pongpangan Foundation.

Siriporn Skrobanek. 1985. "In Pursuit of an Illusion: Thai Women in Europe." *Southeast Asia Chronicle* 96:7–12.

Standing, Guy. 1989. "Global Feminization through Flexible Labor." *World Development* 17(7):1077–95.

Tambiah, Stanley J. 1970. *Buddhism and the Spirit Cults in North-East Thailand*. Cambridge: Cambridge University Press.

Terweil, Baas J. 1975. *Monks and Magic: An Analysis of Religious Ceremonies in Central Thailand*. London: Curzon Press.

_____. 1979. "Tattooing in Thailand's History." *Journal of the Royal Asiatic Society of Great Britain and Ireland* 1979(2):156–66.

Textor, Robert B. 1961. *From Peasant to Pedicab Driver: A Social Study of Northeastern Thai Farmers Who Periodically Migrated to Bangkok and Became Pedicab Drivers*. New Haven, CT: Yale University Southeast Asia Studies, Cultural Report No. 9.

Thitsa, Khin. 1980. *Providence and Prostitution: Image and Reality for Women in Buddhist Thailand*. London: CHANGE, International Reports.

_____. 1983. "Nuns, Mediums, and Prostitutes in Chiang Mai: A Study of Some Marginal Categories of Women." Occasional Paper No. 1. Kent, UK: University of Kent at Canterbury, Centre of Southeast Asian Studies.

Thongchai Winichakul. 1994. *Siam Mapped: A History of the Geo-Body of a Nation*. Honolulu: University of Hawaii Press.

Thorbek, Susanne. 1987. *Voices from the City: Women of Bangkok*. London: Zed Press.

Tongroj Onchan. 1990. *A Land Policy Study*. Bangkok: Thailand Development Research Institute.

Tsurumi, E. Patricia. 1990. *Factory Girls: Women in the Thread Mills of Meiji Japan*. Princeton, NJ: Princeton University Press.

Turton, Andrew. 1980. "Thai Institutions of Slavery." In James Watson, ed., *Asian and African Systems of Slavery*, pp. 251–92. Oxford: Blackwell.

_____. 1984. "Limits of Ideological Domination and the Formation of Social Consciousness." In Andrew Turton and Tanabe Shigeharu, eds., *History and Peasant Consciousness in South East Asia*, pp. 19–73. Osaka, Japan: National Museum of Ethnology. Senri Ethnological Studies No. 13.

_____. 1987. *Production, Power and Participation in Rural Thailand: Experiences of Poor Farmers' Groups*. Geneva: United Nations Research Institute for Social Development.

_____. 1989a. "Local Powers and Rural Differentiation." In Gillian Hart, Andrew Turton, and Benjamin White, eds., *Agrarian Transformations: Local Processes and the State in Southeast Asia*, pp. 70–97. Berkeley: University of California Press.

_____. 1989b. "Thailand: Agrarian Bases of State Power." In Gillian Hart, Andrew Turton, and Benjamin White, eds., *Agrarian Transformation: Local Processes and the State in Southeast Asia*, pp. 53–69. Berkeley: University of California Press.

_____. 1991. "State Poetics and Civil Rhetoric: An Introduction to *Thai Constructions of Knowledge*." In Chitakasem Manas and Andrew Turton, eds., *Thai Con-*

structions of Knowledge, pp. 1–14. London: School of Oriental and African Studies, University of London.

Urry, John. 1995. *Consuming Places*. London and New York: Routledge.

Uthai Dulyakasem. 1991. "Education and Ethnic Nationalism: The Case of the Muslim-Malays in Southern Thailand." In Charles F. Keyes, ed., *Reshaping Local Worlds: Formal Education and Cultural Change in Rural Southeast Asia*, pp. 131–52. New Haven, CT: Yale University Southeast Asia Studies.

Van Esterik, Penny, ed. 1982a. *Women of Southeast Asia*. DeKalb: Center for Southeast Asian Studies, Northern Illinois University.

———. 1982b. "Laywomen in Theravada Buddhism." In Penny Van Esterik, ed., *Women of Southeast Asia*, pp. 55–78. DeKalb: Northern Illinois University, Center for Southeast Asian Studies.

———. 1984. "Rice and Milk in Thai Buddhism: Symbolic and Social Values of Basic Food Substances." *Crossroads* 2(1):46–58.

———. 1988. *Gender and Development in Thailand: Deconstructing Display*. Toronto: York University, Department of Anthropology, Thai Studies Project.

———. 1990. "Foreign Bodies, Diseased Bodies, No Bodies: Thai Prostitution and Gender Identity." Paper presented at the Conference on Sexuality and Gender in East and Southeast Asia, University of California, Los Angeles.

———. 1996. "The Politics of Beauty in Thailand." In Colleen Ballerino Cohen, Richard Wilk, and Beverly Stoeltje, eds., *Beauty Queens of the Global Stage: Gender, Contests and Power*, pp. 203–16. New York and London: Routledge.

Vandergeest, Peter. 1989. "Peasant Strategies in a World Context: Contingencies in the Transformation of Rice and Palm Sugar Economies in Thailand." *Human Organization* 48(2):117–25.

Wallace, Anthony F. C. 1972. *Rockdale: The Growth of an American Village in the Early Industrial Revolution*. New York: W. W. Norton and Co.

Warr, Peter G. 1993. "The Thai Economy." In Peter G. Warr, ed., *The Thai Economy in Transition*, pp. 1–80. Melbourne, Australia, and Cambridge, UK: Cambridge University Press.

Williams, Raymond. 1977. *Marxism and Literature*. Oxford: Oxford University Press.

Wilson, Constance M. 1983. *Thailand: A Handbook of Historical Statistics*. Boston: G. K. Hall and Company.

Wolf, Diane Lauren. 1992. *Factory Daughters: Gender, Household Dynamics, and Rural Industrialization in Java*. Berkeley: University of California Press.

Wyatt, David K. 1982. *Thailand: A Short History*. New Haven, CT: Yale University Press.

INDEX

ABOUT THE AUTHOR

Mary Beth Mills is an associate professor of anthropology at Colby College in Waterville, Maine.